PELICAN BOOKS

THE PSYCHOLOGY OF PLAY

Dr Susanna Millar took her degree in psychology at
Birkbeck College while working as a teacher. After
engaging in experimental research she obtained her
doctorate in psychology from London University.
Concurrently she held a Fellowship for Training from
the National Association for Mental Health, and then
worked as a psychologist to the Education Committees
of Wakefield and Oxford. Shortly after her marriage
she became a part-time lecturer in child development
at Birkbeck College for three years. Recently, Lady
Margaret Hall whose psychology students Dr Millar
supervises, has elected her to an Honorary Research
Fellowship for three years. Dr Millar is currently engaged on a research project, supported by the Social
Science Research Council, at the Institute of Experimental Psychology, University of Oxford.

a Pelican Original

The Psychology of Play

Susanna Millar

PQR617042

THE PSYCHOLOGY
OF PLAY

SUSANNA MILLAR

PENGUIN BOOKS

Penguin Books Ltd, Harmondsworth, Middlesex, England
Penguin Books Inc., 7110 Ambassador Road, Baltimore, Maryland 21207, U.S.A.
Penguin Books Australia Ltd, Ringwood, Victoria, Australia

—

First published 1968
Reprinted 1969, 1971, 1972, 1973

—

Copyright © Susanna Millar, 1968

—

Made and printed in Great Britain by
Cox & Wyman Ltd,
London, Reading and Fakenham
Set in Monotype Baskerville

TO FERGUS

CONTENTS

EDITORIAL FOREWORD

THIS book can be commended to all parents and to teachers as well as to students engaged in advanced studies in Psychology and the Social Sciences. It is a book which though easy to read may well have been difficult to write. There are certain topics – Play is one Humour is another – in writing a book on which a scientific, scholarly approach must be combined with the lightness of touch appropriate to the subject. A learned treatise on Jokes could be admirable in some ways, but it would be faintly ridiculous. A book on Play should be scholarly and scientific but it must be written with appreciation of the fact that play is generally (though not always) the enjoyment of fun. Susanna Millar, in this book has met that very exacting requirement. It is accordingly a very readable, trustworthy, scholarly study, immensely erudite, perspicacious and judicious. There are many quite plausible theories of play and in this book each is given a fair run for its money. But there is no yielding to the temptation to look for an all-embracing theory which covers everything that can be called play. The recapitulation theory, that in development the individual passes through the several phases in the history of his species, has plausibility. It accounts for the child playing an Indian with bows and arrows, but it breaks down when the 'Indians' install television sets in their wigwams and discard their bows and arrows for guided missiles. The theory that play is preparing for mature life is all right when applied to puppies and kittens and to some games of human children. It breaks down if it is suggested that old gentlemen playing bridge in their clubs are preparing for life in the Hereafter. No, the author of this book does not try to provide a theory to cover all forms of play.

Nor does she succumb to the temptation to moralize and preach sermons. Certainly, playful behaviour raises many important moral issues. Peace-loving parents have qualms in allowing their bloodthirsty children to play with toy soldiers, and they have qualms about some of the sexy sorts of play to which their children may be prone. Susanna Millar knows all this, but she does not take advantage of her position to air whatever may be her own views on the moral questions. The note she strikes in her first paragraph (about the child who agreed to accompany his parents on an Aldermaston march provided he could bring his own lethal weapon) is a note that recurs throughout the book. The relevant facts are stated, so far as they are known. On the basis of these facts sensible parents and teachers can arrive at their own conclusions.

C. A. MACE

AUTHOR'S FOREWORD

WHEN I was asked to write a book on the psychology of play, I remembered a cartoon of a hapless couple on an Aldermaston peace march whose child refused to go with them unless allowed to hold a vicious-looking toy-rocket. Whatever the moral, the cartoon implied an assumption about human behaviour. One of the questions psychologists have to answer is whether such assumptions are justified, and what evidence there is for them.

Psychologists cannot go to ordinary language for their definitions. The fact that there is a common word for a number of activities does not guarantee that they can all be explained by one mechanism, or that the same set of conditions determines them all. It merely shows that people have not found it necessary to distinguish them for ordinary purposes. The term 'play' has long been a linguistic waste-paper basket for behaviour which looks voluntary, but seems to have no obvious biological or social use. Such a category is too vague for the purpose of scientific study. At the same time, it is unsatisfactory to restrict the meaning of a common word arbitrarily. This simply results in a confusion of different definitions. Common-sense questions about any human behaviour do need answering. But they have to be 'unpacked' before the behaviour can be studied in a way that precludes mere speculation. To do this for play, I have described theories that have been held about play, and have tried to piece together what is actually known about various forms of it from observational and experimental studies. Such a mosaic is bound to be incomplete as yet, and the patterns emphasized may not be those which emerge ultimately as most salient. But at least it will be possible to ask sensible questions about the missing pieces.

Since this book is intended mainly for the general reader, the discussion of theories and experiments has been kept at a simpler and less technical level than would be necessary for students of psychology. For the use of the latter, I have included a fair number of references to scientific articles and books for details of experiments and technical points. The first two chapters deal mainly with theories which have influenced psychological thinking about play in the past. They should also serve as an introduction to the subject for non-psychologists. The third chapter surveys examples of play among animals of different evolutionary 'standing', while the remaining chapters are concerned with various human play-forms at different levels of child development.

This book was written over a period of three years, substantially completed in December 1966 and given to the Publishers in June 1967.

I wish to thank Professor R. C. Oldfield, Professor L. Weiskrantz and the staff of the Institute of Experimental Psychology of Oxford University for the use of the library and Institute facilities, and Dr D. J. McFarland for valuable criticisms of parts of the manuscript. To my husband I owe more than gratitude for his constant encouragement and patience.

CHAPTER ONE

HISTORICAL INTRODUCTION

As I write, my one-year-old is standing in the middle of the room, looking at the world upside down through his legs, the three-year-old sits at a small table, her head earnestly bent over sheaves of paper. She, too, is writing a book. Her pen had to be the same colour as mine, her sheets of the same shape, and every now and then she looks up to make sure that her scribbles resemble mine. A peaceful scene which will not last long but, while it does, typifies some of the range of behaviour called play. Young monkeys look through their legs as infants do, and throughout history children have cooked, washed and scribbled in imitation of their elders. Yet it is only comparatively recently that any serious attention has been paid to such activities, or that there has been any idea that they might provide valuable clues to understanding children, and the motives that lead humans and animals to behave as they do.

It is, of course, always tempting to find echoes of modern notions in the past. Plato is often cited as the first to have recognized the practical value of play from his prescription in the Laws to distribute apples among boys to help them learn Arithmetic, and to give real miniature tools to those three-year-olds who were later to become builders. Aristotle too thought that children should be encouraged to play at what they were to do seriously as adults. Following the great educational reformers, from Comenius in the seventeenth, to Rousseau, Pestalozzi and Fröbel in the eighteenth and early nineteenth centuries, teachers increasingly accepted the idea that education should take account of the child's natural interests and stage of development. This culminated in Fröbel's stress on the importance of play in learning. An unhappy childhood led him to take an interest in young children, and his admiration for the romanticist philosophy of Schelling made the idea of freedom and self-expression almost an article of faith with him. His sympathy for children, and his practical experience as a teacher, enabled him to realize that the kind of play children enjoy, and the toys they find most attractive could be used to gain their attention, and to develop their capacities and knowledge. His ideas were of great practical value. But there was little systematic knowledge of child development in Fröbel's time, and his conception of play as the 'unfolding of the germinal leaves of childhood' does not explain anything.

The first formulations of theories of play were to be left to the mid- and late-nineteenth century under the influence of evolutionary theory. If the main activities of living things were directed to satisfying bodily needs – to the serious business of preserving life and the species – what function could be assigned to play? An early, perhaps rather simple-minded answer was that it had its use as recuperation from work. The idea had already occurred incidentally in some seventeenth-century writings, but is usually associated with two nineteenth-century German thinkers, Schaller and Lazarus, who both wrote books on play. Schaller thought that play restores powers that are nearing exhaustion. Lazarus contrasted play with work and with idleness, and advocated active recreation as a restorative. A game of football or darts, even painting the garden gate may act as relaxation. But this will not do for the activities of the young. No strenuous work precedes the kitten's jumping after a ball. Puppies romp until they are tired, and then start the game all over again.

Surplus Energy

The incessant running, jumping, and tumbling about, characteristic of young children and animals seems to call for a different kind of explanation. The English philosopher, Herbert Spencer, writing his monumental *Principles of Psychology* in the mid-nineteenth century, elaborated what is now known as the 'Surplus Energy' theory of play. In its simplest form, the notion that children play to 'blow off steam' was probably current long before. Spencer originally got it from the philosophical and aesthetic writings of Friedrich von Schiller, although he charmingly confesses that he could not remember the German poet's name. Schiller called play the expression of exuberant energy, and the origin of all art. Spencer, nearly a century later, also considered play as the origin of art, and as aimless expression of surplus energy, but gave this a typically evolutionary twist. He argued that the lower an animal is on the evolutionary scale, the more its energies are taken up with finding food and escaping from its enemies. Play evolved in the higher animals, since with their greater range of skills they needed to spend less time on keeping themselves alive, and were, nevertheless, better fed and healthier, and so had more energy available.

The notion of a surplus of energy conjures up the picture of a water or gas system in which the store discharges into various channels, and might overflow if the pressure builds up, and is too much for any one outlet. This sort of analogy was used a great deal in psychological theories in the early part of this century, but has been found rather inadequate. As an explanation of play obvious objections spring to mind. Play can act as an incentive. A child, tired from a long walk, will perk up and trot home rapidly if he is promised play at the end of it. Excess energy is not needed for play. A baby will yell for toys when by all other signs it is badly in need of sleep and rest. The amateur footballer is not more energetic than the professional. Actually, Spencer's own theory was not as crude. His detailed explanation rests on speculations about the physiology of fatigue in nerve-centres. These, according to him, disintegrate by being used, and need time to be restored. A nerve centre which has been at rest for any considerable period of time will become physically unstable. It will then be over-ready to respond to any kind of stimulation, and issue in the kind of action appropriate to that particular centre. This accounts for the imitative element in play. When no opportunity for serious fighting has occurred for some time, the animal engages in simulated fights – or plays chess if he is a man. In addition, competition based on egoistic feelings, will, if unemployed, issue in play. Spencer's ingenious physiological speculations are out of date. Nor does his theory cover all the facts. The office worker or business executive does not necessarily use manual skills in his free hours. A boxing champion may be a leisure-time student of Shakespeare, but this is less likely than that the mathematician plays chess which involves similar skills in play to those used in work.

Nevertheless, the facts for which Spencer tried to account do need explaining. No one who has seen a class of healthy eight-year-olds released from an Arithmetic lesson can doubt their need to move and shout. Solemn adult audiences will shuffle their feet and clear their throats between the movements of a piece of music. Charles Darwin, in his *Expression of the Emotions* (1872), noted that intense joy and pleasurable excitement make people dance, clap their hands, stamp and laugh. Some sort of surplus energy theory was held by many subsequent writers for these reasons, and the notion continues to crop up. It has often been used as an argument for providing playing-fields and gymnasia. But few of the later formulations are as sophisticated in the attempt to connect physiological, psychological and social facts as that of Spencer.

Recapitulation Theory

Evolutionary theory in the nineteenth century gave a tremendous impetus to child study, as to all biological sciences. Spencer's earlier writings were too speculative, and some say too badly written, to make much impact. But Charles Darwin's massive evidence in his *Origin of Species* (1859) could not be disregarded. Interest in man's development from lower species led to an interest in the development of the newborn baby to adult human. The emphasis shifted from speculation to observation. Proud fathers, not least among them Darwin, began to record their infants' development with the seriousness and scientific rigour previously accorded only to beetles. There were few systematic studies of children before this. The earliest was an investigation by a German called Tiedemann in 1787. But the beginning of Child Psychology is usually traced to Preyer, a German physiologist whose first-hand systematic observations on the development of his baby son from the reflexes present at birth to more complex behaviour were carefully recorded. His *Mind of the Child* appeared in 1882 and was a textbook for many years. A spate of baby biographies followed in its wake. Another 'father' of child psychology was G. S. Hall, an American professor of Psychology and Pedagogy. His twin interests in evolutionary theory and in education (he had been a private tutor before studying under the great philosopher-psychologist William James) led him to study children. For the first time a serious scientist concerned himself with such questions as the kind of dolls children prefer, or how soon they are given names. His 'Recapitulation Theory' of play rests on the notion that children are a link in the evolutionary chain from animal to man, and pass through all the stages from protozoan to human in their lives as embryos. Some of the stages through which the human foetus passes from conception to birth are similar to the developmental sequence of structure and behaviour from fish to man. This seemed to provide evidence that individual development (ontogeny) repeats that of the race (phylogeny). Hall extended the idea of recapitulation to the whole of childhood in a famous book on adolescence in 1904. The child relives the history of the race as the embryo relives that of its more remote ancestors. The experiences of his ancestors are handed on, and the child re-enacts in play the interests and occupations in the sequence in which they occurred in prehistoric and primitive man.

The recapitulation theory was able to give a more detailed account of the content of play than other attempts. Children's delight in playing with water could be connected with their fishy ancestors' joys in the sea; their insistence on climbing trees and swinging from branches showed vestiges of the life of their monkey-like forebears. Boys aged between eight and twelve years like fishing, canoeing, hunting, tent-building, and they enjoy doing these things in groups. The analogy with primitive tribal life was very tempting. Unfortunately, the theory was based on the assumption that skills learned by one generation, and the cultural experiences it has, can be inherited by the next. This Lamarckian view of evolution was not supported by greater knowledge about the function of genes in heredity. Most Western geneticists reject the notion that acquired characteristics can be inherited – at least in any form which could make Hall's recapitulation theory plausible. There is no tidy linear progress from 'primitive' to more complex civilizations. Nor are children miniature adult savages. Riding bicycles and using toy telephones is hardly a rehearsal of ancient experiences. But theory does not have to be correct to be of use. Hall's recapitulation theory had the excellent effect of stimulating interest in children's behaviour at various ages.

The Practice of Skills

A different theory was put forward by Karl Groos, a professor of philosophy at Basle, in his books on the play of animals in 1896, and on the play of man in 1899. He became interested in play as a possible basis for aesthetics. Impressed by Weissman's investigations which first made it doubtful that acquired characteristics can be inherited, Groos based his explanation entirely on the principle of natural selection put forward by Darwin as one of the main agencies of evolution. Those animals survive who are best fitted to cope with prevailing conditions, and whose offspring can adapt to changing ones. If animals play, this is because play is useful in the struggle for survival; because play practises and so perfects the skills needed in adult life. The infant continually moving hands, fingers, toes, babbling and crowing, learns to control its own body. The kitten stalking and chasing balls of knitting wool becomes adept at catching mice. Only animals endowed with detailed instinctive patterns of behaviour which are perfect on first trial have no need to play. The parasitic solitary wasp emerges from the worm on which it was deposited as an egg by a mother wasp it has never seen. Yet it repeats its mother's performance flawlessly: finds a worm for its eggs, paralyses it by an expert sting, and so provides fresh food for the grubs which will emerge long after it has flown away. In complex and changing environments, such rigid inherited patterns of behaviour are uneconomic. Natural selection favours adaptable animals whose instincts are sufficiently fragmentary and plastic to benefit from experience. Such animals must practise and perfect their incomplete hereditary skills before a serious need to exercise them arises. They must play. Play, the generalized impulse to practise instincts, is closely connected with imitation – another generalized instinct which replaces the need for a large number of specialized, rigid ones. To learn by imitation is important for those young whose hereditary modes of action are scanty. The more adaptable and intelligent a species is, the more it needs a period of protected infancy and childhood for the practice gained in play and by imitation.

In support of his theory Groos collected an enormous number of examples from books, periodicals and his own observation. Most persuasive for the practice theory of play are the stories of play-fighting. The teasing and tussling of the young of many species seems well explained as practice of an instinct for future use. The objection that fighting and playing at fighting differ in that animals do not harm each other in play, and renew the game rather than kill or run away, is not serious. A species that practised its skills by killing off all but the strongest animals in infancy would soon die out. Actually, Groos regarded many forms of play-fighting not as preparation for life and death struggles, but as practice for courtship contests among the adult males of many species after which the female yields to the victor without resistance.

The play of mature animals is less easily accommodated by

a theory that play is an instinct to practise instincts for use in adult life. No doubt practice benefits even adults, and Groos's point that they continue to play because play in youth has been pleasant recognizes the learned element in play. But it weakens the original theory. Moreover, Groos's excellent classification of the play of animals and humans includes not only fighting and love-play, but also movement, recognition, remembering – in fact nearly all the functions of an organism. Calling all these 'instincts', and assuming two special instincts to practise them seems excessive. If living organisms exercise all their functions and skills, it adds nothing to say that they have an instinct to do so. The value of Groos's theory lay in showing that activities defined as aimless and useless could have a serious biological purpose. In a modified form, without assuming a special instinct, the theory that play is practice is still frequently regarded as valid.

Play as an Attitude

Play may be useful, but it is also connected with laughter and fun. Darwin mentioned how frequently children laugh when playing. James Sully in his *Essay on Laughter* in 1902 suggested that laughter acts as a sign of play, and is essential to a social activity involving a playmate. Teasing and tickling are mild attacks, and would be regarded as such, but for the accompanying laughter which informs the participants that no serious harm is intended. Sully speaks of the play-mood, or playful attitude in which laughter is an element. It is an attitude of throwing off restraint, and pleasure and enjoyment are essential to it.

There are advantages in regarding play as an attitude. Groos showed that almost all the natural functions of an organism may be used in play. Play cannot, therefore, be a special kind of activity with characteristics that distinguish it from other activities. This difficulty is avoided by classifying the mood of the person rather than what he is doing. Unfortunately, the criteria for deciding when an animal or young child is happy or pleased are difficult to apply, and observations of children show no invariable connexion between obvious pleasure and play. A three-year-old trying to build a complicated house of bricks is absorbed, furious if a younger brother knocks it over, disconsolate if it does not succeed, but he is neither hilarious nor particularly 'playful' about it. On the contrary, he shows every sign of being very serious. We assume that he enjoys building the house simply because he need not have done it. He chose it himself. Freedom of choice, not being constrained by other people or by circumstances, is a hallmark of play, although it provides no absolute distinction. People often freely choose what work to do to earn their living. In one of Trollope's novels, Planty Palliser, the immensely rich heir to a dukedom with more choice of activities than any child, devotes his time to working on his pet scheme for putting the nation's finances to rights, and considers all the usual pastimes of hunting and parties as unwelcome interruptions. Skipping with a skipping-rope certainly ranks as play, but not when the World Heavyweight Champion does it before an audience for pay, even if he loves doing nothing better than skipping.

Nevertheless a certain degree of choice, lack of constraint from conventional ways of handling objects, materials and ideas, is inherent in the concept of play. This is its main connexion with art and other forms of invention. Perhaps play is best used as an adverb; not as a name of a class of activities, nor as distinguished by the accompanying mood, but to describe how and under what conditions an action is performed.

The gallant attempts to provide direct, comprehensive theories of play are inadequate partly because they attempt to define and treat play as an activity with a common core and with characteristics that distinguish it from all others. Actually each emphasizes a different aspect of play. The recreation theory is mainly about the leisure activities of adults. It is an attempt – even if a poor one – at psychological explanation. Spencer's surplus energy theory is most plausible about lambs frisking and the stampede of small boys. His account is in terms of physiological function – the action of nerve centres and the like. Hall tried to explain how play varies with age, and why certain forms of it seem to recur over differences in space, time and culture. Groos attempted to account for the fact that it is mainly the young of a species who play, and that such play is characteristic of the activities of the species to which they belong. Further advances in understanding the conditions which determine play could come only from seeing it as an aspect of a whole range of human and animal behaviour which needed to be explored systematically. This came to be the province of psychology.

CHAPTER TWO

'PLAY' IN PSYCHOLOGICAL THEORIES

PSYCHOLOGY had been part of philosophy, physiology, medicine, education, or zoology before it gradually became a separate empirical science in the nineteenth century. The questions asked and the methods of investigation were at first bound to be different for the physician wishing to cure abnormal behaviour, the physiologist relating behaviour to the functioning of the central nervous system, the teacher in quest of methods, the zoologist studying the behaviour of animals who cannot talk, and the inheritors of a philosophy concerned with human experience and phenomena as they appear to man. Inevitably a number of differeht 'schools' of psychology(387) had developed in the early part of this century. To those who considered the investigation of human behaviour to be almost impious, these differences in theory and method were merely proof of the impossibility of the attempt. In science, however, it is neither new nor detrimental to progress that early explanations of a relatively small range of facts should be extended by their protagonists to cover the whole subject and so clash with other hypotheses designed to answer different questions. The early theories led to advances in formulating questions and methods of investigation as a result of which modern theories tend to be less all-embracing and more easily tested. The problem of play was not central to any of the theories, but some of them influenced subsequent conceptions and investigations of play. These will be discussed below.

Psychoanalytic Explanations of Play

Psychoanalysis was evolved by Sigmund Freud at the end

of the nineteenth and the beginning of the twentieth century as a method of treating mental illness. The use of play in adapting this technique to disturbed children was incidental. The assumption behind it, however, might be seen as a brilliant logical error which led to concern with behaviour hitherto mainly thought of as chance, or useless, actions. No behaviour can be considered as uncaused. To Freud this meant that all, or at least most, behaviour is motivated. Not that Freud would have looked for a man's motive in falling down when hit by a brick; but if the man was subject to many such accidents, he would have examined the man rather than the brickwork. Slips of the tongue, forgetting one's wedding anniversary, dreams, and the play of children were not chance occurrences but determined by the individual's feelings and emotions whether he was aware of them or not.

Freud was a neurologist by training(186). He later studied under Charcot in Paris and Janet at Nancy, who both used hypnosis in the treatment of hysteria. During hypnosis, patients were told that their symptoms would disappear. This treatment seemed particularly appropriate for the majority of Freud's patients who showed no evidence of neurological damage. But Freud soon found it inadequate. Cures were seldom permanent, and not everyone could be hypnotized. In collaboration with a colleague, Breuer, he experimented with questioning patients about their symptoms under hypnosis, encouraging them to talk freely. This 'talking out', or cathartic method was apparently often followed by relief. It was supposed to work by releasing pent-up emotions(46). Later Freud abandoned hypnosis altogether, merely encouraging patients to say whatever came into their mind. He finally made only one rule which was to govern their spontaneous talk: they must say everything as it occurred to them, even if it was trivial, painful or embarrassing(126a). This was the method of free association – the main tool of psychoanalysis. It assumed that thoughts and feelings which occur when the speaker lets 'his mind wander' are associated with, and determined by, significant events and feelings which had been forgotten (repressed) because they were painful or shameful to the patient's idea of himself. They could, therefore, only come up in a disguised form, symbolically, or as trivial memories. It was the business of the physician to make the patient aware of their significance so that he could face hitherto unrecognized feelings and conflicts and integrate them with the rest of his experience. The symptoms, brought about by unrecognized urges without legitimate outlets, would then disappear. Some of Freud's successors used free play as interchangeable with verbal free association in the treatment of children.

Freud's clinical successes with his method appeared to him to justify the explanations he evolved and altered over a number of years. He started with the assumption that human behaviour is determined by the amount of pleasure or pain to which it leads. Pleasurable experiences are sought, painful ones avoided. When unchecked by facts or the demands of others, human behaviour and thinking is motivated by the wishes of the individual. In play, in dreams, and in phantasy(123) checks from hard facts do not operate; they are determined by wishes. The child distinguishes play from reality, but uses objects and situations from the real world to create a world of his own in which he can repeat pleasant experiences at will, and can order and alter events in the way that pleases him best. The child wants to be grown up, and to do what adults do. In play this is possible. The little girl wields authority among her dolls which is denied to her in reality. The student sees himself in phantasy as a brilliant professor, acclaimed by the world for his discoveries. From there to imaginative production is but a step. Art is an elaboration and refinement of day-dreams.

Freud was impressed by the frequency with which patients' conflicts and anxieties appeared to be connected with sexual experiences in their early childhood. Most of these turned out to be phantasies. He explained this by assuming that sexuality begins much earlier than puberty. The fact that respectable patients often showed unwelcome signs of being in love with their therapist he held to be due to a transfer to the therapist of forbidden and obliterated sexual wishes which had remained fixed at an infantile level and impeded normal development. Freud used the term sexuality in a much wider sense than common to include all manifestations of striving for pleasure. He assumed a basic instinct, Eros or Libido – generally speaking, an urge to live – as the source of all motivation, part of it checked, transformed and redirected by the necessity to come to terms with reality.

Freud postulated a direct sequeuce from the infant's sucking and mouthing when no longer hungry, and the child's apparent satisfaction in bodily sensations to the more unequivocally sexual urges of puberty. Sexuality in the infant was not considered the same as in the adult. Until maturity the sexual instinct or libido would go through a number of stages, innately determined by heightened sensitivity in special bodily zones at different ages. In the first year of life an infant's activities centre on the mouth. Even when not hungry he mouths, sucks, bites and explores objects with his mouth. This oral stage is succeeded by an anal stage. The two-year-old enjoys urinating, defaecating and associated activities. In the third year, genital sensations predominate. The child's pleasure in sensations from his sexual organs is no longer centred entirely on himself. With growing awareness of sex differences it becomes related to other people, especially the parent of the opposite sex. This is the famous Oedipal stage during which the boy is said to love and wish to possess his mother, and to regard his father as a feared and hated, although also loved, rival. The anxieties generated by this conflict are supposed to be resolved by a compromise. The boy cannot replace his father, but he can be like him. He begins to identify himself with his father's commands, prohibitions, standards and social values, and makes them his own. This 'interiorization' of social values, given additional impetus by unexpressed anger, marks the beginning of what is commonly called conscience. The process is consolidated during the following 'latent' period until puberty. A somewhat similar development is supposed to follow in the girl who resolves her conflict over loving and hating her mother by identifying with her and so assuming her social role as a girl and woman.

The picture of libidinal development is that of a stream which must find an outlet. It may unconsciously be canalized, or redirected (sublimated). But if it is dammed up, it will run a subterranean, unrecognized (repressed) course, and erupt in unsuitable places. Over-indulgence as well as frustration may produce this, fixing the libido at one or other of the developmental stages. The stability and resilience of his inherited biological make-up, and the degree and frequency of traumatic experiences at vital developmental stages would determine the extent to which an individual can withstand later stress, or will break down into neurotic illness. But even the healthiest child of the most enlightened parents will experience frustrations and conflicts in developing from an infant, with insistent, chaotic urges, to an adult who can defer his satisfactions and adapt them to what is socially acceptable. To resolve the conflicts, disturbing feelings or wishes may be repressed so that the child is no longer aware of them, or they may be transformed into their opposite. The child, for whom indulging in anal messes is made too frightening, may become obsessively clean and meticulous. Alternatively, disquieting feelings may be attributed to others or even to objects. A good deal of play is supposed to be projection of this kind. Not oneself, but dolls, imaginary companions, evil witches or wizards behave maliciously; roast the mother doll on the stove, and kill everyone in sight. It is other people who are naughty, or tell one to do wrong. Another way of dealing with frightening wishes is to substitute an object which makes them harmless. Immersing the baby-doll in water, or throwing it against the wall relieves the jealous brother's feelings without harming the new baby. Unless anxiety is so great that all play is inhibited, the wishes and conflicts of each developmental stage will be reflected in the child's play, directly, or by substitute, symbolic activities. Blowing bubbles may go back to oral over-indulgence or frustration. Sand and water-play are acceptable substitutes for 'soiling and wetting'. A child may express his feelings openly in play, like the two-year-old girl who was observed to dance about, holding a toy broom in the correct position, and chanting happily 'I've got a peenah (penis)' after having had sex differences explained to her. Usually the substitutes would be more obscurely symbolic. Thwarted interest in pro-creation may give rise to interminable pseudo-questions at the genital stage. In the period of identification, the boy will pretend to be his father or a bus driver, the girl will play at being mother. Unsatisfied urges may be redirected into socially acceptable channels. According to Freud, the im-petus to seek knowledge, and to produce art and civilization derives from the sublimation of libidinal impulses.

Freud's early view that in play events are so altered as to fit in with the child's wishes did not later seem to him to account entirely for the frequency with which unpleasant experiences are repeated in play. Children who greatly dislike taking medicine dose their dolls and teddies. A fright-ening accident or fire witnessed by them will be graphically re-enacted. In a later formulation of his theory(126) Freud refers to a hypothesis by the German physiologist, Fechner, who was one of the great early names in the school of psy-chology concerned with psycho-physical and physiological problems. Fechner in 1873 applied the recently discovered principle of conservation of energy to living organisms. Organisms, in order not to disintegrate into their physical surroundings, must keep their internal conditions in as constant and stable a state as possible. This is the principle of homeostasis, held in one form or another by most biolo-gists(36). Fechner assumed that events occurring in an organism give rise to pleasure in so far as they contribute to the organism's stability, and to pain if they upset this stab-ility. Consequently, if the organism is excited by external stimuli, it must act to restore the previous condition. Freud's view was that organisms try to keep the level of nervous tension as low as possible, and that all increases in excitation are felt as unpleasant, decreases of excitation as pleasurable.

Exciting events, i.e. unpleasant tensions and conflicts are repeated in phantasy or in play because repetition reduces the excitement which has been aroused. Play enables the child to master the disturbing event or situation by actively bringing it about, rather than being a passive and helpless spectator. Playing to master disturbing events is still an explanation in terms of striving for pleasure and escape from pain, since the repetition is held to reduce the unpleasant disturbance. In his final speculations Freud assigned to the impulse to repeat a status equal to libidinal strivings. According to this, the impulse to repeat, and hence play, are part of the urge to restore an earlier, more stable, condition of the organism. There is no state so stable and quiescent as death. In addition to the urge to live, Freud now postulated an instinct impelling the organism towards death and destruction. Very few even among Freud's followers accepted these later speculations, the paradox that the aim of living is to die, or that play is a manifestation of compulsive repetition. But his view that play is due to an impulse to master events had wide currency.

Explanations in terms of some kind of 'energy' which is not the same as energy in physics have gone out of fashion (this will be discussed in the following section). But psychoanalytic theory was never in the main stream of academic psychology. The most cogent reason for this is the difficulty of testing Freud's hypotheses experimentally. Freud mainly dealt with the individual human moral predicament which is difficult to re-create in the laboratory. Psychoanalysis cannot provide these tests. It is essentially a method of clinical diagnosis more allied to detective procedures than to experimental methods which, ideally, specify the conditions under which a given behaviour will occur, and test this by varying these conditions systematically. Free association includes no sufficient check on bias in the therapist's interpretation or on compliance by the patient. Nevertheless, Freud greatly influenced psychological thinking. His impact on child psychology was probably due to the fact that his description of the child's emotional and social development provided a coherent framework for a number of isolated facts at a time when there were few or no coherent explanations of these. His emphasis on the effects of early experiences, on the influence of various types of discipline of feeding, weaning, toilet training, on social behaviour, gave rise to a number of inquiries by investigators who did not necessarily accept his theories.

Freud's explanations of phantasy and play as the projection of wishes and the re-enactment of conflicts and unpleasant events in order to master them led to techniques of personality assessment based on the assumption that play and phantasy reveal something about the inner life and motivation of the individual. Imaginative play with dolls, making up stories to pictures or inkblots and other projective devices have been used both for clinical diagnoses and in research (262: ch. XV & XVII).* They have also been severely criticized.

The most direct influence of Freud's views on play was on the various forms of therapy for disturbed children which derived from psychoanalysis. Most of these used spontaneous play: some as a substitute for the verbal free association of adult therapy, others as a form of catharsis, or as an aid to communicating with the children, or simply in order to observe them. Play-therapy will be discussed in a later chapter. Until recently the majority of publications on children's play have been almost entirely concerned with the use of play as a technique for personality research, and in the diagnosis and treatment of disturbed children.

Other Instinct Theories; Ethological Investigation of 'Irrelevant' and 'Useless' Behaviour

A good deal of both animal and human behaviour invites description in terms of striving towards goals or satisfying needs which fulfil definite functions in keeping the individual or the species alive. In some animals these patterns are rigid

* All numbers in brackets refer to items in the bibliography. Roman numerals following a colon refer to the preceding number.

and stereotyped and unlearned. In others, especially the higher mammals and man, they are subject to learning and experience, but can, nevertheless, not be explained in terms of reasoning or foresight on the part of the individual. 'Instinct' served as a portmanteau term for these.

At the turn of the century, the picture of an energy store in analogy with gas and water as sources of power was often used to describe the workings of instincts. The English psychologist, William McDougall, for instance, listed fourteen major instincts, drawing their force from a common energy pool but each having a separate channel or motor-mechanism directing the energy to its own goal. Play occurred as an overspill from the pool into all the existing channels. An instinct consisted in an inherited tendency to act in a certain way, attended by a characteristic emotion, and an innate tendency to notice features of the environment relevant to its goal. Instincts were thought to combine in various ways through learning and experience into lasting attitudes and sentiments which motivate adult behaviour. The forceful simplicity of McDougall's account showed up the difficulty of the instinct concept better than most. For instance, if primary instincts are due to organic deficits, vitamin deficiencies and heat loss must be included with hunger and sex as important instincts, while curiosity becomes the odd man out. Yet the tendency to explore is almost universal. More difficult still, any number of lists of instincts could be, and were, produced.

The study of animal behaviour in its natural setting and its analysis under experimental conditions (ethology), especially the investigations of K. Lorenz and N. Tinbergen(361), at first gave the instinct and energy type of theory a new impetus, but they also transformed it. Ethologists have not, until very recently, been specifically concerned with play. But the detailed study of the conditions which determine biologically useful behaviour also necessitated the study of biologically 'irrelevant' and 'useless' behaviour to which play belongs.

Vacuum Activities

In a now famous fish, the stickleback, occupying a territory, fighting intruding males, nest building, mating and the
care of offspring occur in sequence, and each phase of the
sequence depends upon the presence of appropriate stimuli.
Tinbergen showed that only intruding males with red
'nuptial' markings are fought by the male stickleback about
to mate. The red colour is the important cue. Whether
fighting will take the form of chasing or biting depends on
yet other stimuli. The intruder is bitten only if he slaps the
territory owner in a fashion which can be imitated with a
glass rod by the experimenting ethologist. After the fish has
established his territory, and built a nest, he performs a sort
of zigzag dance, but only on seeing a female with a swollen
abdomen (containing eggs) whom he conducts to the nest
by the dance.

On occasions, however, sticklebacks apparently dance
in a completely empty tank; a somewhat useless procedure
which may appear to be performed 'for fun'. Hand-reared
female canaries who have never been given material for
building nests make appropriate nest building movements
when in breeding condition even in empty nest-pans (164).

These sorts of behaviour were originally called 'vacuum'
or overflow activities. It was supposed that, in certain circumstances, internal conditions such as hormone production
and the like would build up to such an extent that the innate
stereotyped motor patterns which normally end a behaviour
sequence (e.g. mating, eating: the 'consummatory' acts)
would be released by less appropriate stimuli than those
normally necessary, or would go off without any stimuli at
all. Whether 'vacuum behaviour', in the sense of behaviour
not influenced by any external stimuli at all occurs, would
be difficult to establish. In many cases, behaviour which
appears to be useless, or irrelevant turns out to have quite
specific stimuli and uses. Beach(25), commenting that to
call an action 'play' is frequently merely a confession of
ignorance, refers to a species of fish who have the habit of

leaping over sticks and other objects floating in the water. This looks like an enjoyable game. Actually it scratches parasites off the fishes' back.

Displacement

Investigations of another type of apparently irrelevant or inappropriate behaviour called 'displacement' activities, also show this. It sometimes happens that an animal, engaged in some biologically useful activity, suddenly turns away to do something quite different. Fighting cocks peck at the ground as if feeding, a herring gull may interrupt a fight to pluck at nesting material, and some birds wipe their bills or preen themselves during courtship. The interpolated or 'displaced' activity is normally part of quite a different biological sequence from the ongoing one. It often belongs to general body-cleaning. Displacement has been shown to occur particularly when the ongoing activity is checked or two incompatible reactions are equally aroused. The male stickleback fights other males on his home ground, but flees from them outside his territory. At the boundary of his territory, where he has to be equally ready for either of these incompatible responses, a male upon seeing another frequently shows digging movements as if building a nest. Such 'displacement' digging has been produced experimentally by making a red dummy 'attack and defeat' a male in his own territory and then holding it still. The routed male will return and just before he renews the fight he 'digs'. Tinbergen originally held that the incompatible responses (e.g. fleeing and fighting) hold each other in check, so preventing a discharge of excitation through either response. Energy generated in centres controlling each of these activities within the central nervous system, further charged both from higher centres, and from various internal and external sensory stimuli, would 'spark over' or be displaced on to the centre of another instinctive activity and so find an outlet. However, it has been shown that when birds stop in the middle of some activity to preen their feathers it is not merely because the ongoing activity has received some temporary check, but also because the stimuli which normally call out preening are actually present. Chaffinches, when offered food and frightened at the same time, will show more signs of preening, scratching and other forms of grooming if their feathers have been sprinkled with water(309).

'Intention Movements'

Movements, unrelated to the presumed 'goal' of an activity can occur where some, but not all the conditions for the total activity are present. For instance, keen hunting cats were given one mouse after another. The effect of different degrees of satiety showed in the order in which different activities dropped out. First the cats stopped eating, but still killed the mice. Then killing stopped, but they still stalked and caught the mice. Later the cats no longer bothered to catch the mice, but continued stalking, especially those farthest away while ignoring those that ran over their paws (224). 'Toying' with food often occurs when animals are no longer hungry but food is still present. Doves eat less than normal when thirsty, but continue to show some feeding behaviour. They pick up food in their bills, drop it again, return to the food and 'play' with it, but eat less(232). These forms of intention movements are sometimes called 'play', but only in the extended sense of 'toying' with something.

Incomplete Activities in the Young

Another useless, out of context, and apparently bio-logically irrelevant activity occurs during the development of an individual. Parts of the adult mating pattern are present in many mammals before they are sexually mature, and the play of young mammals often includes these(26). Very young birds may show the 'quivering' movements made by adults to fasten twigs in the nest, but which are without function in the young bird. In the normal adult

sequence exploring and seeking appropriate objects precedes eating, building, mating, etc., which end each part of
a sequence. In the young, these stereotyped movement
patterns occur without any evidence of 'need' or seeking a
goal. It is only during the course of development that they
come under the control of appropriate stimuli, and become
integrated into a complete sequence. Newborn chicks can
peck perfectly, but have to learn which objects are edible.
Yet they peck at round rather than triangular shapes(109).
This must make it easier for them to learn to peck at grains
rather than inedibles. Young birds are able to make drinking
motions before ever having drunk water. Such learning is
often innately favoured. The young respond to generalized
characteristics of the objects they learn to select. A combination of brightness, reflection, and movement of a surface
elicits drinking motion in young birds even if it happens to
come from a mirror rather than water and so makes the
attempt irrelevant. The play-like pouncing reported of an
owl which had been reared without experience of live
prey(359) may depend on an innate sensitivity to certain
general characteristics like movement and size which are
narrowed down to appropriate objects with experience.
The typical play of kittens, like chasing and pouncing upon
balls of knitting wool may be of this type.

'Surplus Energy'

The function of external stimulation in 'irrelevant' behaviour is only one aspect of the problem. Appropriate
stimuli fail to arouse a response unless the necessary
internal conditions are present. Seasonal and maturational
variations in hormone production alter the threshold at
which given external stimuli become effective in reproductive activities. Activity in the central nervous system and
brain is involved. As these conditions are becoming known
in detail, the relation between innate movements, the condition of the organism's central nervous system and the
external stimulation is no longer usefully or correctly

described in terms of building up and spilling over of energy (163, 289, 397).

The concept of surplus energy has died hard probably because it carries with it the suggestion of felt urges, observed persistence of behaviour in the face of obstacles, the undoubted fact that organisms are physical systems which use physical energy, and because it seems to answer the question why organisms act. However, organisms do not have to be prodded into action. They are active by virtue of being alive. The relation between a felt urge, bodily arrangements for mobilizing and using energy, innate movement patterns and biological usefulness are understood all the better for being analysed separately. Neither the facts of biologically useful nor of irrelevant behaviour require, or are well described by, instinct-energy explanations(165). Concepts of instincts can now be seen for what they are: labels attached to classifications of behaviour patterns in terms of their individual end-states such as eating, fighting or mating; or in terms of their biological function: reproductive activities, body-surface maintenance and so forth. More recently, classifications tend to be in terms of the homeostatic systems which regulate the energy exchanges between the organism and its environment. For instance, the regulation of body temperature, or of water-balance are conveniently classed as systems in terms of the mechanisms required for their control.

What is included in a classification of a given behaviour may vary with how much is known about it, its prevalence in a species, the conditions sufficient and necessary for its occurrence, and the frequency with which it occurs in a given context. For instance, Tinbergen found that the displacement digging, i.e. pseudo-nest building of the male stickleback at the boundary of his territory, functions as a threat to other males. Some of the love-play of animals which commonly occurs when one of the partners is not sufficiently aroused often includes 'displaced' activities. It has been reported that a male corncrake, after twenty-three attempts to copulate with a stuffed female, went off to find a caterpillar, and offered it to her as an inducement(8).

It has been suggested that 'vacuum' and 'displacement' activities should be distinguished from 'true play', because, playful activity is not tied to specific goals or biological necessities, but occurs only when activities have become detached from the main course necessary for the maintenance of the animal and its species(359). It is doubtful whether such distinctions can be applied rigidly. Some activities, usually called play, have some of the hallmarks of biologically necessary behaviour which occurs out of context or out of sequence(181). There is no need to prejudge the issue on questions about play which are just beginning to be investigated. If all instances of what in ordinary language is called 'play' turned out to be parts of biologically useful behaviour patterns occurring under specifiable conditions, this would advance our knowledge, but hardly necessitate a change in ordinary language.

Learning Theories and Play

The main effect that learning or behaviour theory has had on the psychology of play is that the subject as such no longer exists. The position, as expressed by Schlosberg in 1948(319), is simple. Play is a totally vague, scientifically useless concept. It covers a motley of behaviours which ought to be investigated separately. According to Schlosberg, some of the established findings from experiments on learning will be found to explain different types of play. For instance, in the early stages of learning to discriminate one coloured lamp from others, the learner will press the key reserved for that lamp also in response to other lamps near it in colour or position. It is known that, by and large, children make more such mistakes than adults. They discriminate less well, or generalize more(243). Schlosberg thought that a number of instances of play could be explained in this way. A puppy chasing a rolling ball is making a generalized response to a small moving object. In general, too, an action which is rewarded by food, praise or other learned incentives, tends to be repeated when some of the circumstances in which the original learning took place are present. A pat on the head for the dog who brings a ball to his master reinforces the dog's behaviour so that retrieving the ball will be set off by the sight of the ball or the master. A child may climb a tree or try to balance a ball on his nose because he has received praise for similar activities in the past. The expectation of being applauded for competence as well as other learned social incentives may account for a good deal of play. 'Look at me, Mummy, look what I can do!', is a well-known accompaniment of young children's play. Schlosberg suggests that some play may also be explicable in terms of a lowered threshold in rested animals to stimuli which would be too weak to arouse a response in a tired or preoccupied one, and refers to the possibility that some kinds of play fall into the category of out-of-sequence behaviour of the kind studied by ethologists.

The view that play needs no special explanation other than that found to hold for behaviour in general unfortunately also resulted in a dearth of experimental studies of the conditions under which various types of play actually occur. However, a revival of interest within the last fifteen years in curiosity and the role of attention in learning, is promising to contribute to our knowledge of another aspect of play: play as a response to novelty and change.

Russian Studies and the Orienting Reflex

American learning theorists of the 1930s and 1940s were most influenced by two types of earlier investigations: the conditioned reflex studies of the Russian physiologists Bechterev (1857–1927) and Pavlov (1849–1919) on the one hand, and the puzzle-box experiments of the American E. L. Thorndike (1874–1949) on the other. As is well-known, Pavlov, in his studies of the digestive system of dogs, found that flow of saliva, an unlearned reflex response to food in the mouth would, with repetition, occur at the sight of the food-dish alone, or even on hearing the footsteps of the attendant bringing it. The unlearned reflex had become 'conditioned' to a new stimulus which signalled the food. The effect, confirmed by innumerable well-controlled experiments, was taken as a paradigm of all learning, from the simplest to the most complex. If a tone is paired with food, the dog will salivate to all kinds of tones. The response generalizes. If one tone is paired with food while another is sounded without it, the dog will learn to discriminate between them. He will come to respond to the correct one only, since conditioned responses which are no longer followed by the original unconditioned stimulus gradually undergo extinction. Pavlov found that whenever something novel was introduced, however apparently irrelevant, it would interfere with whatever the animal was doing. The animal would stop, become alert, prick up its ears, and turn in the direction of the new stimulus. Pavlov called it the investigatory or 'what is it?' reflex, and considered it the basis of exploring, and essential to stable conditioning or learning (277).

The 'orienting' reflex, as it is now usually called, has been studied extensively in Russia in recent years(339). It is a response to any new stimulus, and has two main effects: a general one of alerting or arousing the individual, and more specific effects which increase sensitivity to receiving specific sensory stimuli and expose the organism to the maximum information while inhibiting ongoing activities and related stimuli. If the novel stimulus is not followed by food, danger or anything of significance to the animal, the reaction subsides. If further changes or significant events follow, the orienting responses go on much longer. The discrimination and selection of stimuli which is essential before any new association can be formed depends on the presence of orienting reactions, according to these investigators(228).

On this theory, curiosity, exploration, the urge to investigate is traced to the orienting reflex, the unlearned response to novelty or change. Since this means that the animal may attend to stimuli other than those already connected with rewards or dangers, 'aimless' investigations, and hence some aspects of play are not difficult to explain by it. However, the orienting reflex had not yet come into prominence when the American behaviourists first encountered Pavlov's work.

Motivation in American Learning Theories

The early behaviourists, especially Watson, regarded explanations in terms of instincts as sterile, and were violently impatient of the current introspective method which had produced inconclusive arguments, and was useless with children and animals. The objectivity and experimental precision of Pavlov's methods, his description of results in terms of observable bits of behaviour and physiological mechanisms, and the fact that his theory explained behaviour in terms of learning, assuming only a minimum of unlearned reflexes, could not fail to make an impact on Watson and the later learning theorists who were influenced by him.

The learning theory put forward by Guthrie in 1935 was closest to Watson's adoption of Pavlov's system. It postulated a simple association between a response, thought of as some movement, or glandular secretion, and any stimulus, or combination of them, which has accompanied it, as the principal law of learning. Motivation was irrelevant to this. The movements, internal or overt, of a hungry animal are different from those of a satiated one, and so become associated with different cues. Reward improves learning not *qua* reward, but because it ends a given series of movements, and so preserves the connexion between it and whatever the animal was doing last from disintegrating by interference from other movements. Aimless behaviour presents no difficulty on this account. Guthrie's ingenuity made it account for purposeful actions too.

The most influential learning theory in English-speaking countries, that of C. L. Hull(173), was more affected by Thorndike's assumption that reward is important in learning. The typical 'trial and error' learning cats exhibited in Thorndike's puzzle boxes provided an alternative learning paradigm to Pavlov's conditioning procedure. The cats at first appeared to move randomly, accidentally hitting the puzzle device which opened their cage door to food and freedom. Hitting the puzzle device gradually improved with the number of successful trials. Thorndike describes this by assuming that connexions between stimuli in the box and responses are strengthened by being rewarded.

Hull's carefully worked out system of postulates, based on empirical findings, and formulated so that testable deductions could be made, was far more elaborate and precise. It assumed that reward is essential to learning. Behaviour is motivated by primary drives, i.e. physiological deficits like hunger which give rise to strong internal stimuli. Reward consists in the reduction of a drive state aroused by physiological needs and the stimuli to which they give rise. A typical experiment, with variations too numerous to be mentioned, is that of hungry rats running through cages, constructed in the form of mazes, to goal-boxes containing food. Being hungry – measured by the number of hours a rat had been deprived of food – and getting some food at the end of the run, are essential to learning the maze. The food reduces the hunger-drive and so reinforces the connexion between the cues of the correct alleyways (their position, brightness, etc.) and the running responses which were instrumental to getting the food. It has been shown that the presence of some originally quite innocuous cue, if it became associated with pain, was sufficient for the rat to learn a new puzzle device which allowed it to avoid it. So a whole array of 'secondary' drives could be learned(248). Praise, being given money or toys are secondary rewards which have become effective through previous learning based on the reduction of some primary drive. The child learns to imitate his parents and older children because matching his behaviour to that of the older and stronger has led to desirable results more often than not in the past(247). The long period of human childhood during which needs are satisfied by the mother and other people will give rise to secondary motives which make verbal and social incentives effective. Nor is it necessary that the original reward should actually be given every time a child engages in a particular activity. It is sufficient if some of the external cues or internal stimuli connected previously with reduction of drive are present. Stimuli produced by the animal's own responses may mediate, acting as signals for rewards(273). On this theory, behaviour like play which is engaged in without apparent reward is explained as reinforced by secondary, learned cues signalling rewards, or mediated by stimuli produced by the animal's own responses.

Skinner's(331) learning theory is more concerned with laws describing how stimuli, responses and rewards (reinforcements) vary with each other, than with the mechanisms by which learning is achieved. He distinguished between responses elicited by stimuli, and 'operant' behaviour which occurs anyway but is 'shaped' by being reinforced selectively. He showed that one of the factors which keeps a habit going is the rate and timing of reinforcement during learning (113), especially if this is irregularly spaced (not easily predicted by the learner). A bird, learning to peck at a lever that brings it food pellets at every peck will quickly stop pecking when food no longer follows. If, however, the food pellets have previously come at irregular intervals, the birds will go on pecking much longer. It has been suggested that this is much more like the child's situation. No parent can reinforce (praise, reward) a given behaviour each time it occurs. Apparently unrewarded behaviour may simply be behaviour carried over from previously irregular rewards. Rewards given at regular short intervals without any reference to actual behaviour, may produce odd and senseless actions, on the other hand. Hungry birds were given bits of food at regular short intervals regardless of what they were doing. The result was that whatever movement the bird happened to make when the food-tray appeared eventually became conditioned to it. By the end of the experiment some birds were bowing, others tossing their heads until the food-tray reappeared, and continued this for 10,000 more times after it had been removed permanently(330). Possibly some play develops in this way.

Learning and Attention to Change

The question whether reward, in the sense of reducing drive, is the *sine qua non* of learning has long given rise to some interesting issues about learning. Here only its relevance to problems about play can be mentioned. Exploring and playing with objects 'for their own sake' occurs precisely when the animal appears most comfortable and least driven by physiological needs and their derivatives. On Hull's assumption this either cannot lead to learning, or if it does, must be due to secondary drives.

Tolman, another of the great learning theorists of the 1930s and 1940s(362), held that reward aids performance rather than learning. A rat will learn a good deal about a maze even if it is not hungry and gets no food. This shows in the superior performance of these animals in learning to run from the entrance to food-box when they are hungry, over animals without previous experience of the maze. That learning can occur in these conditions is now generally accepted(354) although animals learn better when they are moderately hungry or otherwise motivated, and get a reward.

Reformulated, Hull's theory can account for this by assuming separate effects of drive on learning and performance(174). A very small amount of reward or secondary reward is sufficient for learning. Simply seeing the food when not hungry would do. But for performance, strength of habit plus strength of drive are required.

However, an increasing variety of facts was awkwardly accommodated by the original theory. For instance, rats given an equal choice of entering one of two arms in a Y-shaped maze, prefer the arm which presents some novelty or change, when there is no other reward. It was shown that this was not due to a fatigue-like process inhibiting the last movement made from being repeated, as would be predicted by another of Hull's postulates(137), but rather a response to change in the external stimulation(345). A series of experiments on monkeys by Harlow and Butler showed that these animals will learn puzzles for no other reward than the opportunity to do another one. If placed in uniformly lit covered boxes, they will open an aperture in the box many times to look at another monkey or an electric train, or merely for the chance to look out(62, 63, 149). Even baby monkeys who had had as yet no solid food or any experience which would associate handling objects with the reduction of a primary drive, would manipulate small puzzles put at the end of their cages almost endlessly(150). Harlow postulated exploratory and manipulative 'drives' to account for the fact that learning occurred under these conditions. This suggests that external stimuli motivate behaviour in the same way as internal stimuli from physiological deficits. But exploration and manipulation 'needs' do not fit in easily with the notion of drives aroused by physiological deficits which have to be made good. To classify exploring, manipulating and play with sex and hunger merely makes the concept of drives as useless as the older notion of instincts. Nor does it help to explain a variety of other findings which make 'drive-reduction' as the sole explanation of motives difficult. Hungry animals and humans will work for food and, within limits, work more assiduously the more they have been deprived of it. But animals, with lesions in specific areas of the brain, and many rich men and women over-eat(352). Animals will learn if given saccharin solutions as rewards although these cannot make good a food-deficit. Increasing the 'drive' for water by injections of salt-solution increases drinking, but does not necessarily increase learning something in order to get water(161). More rather than less stimulation may be sought. Rats, pigeons, cats and men with electrodes implanted in special areas of their brains will repeatedly and persistently press buttons which turn on electrical currents and so give themselves mild shocks(270, 271, 154). 'Boredom' can have quite spectacular effects. The evidence comes from adults placed on comfortable beds in soundproof, silent rooms, wearing ear-plugs, goggles which diffuse the light and so effectively prevent perception, cylinders encasing their arms and legs which restrict sensations from body movements. The majority of the paid volunteers (psychology students) intensely disliked the experience (115: ch. V, 398). Some could not continue it beyond the first few hours, others sought stimulation by whistling or trying to move. A feeling of not being able to control their thoughts, hallucinations and distortions of perception were reported in the original experiments.

Less extreme symptoms of fatigue, restlessness and irritability together with loss of efficiency occur with long-continued, repetitive tasks such as monitoring radar screens where signals appear at infrequent and irregular intervals. Introducing changes in the task or in the situation improves performance almost immediately(49). Slight changes, such as different illumination, sends up the rate of bar-pressing in rats(161), and production in factories, for a while. Changing back to the original illumination after an interval has the same effect. Given a choice, adults look more often at incongruous pictures, such as four-footed birds, than at ordinary ones, prefer complex to simple drawings, and patterns which are surprising because they differ from preceding ones(34).

According to Berlyne(34), investigation, exploration and manipulation are called out by relative novelty, change, surprisingness, incongruity, conflict, complexity and uncertainty in the stimulation. These arouse the organism's mechanisms for emergency action. Absolute novelty may be ignored as meaningless; abrupt change may be avoided, but relative novelty which fits partly but not wholly with what has been experienced before; change from what has gone before; incompatibilities in a present pattern; conflict due to simultaneously aroused but incompatible responses, or uncertainty due to discrepancies in expectation, alert the individual. The arousal is reduced by exploration and investigation. The process of becoming alerted may become pleasurable because it has been followed by a reduction of excitation, and is, therefore, associated with reward. Suspense, even moderate fear, may be enjoyed as thrills.

There are other possible explanations. Organisms may need some 'optimal' amount of stimulation rather than a reduction of drive. Consequently, if the level of incoming stimulation is too low, they will seek to enhance it or reduce it if it is too high. Exploration or play may belong to the former category, or possibly exploring may reduce arousal, while play enhances it, and is a response to boredom or lack of stimulation. It has been suggested that an optimal level of stimulation does not only depend on the amount of actual stimulation, but also on the organism's ability to deal with it – classify or code it in some way(87).

The emphasis shifted from questions about degrees and kinds of motivation to questions about stimulus conditions; from questions as to why the rat runs into a given alley of a maze to what sort of alley it runs to most; in what kind of stimulus arrangements it will learn most quickly, and be able to transfer that learning to a new problem. Noticing external cues came to be considered essential in the chain of responses to be shaped by reinforcements(388). Questions about learning involve questions about attention and the kind of stimuli upon which an animal is most likely to act(234, 344). One class of these is the 'eliciting' stimuli of the ethologists, determined by the organism's structure and early learning. Another is the cues which have acquired signal value from conditioning and association with reward studied by the learning theorists. Another dimension of stimulation, long recognized as important, is its intensity. There may also be a preferred mode of sensing. Sounds may prevail over sights for a species – other things being equal; or colour may win out over black and white. Novelty, and the appreciation of change and differences generally, whether in the external stimulation itself, or enhanced by discrepant expectation, are those most frequently mentioned in connexion with exploring and investigating.

Whether play is determined by the same stimulus characteristics as exploring; how timing of changes and repetition, or characteristics such as complexity and surprisingness affect play, and whether all play is equally dependent on these are still mainly questions for study, and will be considered further later.

The Contribution of Gestalt and Field Theories

Three German psychologists, Wertheimer, Koffka and Köhler, investigating perception in the early twentieth century, were mainly responsible for the description of psychological processes in terms of 'Gestalten' (literally, figures or configurations). A number of their experimental findings did not fit in with the older view which explained perception in terms of separate sensations. A rapidly presented series of static pictures showing successive movements of an object or a person is perceived as a moving object or person. A spot of colour on white paper is seen as a different hue when it is put on a black or grey or differently coloured background. Animals taught to choose a medium grey rather than light grey box for food, and then given a choice of the medium grey and a dark grey one, will prefer the dark grey, showing that they were influenced not by the absolute colour of each, but by the colour relation between the boxes. Rapidly presented incomplete circles are seen as complete circles. Such findings led to the Gestalt school of view that animal and human behaviour is a function of the total pattern or situation at any given moment rather than of separate stimuli.

In a book in 1924(197) Koffka applied Gestalt school principles to child development. One of these implies that a response is aroused as soon as a perception occurs because both belong to a single configuration. Seeing a piano and striking the keys belong to one pattern; so the perception immediately arouses the response. Passing by a door-bell makes the child want to ring it. There is an immediate structural connexion between the perception of a given pattern and an action appropriate to it. This accounts for imitation: the baby's babbling in response to talk, the pet chimpanzee or the toddler dusting furniture, or putting on lipstick. Perceiving the result arouses the impulse to the same action in the beholder because the action is part of a total pattern. Imaginative play occurs because the child's world is less differentiated than that of the adult. The child sees no contradiction in cuddling or stroking a stick as if it were a baby. A stick or a doll can be stroked, and the fact that its other features do not correspond to the concept of a baby is as yet irrelevant. The child does not 'animate' his world. He merely has not yet learned to distinguish what is alive from what is not. His perceptions are less differentiated and hence evoke actions which, to the adult, seem inappropriate.

Kurt Lewin (1890–1947), originally a member of the Berlin Gestalt school, extended and elaborated many of their concepts in his *Field Theory*(217). The behaviour of an individual depends on the total situation in which he finds himself. His responses will vary with his age, personality, present state, and all the factors present in his environment at any given moment. Whether a balloon is a coveted toy or looks dangerous will depend on the child's age and development, as well as on the context in which he sees it. A child may be negative in one situation, shy in another, at ease in a third. His mother's presence may, for the young child, transform a frightening situation into an enjoyable one. The child's world is different when he is tired or hungry. It is different for him at the age of two than it is when he is four years old, even if the physical characteristics of the environment remain the same. Psychology, according to Lewin, is not the only discipline in which a totality of mutually interrelated facts have to be analysed. This is the case in physics too. A physical field is described in terms of mutually interrelated forces. In analogy, the total psychological situation, the facts about a person and his environment, may also be regarded as a field of forces. Its dynamic structure can be described in terms of the mathematical concepts of topology – the geometry of space. Vectors in the physical field define forces through properties such as direction and strength. The direction of a child's actions will be determined by positive and negative 'valences' in the psychological field.

A toy which has a positive valence is one which is approached, an object with a negative valence will produce withdrawal. Interest, for instance, becomes graphically a situation in which there is a toy in a given place. Its attractiveness can be measured in terms of the number of moves the child makes in its direction. It is possible to discover the effects of obstacles on his behaviour by literally blocking the child's direct path to an attractive toy. The younger the child, the less differentiated are his needs, the part played by family, friends and activities. Development is in the direction of greater differentiation. The boundaries in the infant's psychological field are less firm than in the adult's. He is more easily influenced. There is also a 'vertical' stratification into planes of reality and various strata of unreality. The most unreal of these are the planes of dreams and wishes where the individual can do as he pleases and what is wished for is obtained in phantasy. Some of the peculiarities of children's play result from confusing reality and wishes. The meaning of objects and the child's own roles are fluid. A piece of cardboard, caressed as a baby one minute, may be torn up the next. Since objects have not yet a fixed character, substitutes are more acceptable, although this varies with different situations.

Gestalt and Field theories are not generally accepted as adequate models today, although the Gestalt school's experiments helped to revolutionize theories of perception and thinking. Translating psychological problems into questions of the direction and force of various subgroupings in a geographical field produced some interesting experiments. Those concerned with the effects of barring a child from attractive toys he can see, and with the conditions under which children will accept substitute objects for the purposes of play, will be mentioned later.

Jean Piaget's Theory of Play

Demands on child psychologists for practical advice over educational and behaviour difficulties led to investigations of play mainly as a tool in educational and therapeutic techniques. Explanations were taken eclectically from available theories, mainly neo-Freudian or neo-Hullian (216). Psychologists studying normal development, on the other hand, were largely concerned with factual description and classification. The child psychologist Stern divided play into individual and social play, each of these having sub-categories. Individual play includes mastery of bodily activities like running and jumping, mastery of objects in constructive and destructive games, and transformation of objects and people by impersonation. Social play includes games of imitation and fighting. Another child psychologist, Charlotte Bühler(56), classified play into functional games using the child's sensory-motor apparatus, games of make-believe and illusion, passive play such as looking at books, and games of construction. These, as well as definitions of play in terms of the pleasure that the child takes in his own functions, and in the pleasure of 'being a cause', are essentially chapter headings.

A major exception to this is the developmental psychology of Jean Piaget (b. 1896), who is professor at the University of Geneva, and director of the Institut Rousseau. Originally a zoologist studying snails, he had already started his immense number of publications at the age of ten(116). His biological training and his interest in philosophy, especially in the theory of knowledge, led him to study the intellectual development of children in the belief that the logical analysis of 'knowing' can be illuminated by facts about how children actually come to think logically. In turn, especially in his later investigations, he uses logical models to analyse his findings on children's reasoning at various ages.

Piaget's theory of play is closely bound up with his account of the growth of intelligence(283). He postulates two processes which he believes to be fundamental to all organic development: assimilation and accommodation. The simplest example of assimilation is eating. Food is changed in the process of being taken in and made part of the organism. Accommodation is the organism's adjustment to the external world, as for instance in posture; changing course to avoid an obstacle, or contracting eye-muscles in bright light. The two processes are complementary and involve each other. If the food particles to be assimilated are large, the animal has to open its mouth wide. A number of physical and chemical processes go on in the organism accommodating it to the type of food received, at the same time changing what is being digested. Piaget uses the terms assimilation and accommodation in a wider sense to apply to intellectual processes. Assimilation refers to any process whereby the organism changes the information it receives, in the process of making it part of the organism's know-how. Information is, as it were, digested. Accommodation means any adjustment the organism has to make to the external world in order to assimilate information. Intellectual development is due to the continual, active interplay between assimilating and accommodating. Intelligent adaptation occurs when the two processes balance each other, or are 'in equilibrium'. When they are not, accommodation or adjustment to the object may predominate over assimilation. This results in imitation. Alternatively, assimilation – fitting the impression in with previous experience and adapting it to the individual's needs – may predominate. This is play. It is pure assimilation which changes incoming information to suit the individual's requirements(285). Play and imitation are an integral part of the development of intelligence, and, consequently, go through the same stages.

Piaget distinguishes four major periods in intellectual development; each with a number of sub-stages. From birth until about eighteen months is the sensory-motor period. According to Piaget, the infant starts with uncoordinated impressions from different senses which he is as yet unable to distinguish from his own reflex responses to them. During this time he gradually achieves the sense and motor coordinations and adjustments necessary to perceive and manipulate objects in space and time and to see causal connexions between them.

In the next major period, the representative stage, from

the age of about two to seven or eight, these achievements are repeated on the symbolic and verbal plane. From merely being able to envisage objects in their absence, the child learns to symbolize a whole universe of objects and relations between them. But he is as yet unable to regard these from any point of view except his own. This 'egocentrism' is not egotism or selfishness, but forced attention to one aspect of any event. This makes it impossible to reason logically, since logical operations involve being able to reverse the constituents in a chain of reasoning, and seeing their implications from a number of standpoints. At this stage, the child cannot group objects on the basis of their common characteristics. He classifies 'syncretistically', placing one object with another because something about each happens to catch his attention. Reasons for actions are given in a similar fashion: a balloon flies because it is red, and has string on it. Concepts of number, quantity, time, space and causality are pre-logical. If two identical jars are filled to the same level with some liquid, and one of them is emptied equally into two further identical jars, the young child will deny that the liquid in the two jars is equal in amount to that in the first jar because he attends only to one aspect – the height of the water level in the jars. He is incapable as yet of mentally performing the operation backwards: pouring the liquid in the two half-filled jars together in imagination.

In the third major stage at the age of eleven or twelve, the child becomes capable of reversing operations mentally but only on concrete instances. With development, attention becomes 'decentred'. Mentally reversible operations become first possible, then coordinated with each other so that a given relationship comes to be seen as an instance of a whole class. It is only in adolescence that these operations become completely abstracted from all concrete instances, and formal logical argument to which facts are irrelevant can be conducted.

At each stage, concepts are developed with experience through the interplay and balancing of assimilating and accommodating activities. Experience alone is not enough.

There are inherent limitations on development at each stage, partly due to the stage of maturity of the individual's central nervous system(179), partly due to his experience of both the physical and the social environment. Cooperation with others, and, later, interchange of ideas, are important because they make the individual look at things from several different viewpoints. This is essential to seeing logical implications and contradictions.

Play starts in the sensory-motor period. Piaget's account of this is based on the detailed observations and ingenious, if not methodologically flawless, experiments on his own three children between 1925 and 1929(284). According to Piaget, the newly born infant does not perceive the world in terms of permanent objects which exist in space and time. Judging by the difference in the baby's reactions, a bottle out of sight is a bottle lost for ever. A moving point of light may be followed while it is in the line of vision, but there is no reaction when it disappears. When the infant, a little later, sucks not only in response to having his mouth stimulated, but also makes sucking movements in the void, and continues to stare at the point at which an interesting sight vanished – this does not count as play yet, because it merely continues the pleasure of feeding or looking. The infant's behaviour now goes beyond the reflex stage. New elements become embodied in the circular reaction between stimuli and responses, but the infant's activities are still only a repetition of what he has done before. Piaget calls this 'reproductive assimilation': doing what was done before when such actions are well within the infant's capacity. Such repetition 'for its own sake' is the forerunner of play.

Early sensory-motor development is not, in fact, adequately described in terms of separate reflexes which are extended by experience. Some coordination between some sense receptors and movements exists already at birth(379), and many of the reflexes present in the neonate are superseded rather than incorporated into later voluntary movements(10, 366). Nevertheless, some assumption of interplay between receiving and adjusting to information is required in any case. The spontaneous 'exercise' of babbling, fist-waving, etc., present in all normal babies, is likely to be concerned in this(6).

Piaget has no need to assume a special impulse for play, since he regards it as an aspect of assimilation, i.e. the repetition of an achievement to fit it in and consolidate it. By the fourth month of life, looking and touching have become coordinated and the child learns that to push the toy hanging from its cot will make it swing or rattle. Once learned the action will be repeated again and again. This is play. 'Functional' pleasure, and 'pleasure in being a cause' arise from the repetition of actions as soon as they are mastered during the successive sub-stages of the sensory-motor period. Having learned to remove covers to find toys and other objects, removing covers and screens itself becomes an enjoyable game for the seven- to twelve-months old. At this time too, an interesting result accidentally achieved will be repeated in an almost ritualized form. Play is no longer mere repetition of what was successful, but becomes repetition with variations. However, it is not until he is between twelve- and eighteen-months old that there is active systematic experimentation. By this time, the various possibilities of what can be done with objects have become coordinated. This allows the child to differentiate his actions from the object to which they are directed. It is the beginning of systematic exploration and the pursuit of whatever is new. In the final stage of the sensory-motor period, action in the absence of objects, and with it, symbolization, pretence and make-believe become possible.

Symbolic or make-believe play characterizes the period of representational intelligence from about two to seven years of age. Piaget's views on this period are based on his observations of children's spontaneous talk and answers to questions, and on more recent experiments on children's concepts of number, space, quantity, and so forth. Initially, thinking takes the form of substitute actions which still belong to the last of the sensory-motor developments. A knotted rag is used as if it were a baby. Actions appropriate to one object are used on a substitute. According to Piaget images result from the bodily adjustments to an object in its absence. Their occurrence without complete, overt movements, is the basis of images. Initially, these interiorized actions stand for the object, as concrete symbols, later they act as signs indicating or signifying the object. Language is a socially ready-made set of signifiers – words – which help this process, but are not essential to it. Symbolic and make-believe play has the same function in the development of representational thinking as practice play had in the sensory-motor period. It is pure assimilation, and consequently repeats and organizes thinking in terms of images and symbols already mastered; for instance, asking questions for the sake of asking, telling stories for the fun of telling them. Symbolic play also functions to assimilate and consolidate the child's emotional experiences. Anything important that has happened is reproduced in play. But what has happened in reality is distorted in play, since no effort to adapt to reality is being made. The peculiar character of make-believe play, however, derives from the peculiar character of the child's intellectual processes at this stage; his 'ego-centric' position and the highly individual character of the images and symbols he employs. During the representative period, make-believe play becomes progressively more elaborate and organized. With growing experience of the physical and social environment, there is a transition to more accurate representation of reality. This increasingly involves sensory-motor and intellectual practice so that play becomes constructive, adapted to reality, and ceases to be play altogether. At the same time, the child becomes more socially adapted and consequently needs to resort less to symbolic substitutes and distortions of reality.

Individual symbols and beliefs become modified through cooperation with others and, partly because of this, reasoning and the use of symbols becomes more logical and objective in the period from eight to eleven. Play is now controlled by collective discipline and codes of honour so that games with rules replace the individual symbolic make-believe of the earlier stage. Although games with rules are socially 'adapted' and survive into adulthood, they still show assimilation rather than adaptation to reality. The rules of the game legitimize the individual's satisfaction in his sensory-motor and intellectual achievement and victory over others, but are not equivalent to intelligent adaptation to reality.

Piaget's theory gives play a clear biological function as active repetition and experiment which 'mentally digests' novel situations and experiences. It affords a coherent description of the development of successive activities from pushing hanging rattles to acting out stories and playing rugger or chess. But there are difficulties. Some of these are due to the fact that Piaget concentrates on what can be inferred about the logical status of children's reasoning from their mistakes, rather than on specifying the conditions under which errors occur. His methods are designed to discover the sequence of actions which lead to mistakes or correct solutions, and this has produced essential data which are not in doubt. But it cannot yield precise information about the specific factors influencing a given finding. This has frequently been criticized.

The assumption that play is pure assimilation allows us to predict that a child will play at whatever activity he has just mastered, and that it will be characterized by distortions of reality to suit the child's needs. It does not specify the extent to which such distortions can be modified by experience at a given age-level. For instance, need they occur at all in a well-adjusted, well-informed five-year-old? Statistical precision about the number of children studied and the percentage of these making a given logical error, computations of variations in the results contributed by systematically rotated variations in the way tasks are presented are anything but characteristic of Piaget's studies. But attempts to translate his studies into more orthodox experimental form are often difficult to interpret in relation to the theory. For instance, by and large, American children reach the stages of reasoning earlier than the ages given by Piaget with his Swiss children. Yet, although Piaget states definite ages at which given cognitive achievements are attained, he implies throughout that experience as well as maturation determine these. A difficult concept, that of specific gravity, was taught in a relatively short time to bright five- and six-year-olds by a carefully planned course. They immersed objects of different materials, sizes and weights in water, weighed the amount of water they displaced and so on(268), and learned the concept by these guided experiences. These five-year-olds were clearly not 'pre-logical' in their thinking. It could be argued that merely the time at which they reached the concept, not the sequence of logical reasoning, had been affected.

Three major assumptions are essential to Piaget's theory. His theory implies that intellectual development proceeds in a sequence which may be accelerated or retarded, but cannot itself be changed by experience; that the sequence is not continuous but made up of stages each of which has to be complete before the next cognitive step can be attempted(178), and that the sequence can be explained in terms of the kind of logical operations involved. There is evidence that, for instance, some number concepts are consistently easier than others(383). It has also been shown, however, that these sequences do not result solely from the type of logical operation involved(45), but may depend on some specific experience – e.g. that of measuring – which children at these ages rarely have in our society. The number of items in a task rather than the logical operation involved in it, may constitute the major difficulty. For instance, Piaget found that children of five are unable to copy the exact sequence of beads in a chain or of doll's clothes on a line. But when the number of beads is reduced to less than seven, younger children succeed. Number of items rather than the ability to follow a sequence must, therefore, constitute a major difficulty in this. A good many of Piaget's descriptions are not in doubt(225, 335) but more evidence is yet needed to decide whether they are best interpreted in terms of a theory of the development of logical structures in the individual by progressive balancing between taking in and adjusting to information. If Piaget is right, whatever factors determine intellectual development also determine the development of play.

Piaget distinguishes between play as repetition of an action already mastered, and repetition of an activity in order to understand it. The latter is investigation or exploration and involves accommodation to reality. In play, on the contrary, reality is adapted to the child's own needs. In its form of 'pure' assimilation play comes to an end at the end of the period of representative intelligence with the waning of 'ego-centrism'.

Comment

Each of the original theories is relevant to a slightly different set of problems about play. Freud's theory concerns the relation between imaginative play and emotion. Piaget deals with play as an aspect of intellectual development. Ethologists are interested in the evolution and biological significance and causation of apparently aimless and irrelevant behaviour. Learning theorists have been uninterested in play, but play involves learning and selective response to stimulation. Questions about emotional arousal, perception, learning and biological and developmental points of view are no longer totally isolated from each other. It is now possible to relate some apparently very different topics. But this does not mean that the same set of conditions necessarily applies to every instance of play. The examples of animal play given in the next chapter will show this to be unlikely.

CHAPTER THREE

THE PLAY OF ANIMALS

A DIRECTOR of the Basle Zoological gardens reported(156) that a bear, during a pause in its training for performances got on to its scooter spontaneously for a few rounds, apparently for no other reason than interest in the activity for its own sake. The elaborate solo dance of the thrush, and bird's song have also been described as evidently enjoyed by the birds for their own sake, and so incorporating an element of play even if the ultimate biological purpose of the activity is courtship or the establishment of territories(8). But the interpretation an activity suggests to the observing human in analogy with his own feelings is not a valid explanation. The spontaneous performance of trained animals, like the Basle bear, is best described as a function of learning. Activities paired with, or made contingent upon incentives like food, drink, or the avoidance of pain tend to be repeated for some time without reward, especially under certain conditions of training (see Chapter Two). The sight of the scooter, an important cue to the bear in his original training, may have been sufficient to make him try a few rounds.

Play is found more frequently, and in more varied forms in 'higher' than in 'lower' animals(25). Since a species' place on the evolutionary tree is in part determined by the complexity of its bodily structures and functions, which, in turn, are linked with capacity to learn and to vary behaviour, there is a likely link between ability to learn and to play. However, this leaves many puzzles. Why do young animals play more than older ones if play is learned? Why does it take specific forms in different species?

The first step in clarifying such questions is to try to classify activities which have been called 'play'. They fall roughly under four headings. One is general activity when this is not a one-to-one response to some immediate stimulus from the environment. The frisking of lambs and kids, the gambolling of puppies, are examples. They are influenced by environmental conditions, warmth and the weather. Reports on a wide variety of animals agree that animals play more under the kind of weather conditions which are best for them. British domestic cattle(54) prefer good weather for their play; lions play more on cool than on hot days(77). Animals play more after just being released from confinement, or when fresh bedding is put into their stalls. More play has been reported of captive animals than of animals in the wild. None of these conditions is sufficient to explain the activity entirely. This does not mean that external conditions, and stimuli which favour the occurrence of play are irrelevant. On the contrary, they constitute an important part of the explanation. But in cases where one, or a very limited number, of external stimuli suffice to explain an activity, the word 'play' is rarely used.

A second group of activities which have been labelled 'play' consists of parts of behaviour patterns which normally lead to the fulfilment of a definite biological function, as for instance, feeding, fighting and reproductive activities when they occur out of context, or without accomplishing this purpose (see Chapter Two). Play-fighting without causing injuries, stalking and pouncing upon unsuitable objects, the sex-play of sexually immature animals are some examples in this category.

Social play is a third category, although it overlaps with the previous one in that it often consists of incomplete parts of biologically useful patterns. Social play, however, involves the interaction of at least two animals, and occurs mainly between members of organized social groups. To this belongs the reciprocal behaviour between mother and offspring when this is independent of nursing, cleaning or care-taking, known as 'parental play'. Wrestling and fighting without injury among the young, mutual sex-play of the sexually immature, and corporate activities in which animals are influenced by each other's behaviour but which apparently have no direct social goal, are examples. Köhler's chimpanzees' rhythmical marching in a circle to the banging of old tins(196) presumably belongs here.

Finally, there is a group of activities which includes investigating and exploring the environment, manipulating, and experimenting with objects. These are called 'play' when the exploration serves no apparent useful purpose, and the manipulation of objects is not engaged in to remove some obstacle blocking the way to food or a mate. Domestic cattle, provided they are not frightened, will sniff, lick, chew and generally investigate any novel object. Newborn foals show little fear, and nuzzle everything unless shepherded away by the mare. Pigs need play-objects like chains or rubber-hoses in their pens to occupy their attention(147). Monkeys and apes are proverbially playful, and even invent games(196).

Some examples of play as general activity, incomplete parts of biologically useful patterns of behaviour, social interaction apparently serving no specific purpose, and exploration and experimentation for their own sake will be given for some species roughly in their order on the evolutionary tree.

Is This Play?

No one, to my knowledge, has ever suggested that the single cell animals, the protozoa, play. Their behaviour depends on immediate stimuli either from without or from within the organism. The amoeba, one of this type, moves towards a weak light, gentle touch, and slight disturbances in the water of the ditch at the bottom of which it lives. Strong light, and violent disturbances make it move away. The chemical state of the fluid around it affects the degree to which it is active. A slight rise in temperature makes it move more quickly(145). Spontaneous activity results from its bodily state. If deprived of food, it becomes active 'searching' for it. It has some rudimentary capacity to learn, or at any rate to adapt to changes in conditions. But new habits are formed with difficulty, and do not last long.

It is not until we get to the arthropods, jointed-limbed animals who have their skeleton on the outside of the body, that some observers have spoken of 'play'. A vast variety of species belong to the arthropods, among them the lobster, crayfish and other crustacea, and a million or two species of insects including ants, bees and wasps. Unlike protozoa, insects have a number of specialized sense receptors, and a ladder-like nervous system, with nodal points controlling the function of the various segments of the body, and a central chain interconnecting these. Some ants, bees and wasps, living in organized social groups, have more highly developed and specialized nervous systems than any other invertebrates. They can learn even relatively complex mazes quite well(359). Their spontaneous behaviour consists of fairly rigid, mainly innate patterns of action, but which also involve some learning. Specific bodily structures, sensory stimuli arising within the organism, the state of the ductless glands, the effect of hormonal action on the central nervous system, and the interplay of all these with the conditions present in the environment, are involved. For instance, a certain species of army ants goes on raiding expeditions. It has been shown that the form this takes depends largely on the inherited equipment of the individual worker, that is, the tendency to change course when touched repeatedly, the secretion of a chemical when excited, and a different response to a trail saturated with this chemical from that to one which is not. The predatory raiding is called out by light. The animals are active in proportion to its brightness (321). The whole operation depends on the physiological rhythm of the queen ant's breeding cycle. When the brood is in the active larval stage, the workers go raiding every day. When it is in the enclosed stage, the colony hardly makes any raids. The difference apparently depends on the amount of stimulation of animals by each other in the nest.

The round and waggle dances of the honey bee are utilitarian, although they look enjoyable. A worker who has found food on a foraging expedition indicates its direction, amount and distance to other workers in the hive by the direction, tempo(127) and number of wagging turns of the characteristic dance she performs on return. Bees near her get excited, follow her dance, and then set off in the direction of the food. Ability to perform the figure eight, basic to the dance, is innate. Untutored young workers forced to forage can perform correctly(218). Following the dance of others, however, on which communication depends, needs practice. Using the sun as an orienting point for flight and in the waggle dance is innate, but the bees have to learn to take the sun's path into account as a directional cue(219).

Social games of the sham-fighting kind have been reported of some arthropods 'on fine, calm days when they are feeling no hunger or any other cause for anxiety' (117: Vol. I, p. 469). Danger immediately stops their play. One extremely aggressive species of termites (*Tetramorium coespitum*) sting and mutilate each other ferociously in battle. In play, however, they hardly sting or get hurt, and some of the characteristic fighting movements are absent. There are transitions between this and real battles in the species. Ants of a colony of *Formica pratensis* have been reported to approach each other with fawning movements that looked like caresses, wrestle together in pairs, then fall back only to start all over again(117). They did not eject poison as they do in battles, and no one got hurt. The protagonists are always workers: females who have been housed and fed differently from the future queens as young larvae, are smaller in size, have very small ovaries, and do not mate. The movement patterns of play differed in some essential component from the movement patterns of real fights.

The higher social insects get to know their territory well in their explorations. The question is whether they ever explore 'for fun'. The different duties of honey bee workers – whether they clean, feed the young, build, or forage for food – depend on their age, physiological state and the needs of the hive. When not working, they feed, rest and spend a good deal of time walking all over the hive, poking their heads into various cells, apparently investigating the state of affairs in different parts(218). Young bees who are normally employed within the hive interrupt these visits with bouts of work where there is some to be done. They cease altogether as soon as permanent work is discovered. If conditions are altered experimentally so that work appropriate to the worker's age is not available, the worker will explore more, and will engage in work for which she is normally too old or too young. These observations have been cited as evidence for an inherited impulse to be active said also to underly play(244). However, assumptions of separate impulses to explain behaviour are never very helpful. Nor would it explain why older workers normally employed in foraging also explore the hive at the end of blossoming time when there is less food to collect, but participate much less often in work when the opportunity arises than younger bees.

Some of the external conditions which stimulate exploration in the higher insects are similar to those for mammals. Changes in stimulation, relative novelty, differences in the surface texture of its run and so forth make the cockroach explore(83). Repeatedly presenting the same bend in a twig or blob of colour on it, diminishes the cockroach's 'curiosity'. There is no reason to suppose that such exploration has necessarily been learned in the course of food-finding. At the same time its title to be classed with exploratory play is questionable; probably merely because there appears to be little spontaneous variation in the cockroach's investigations.

Play in Vertebrates

Play is more frequently recorded of vertebrate animals, although not equally of all species. Vertebrates; fish, amphibians, reptiles, birds and mammals, are animals with a backbone around a continuous nerve tube, and a skull enclosing the brain which, in the higher species, becomes the major controlling and integrating centre for the whole nervous system. This makes highly complex, integrated behaviour possible, although the behaviour of the lowest vertebrates, for instance, fish, is less complex and adaptable than that of some social insects. But fish too can learn and solve simple problems. An amusing account of play in fish is of some shooters (jaculators) who, after becoming accustomed to their keeper and to visitors, discomfited them by rapidly and accurately spitting them in the eye(203).

'General Activity' as Play in Birds

The most lyrical descriptions ever given of play are those of birds. The display of the eastern King-bird just before a thunderstorm has been likened to a 'torrent of splendid verse' uttered by the poet Swinburne under similar circumstances (8, p. 177). The flight acrobatics of ibises, and sheld-ducks suddenly swooping down, twisting and turning, and then reforming again, have been considered play. Eider-ducks repeatedly walk up the banks of rapids in order to launch themselves on the stream 'apparently merely for the delight of the downward rush through the swirling waters' (359, p. 363).

Birds are sensitive to changes in the atmosphere. General excitement, including some of the 'flight frolics', seems to be connected with such changes. It is known, too, that in birds living in groups the behaviour of each influences the others. Preening, mating and display in courting, are facilitated in most species by other animals doing the same. Flight games occur in flocks of birds. Any stimulus change, perceived by one bird which prevents it from settling, or causes it to change direction, could, therefore, have some effect on the rest of the flock. The case of the eiderducks may be quite different. Rapid-shooting may be connected with feather cleansing, or may stimulate the skin so that the bird learns to repeat this rewarding act (see Chapter Two).

Irrelevant Behaviour as Play in Birds

The sequence of reproductive activities and care of the young is often very elaborate in nesting birds. The male establishes a territory from which others are warned off by vigorous singing, courts a mate by the display of beautiful feathers, dancing or singing. Male bower birds build constructions sometimes as tall as seven feet, decorate them with orchids or other flowers, or paint them with fruit pulp or charcoal, or ornament them with a variety of coloured or shiny objects to attract the female. The satin bower bird strews his bower with objects the colour of his mate: bluebells, blue bags stolen from laundries, yellow straw, mimosa sprigs, blue bus tickets or chocolate wrappers. The spotted bower bird prefers shiny objects such as car-keys, broken glass, jewellery, coins, and a few bleached bones. One observer had to retrieve his tableware from a bower near his camp, and another even lost his glass eye to figure among the objects which the male bird would pick up with his bill and wave seductively in front of the female he had lured to his bower.

It has been claimed that painting and decorating the bower goes beyond what is strictly necessary, and that a good deal of it is play. However, in spite of the frequently beautiful effects of these bowers, there is no evidence so far to assume it to be anything beyond the display most birds show as a necessary part of courtship. Male birds whose gonads have been removed do not display or build bowers. Injection of male hormone restores the activity even out of season. On the other hand, birds who do not have access to coloured objects can, nevertheless, achieve copulation. So far there are no hard and fast criteria to decide how much display is 'strictly necessary' to put a female in the right mood. The urge to decorate the bower in the characteristic manner of the species is evidently great. A captive satin bower bird killed and used blue finches when no other blue objects were available. The most intensive dancing, painting and collecting of display objects occurs while the male, who becomes capable of copulation fairly early in the season, waits until the much slower female also becomes ready for it(237). Courtship and loveplay stimulate the mate and lead to synchronicity of the partners. It is therefore an integral part of a biological sequence. Display outside the usual sequence occurs quite frequently in bower birds since, unlike most birds, the male's testes do not metamorphose when the female has left him to rear her young. Occasional display and even building may occur outside the breeding season also in the early stages of the regeneration of the male sex hormone. But it is the mature male who builds the most lavishly decorated bower, and seasonal variations depend on factors connected with hormone production. The claim for bower-decoration to be 'play-like' is, therefore, dubious.

The song of immature birds which has as yet no function in the reproductive cycle has been likened to play in young mammals in that both appear during the animal's development, become integrated into functional patterns later, contain imitative elements, and practise adult activities(7). Unlike the full song, subsong is too quiet to carry over distances and seems to have no communicative function either in establishing and maintaining territory, attracting a mate, or as a signal in feeding or warning against predators. The subsong of the chaffinch is quieter than the full song, and has a different sound pattern(358). The simplest type of subsong is sung by young males in their first autumn, and in late winter and the next spring. Older birds may also sing the subsong in late winter and early spring. This is connected with the seasonal increase of hormone production. The subsong of some young birds, reared in complete isolation from other birds, is normal. This means that there must be some innate determinants of the pattern. Nevertheless learning is involved. The song of experimentally isolated birds alters as they grow older, but is much more restricted and simple than the full song of wild chaffinches. Each community of young birds reared together, but without the opportunity of hearing the song of older birds, develops a distinctive song of its own. These are more elaborate than the song of birds isolated from infancy, but differ from the full song of normally reared birds. The true chaffinch song involves some learning, although chaffinch-like sounds are more easily learned than others. Juveniles, once they have heard the chaffinch song, do not easily forget it, even if they are isolated subsequently, nor can they be taught artificial

songs. But isolated birds may be able to learn some very un-
chaffinch like sounds. A chaffinch may learn as many as six
different songs from different neighbours in its first singing
season, but it cannot add to these later. The period of
'experimenting' with sounds is short and confined to the
bird's early life(358). It is essential for the normal development of singing. A study comparing robins and grosbeaks
raised in complete isolation, but each able to hear its own
voice, with robins and grosbeaks made deaf as nestlings,
showed that the bird's ability to hear its own voice is necessary for normal song development(198). Even if the bird
has heard the adult song, but is deafened in the period before
it sings, it cannot reproduce the song. But once the birds
have heard themselves sing, subsequent deafening does not
affect their song(198a). Different species vary in the extent
to which they are able to incorporate other sounds. Vocal
mimics like parrots, mocking birds, and bower birds seem
to be able to reproduce a large range of sounds they have
heard, and apparently do so more in captivity. This presumably makes their vocal play more variable.

Other examples of irrelevant activities in young birds
which appear as play (see Chapter Two) seem to be mainly
stereotyped movement patterns appearing in the young
before they have been integrated into functional units or
associated with the appropriate stimuli. Nest-building
movements in immature birds, and drinking motions of
chicks in response to mirrors are examples(297). 'Mischievous' behaviour has been reported of some captive
birds. A hand-reared young kestrel(23) when brought into
the living-room apparently loved to pounce on a ball of
paper thrown down for him, or on to the tail of the cat. He
did this repeatedly in spite of being dragged about by the cat.
The same observer reported play by a buzzard he kept. This
bird had a bit of wood which he would repeatedly stoop for,
pick up, drop with a clatter, or carry to and from his perch.
Their owner was convinced by the 'great animation' of the
kestrel and the buzzard during these activities that they were
'undoubtedly at juvenile play'. Pouncing, carrying and

dropping objects is in the nest-building repertoire of these birds, so that this play possibly belongs to the category of 'irrelevant' or out of context behaviour.

Social Play in Birds

The majority of birds are gregarious at least for part of the year, especially after the breeding season when flocking occurs. Some also nest in colonies. Some birds, like the domestic chicken, are highly social(166). Social play in adult birds frequently refers to the corporate flight acrobatics mentioned earlier, and to the communal dancing which is part of the courtship display of some species. Sparring and mock attacks have been reported of young tauraco fischeri, young hornbills and sedge warblers(60), and a form of 'king of the castle' game of two white-necked ravens(251). In this, one of the birds would pick up and brandish a lump of dry cowdung or a small stick. The other would charge up to it and they would wrestle for the object. Beyond the observers' reports that there was an 'element of fun' in these performances, we know very little of the conditions which determined them. Aggression in birds, as in a lot of other animals, does not necessarily mean fighting to death, or even to injury. There are methods of intimidation by threat postures, or singing, which may rout an opponent effectively without the biologically disastrous consequences that continual fighting within a species would have. Fighting in birds is mainly connected with the reproductive cycle involving defence of the territory, competition for a mate and defence of the young. In some species, the young go through a period soon after fledging when they are particularly aggressive. Social birds like chickens have a definite rank within the group, shown by who is allowed to peck whom. This pecking order is established by fighting when the hens first come together, and remains more or less the same after that (105: ch. I). Whether the reported 'tilting matches' of young birds belong to any of these types of activities is not clear.

Play and Exploration in Birds

Birds' brains, containing the major centres for the integration and control of nervous activity, are much larger in total
mass relative to body-weight than in the lower reptiles to
whom they are related(288). Territorial birds seem to be
quite good at learning their home ground, but there is little
evidence of generalized curiosity. There are reports of a
general tendency of birds to peck at, scratch, claw and pull
at objects in their environment. Possibly the behaviour of
the young buzzard who played with a bit of wood (see above),
belongs to such exploration of objects but it is more likely
that it must be classed with 'irrelevant' activities. There
seems no reason to suppose that young birds play more than
older ones.

Mammals

Examples of play in mammals, of kids, and lambs, kittens
and puppies, are well known. Mammals, whose females have
specially modified glands with which to feed the young, have
a longer period of youth than any other animals except
birds. The 'higher' up the evolutionary scale animals are,
the longer is their infancy during which they are protected,
and their needs cared for by adults. This is often considered
the most important condition for play; the fact that they
have nothing else to do. However, the connexion between a
long infancy and variety and frequency of play is not necessarily direct.

General Activity as Play in Mammals other than Primates

Conditions which determine general activity have been
studied experimentally in rats. Selective breeding of active
and inactive rats will produce strains that are far apart in
activity level, so genetic factors must be involved(129). Other
factors which influence activity are health, being hungry,
sexual need, and glandular changes, especially those associated with the sexual cycle in the more active females.

Rats are more active in darkness than in light, in lower, than in higher temperatures, after periods of rest than after enforced activity, and after having been restricted in small cages for short periods. Individuals vary. Inactive rats become more so after rest periods. Prolonged periods of confinement have the opposite effect from short periods. They lessen rather than heighten activity. There is a definite association with age. The very young and the very old are quite inactive, while the peak period of activity, in females, is associated with the onset of puberty. General activity has not, as far as I know, been called 'play' in rats.

Domestic cattle(54), horses, sheep and goats(147) and some captive wild animals(157) show general activity which has been called play. Trotting, cantering, galloping, prancing and bucking not aimed at any object have been observed in adult as well as young cattle. One group of non-pregnant cows being fattened after their first lactation were reported as particularly playful. Good food, good weather and any change in the environment such as the arrival of the attendant, someone running alongside them, being fondled, having itchy places on their skin scratched, favours play. Cold, wet weather, illness or fear inhibit it. Young cattle and young horses play more than older animals. Young horses kick and bite at the doors and sides of their stables, sometimes for hours on end. Short periods of confinement lead to more play, as they do to greater activity in rats, but animals closely confined for long periods show a loss of muscular development and less motor skill than those reared under freer conditions.

Contrary to what would be expected if 'surplus energy' explained play, and to the hypothesis that play occurs because there is nothing else to do, captive lions who have all their needs provided for, are extremely inactive, and get out of condition in consequence(156). Some animals develop stereotyped movements – endless walking to and fro and even biting at themselves(157). The type of living conditions, amount of space, food, access to mates, and so forth are largely responsible for these differences.

A study of captive lions living on a five-acre farm, and trained for circus performance showed that even mature lions may play under these circumstances(77). Suitable weather – cool, brisk days rather than overwhelming heat; early morning or evening rather than the middle of the day; changes in the environment, release from confinement, the sudden appearance of attendants, someone running in front of the enclosure, and the introduction of new animals produced more play.

Females play more than males. This appears to be associated with different phases of their oestrous cycle. Conditions of domestication affect this, increasing the number of periods(391). The breeding of healthy captive animals is affected by space, size of social group to which they belong, an adequate territory or 'home', temperature and familiarity. A strange environment may terrify wild animals literally to death. Mild novelty when the animal is acclimatized encourages breeding (27: ch. XIV), activity generally and also play. So far it is difficult to distinguish between general activity and movement play in terms of the external conditions. The conditions for both seem to be those leading to heightened but not overwhelming excitement. It has been suggested that play functions to decrease the excitement(181).

For mammals, more play in the young than in older animals is generally reported. Lion cubs from the age of about a month onwards increasingly play at rolling, biting and clawing until they are a year old. Later, they play more with each other, but all play becomes infrequent after the age of four. There are species differences. Lion cubs play less than kittens, although the 'more' and 'less' of such reports is often rather vague.

Irrelevant Behaviour as Play in Mammals other than Primates

The play of most mammalian young includes activities which belong to recognizable adult behaviour sequences such as mating, hunting and fighting. One of the best examples of this is the stalking and pouncing play of kittens. Does this help them later to hunt and kill their prey? So far, the evidence shows that the movements used in stalking, and catching different kinds of prey are innate, and gain little from practice in kittens, dogs and a variety of other carnivorous, predatory animals(359). However, recognition of suitable objects for hunting, killing and eating does not seem to be inborn, except in the sense that certain general characteristics of objects, such as their type of movement and size, are innately attention-catching. Rolling balls of knitting wool, and dangling rings may be unsuitable for killing but, in fact, share essential characteristics, such as manageable size and being in motion, with suitable prey like mice and birds. A study of small, extremely active and playful carnivorous mammals of the mongoose variety brings this out very clearly(296). The young, and even adults in captivity, play a variety of running and fighting games with surprise mock attacks on each other. They roll in wastepaper baskets, and slip paper hats on. The movements are no different from those used in 'serious' pursuits. Even the unlikely predilection for putting paper hats over their heads has its counterpart and use in slipping into holes for concealment. Whatever biological use such play has, it is not that of perfecting movements and actions essential for survival in adult life. The movements are pretty well perfect even in the young.

Early experience does, however, have some effects. Kittens brought up in isolation did kill rats, but far less and much later than those reared with their rat-killing mothers (202). Cats brought up together with rats as their cagemates never killed them, and only very few killed other kinds of rats. Kittens reared in isolation seemed to be the most 'playful'. They played the cat and mouse game, mostly without killing their prey, running after the rat, gently holding it, throwing it down, running away for a moment, re-chasing it, patting it or turning it with one paw and giving it up without injury. These isolates too showed most of the other kinds of 'inhibited' responses. They ignored newly introduced prey, or merely looked at it without catching and killing as young raised with their mothers did. Neither did they have the positively tolerant attitude of kittens who had had rats as cage mates. Perhaps this is 'play when in doubt', and belongs to ambivalent reactions when two opposing responses such as attack and flight are aroused at the same time. It could also be a form of exploring. A restricted environment and social isolation during infancy seem to make dogs more ready to explore(356). Only further experiments could decide whether the playful behaviour of the isolated kittens is a form of investigation. It seems to have occurred in circumstances in which normally reared ones hunted and killed. Kittens brought up with rats were tolerant of rats, but also played with them far less than the isolates did.

Pre-pubertal sex-play is common in most mammalian young(26). At twenty-one days of age young rats pursue, mount and clasp other rats although they become fertile only at fifty days. Sexually inexperienced rats can mate as competently as experienced ones, but adverse experience, strange or frightening situations, and isolation in infancy may have inhibiting effects later. Young male foxes who have been frightened by vixens, or male mink who have been fought by the female during initial matings may avoid females thereafter unless they are specially re-trained with gentle females. The effect of pre-pubertal sex-play does not seem to be a question of practising mating responses but it may function as social experience essential for the full mating pattern at maturity for which complex social responses and mutual communication are necessary (27: ch. XVII).

Learning to discriminate appropriate from inappropriate objects to stalk, hunt, mate with or kill may be another biological use of play. This still needs further investigation. Inexperienced male rats, given the choice, mounted the female in heat rather than any other of a variety of other rodents or females not in heat. On the other hand, there are reports that inexperienced bulls and male rabbits attempt to copulate with partners who are biologically inadequate(26).

Typically, in really 'playful' animals, components of a variety of adult behaviour patterns not only occur to 'inappropriate' stimuli, but all rapidly replace each other in response to very similar ones. The young mongoose's so-called 'fighting' play includes parts of sexual behaviour, sexual clasping of the human playmate, gestures used in courting display, glandular secretions as in sexual and other excitement, and defence movements. Bodily contact in 'play-fighting' may call out fighting and defence movements, but might equally elicit sexual behaviour which also depends on touch and physical contact. Possibly, animals do not hurt each other in play-fighting because the situation touches off a number of different behaviour patterns, some of which mutually inhibit each other, or alternate too rapidly for each to be completed, or it may result from the fact that in the young, behavioural units are not as yet integrated into fixed sequences with their appropriate stimuli.

Probably, the term 'play-fighting' covers different behaviour in different species, or even at different ages. Baby bears tumbling over one another, constantly renewing bodily contact with one another, seem to be very differently engaged from some species of puppies who apparently establish in their play who will dominate the other in future.

The 'inappropriate' or 'irrelevant' appearance of parts of adult patterns such as nest-building movements in infancy may have some quite definite function. Preventing the exercise of unlearned activities in the young before they have become integrated into functional patterns may delay or disrupt the integration or appropriate appearance of this behaviour later. Female rats reared with rubber ruffs round their necks which prevented them from washing themselves or licking their genitalia failed to clean and nurse their young in maturity (300: ch. I). If reared without nest-building materials, or any equivalent that could be picked up and carried about in infancy, rats failed to build appropriate nests in adulthood(303). However, the conditions which are necessary and sufficient for the appearance of irrelevant behaviour are likely to vary in different species.

Social Play between Adults and Young

Social play among mammals occurs mainly between young animals, although mothers and other adults do play in varying degrees with their young, and, to a lesser extent, with other adults. The bond which develops between mother and young ensures the survival of the young, and is apparently important for their response to their social group. Lambs who have been separated from their mothers soon after birth and hand-reared, are less gregarious and tend to stray farther from the flock as adults than normal sheep(147). Lionesses, ewes, goats and dog-mothers play with their young, and even cats tolerate the pawing and romping of kittens during the first four weeks of their lives. The play of dog-mothers consists mainly of bodily contact, rubbing the face against a pup, rolling it over, nosing, licking and mouthing it. Puppies tend to beg for play as they grow older much as they begged for food earlier on. Species vary considerably in the degree to which the mothers respond to these overtures. Observations on free-ranging relations of domestic cattle – the moose and the elk – confirm species differences in amount and type of play. Elk-cows, for instance, play the splashing and running games in shallow water with their young that are said to prepare the elk-calves for crossing streams in their spring migrations. As elk-calves grow older they increasingly play these games with each other (300: ch. XVII). Moose-dams, on the other hand, do not play with their calves. Moose-calves stay around their mothers until they are yearlings, and play solitary games. Their integration with the herd occurs later than that of elk calves.

Mammal mothers' response to play changes as their young grow older. Soon after birth, cat-mothers initiate constant contact with their young, adapting their behaviour to them, and even joining in the kittens' play which consists mainly of physical contact, pawing and toying with the mother's tail. By the end of the fourth week, the mother cat tolerates such play much less, and increasingly evades the kittens who pursue her for food and play. (300: ch. IV).

Feeding plays an important role in socializing kittens and puppies. The young will get attached to whoever gives them food regularly. It has been pointed out that feeding is normally itself a social situation involving all the innumerable stimuli of touch, vision, hearing, smell, upon which mutual adjustments are based. (41: ch., XIX). Feeding is not the only basis of attachment for puppies. It has been reported that cocker spaniels, fed mechanically but played with by an experimenter who never offered them food, became very attached to him.

Social Play of Young Mammals

The form of social play varies in different species. Horses, elephants, rhinoceroses and camels play 'flight' rather than 'fight' games with each other. The point of the game seems to be to escape(181). This is apparently true also of rabbits, hares and other animals who use flight as their main defence against predators. It is not yet established whether stimuli which normally frighten them, in a milder form initiate the games. The games of carnivorous and predatory animals incorporate more hunting, pursuit and fighting movements.

The play of young mammals with each other is mostly called play-fighting, although it often consists of a variety of different behaviour patterns. The social relations of young, sexually immature animals are less well defined and established than those of the older ones, so that the young probably call out a variety of sometimes incompatible reactions in each other in rapid succession or even simultaneously. Bull-calves, in quick succession, suddenly frisk about, butt each other, kick, shake their heads, and attempt to mount each other(54). That fighting, sexual, defence and display elements succeed each other rapidly in the 'fighting' play of the mongoose has already been mentioned. The presence of elements calling out incompatible responses typically leads to incomplete, or irrelevant or vacillating responses. It is possible that some such explanation may account for the fact that adult lions who are not, on the whole, particularly playful, will play with members of their group who have just been released into the enclosure after a short absence. Group members who are reintroduced after a long period of segregation are attacked(77), unless special precautions are taken. A stranger introduced into a group, of course, calls out attack in most animals, not excluding humans. Possibly the recognition of a familiar animal checks the impulse to attack, provided the separation has not been too long, and issues in play, that is, stalking and leaping upon the animal without doing him an injury. Alternatively, it may be a form of investigation in response to relative novelty.

Familiarity and all the experiences associated with being reared together are important for later social behaviour. Adult lions fight all the time, unless they have been raised together. Fighting seems to develop with age. Young lion cubs do not fight at all. Older lion children stalk and rush at each other, or play the famous 'king of the castle' game, in which one cub climbs upon some object or eminence, while the others try to dislodge him. Baby kids do not fight each other at first, but play-fighting increases among older age-mates. This apparently helps to determine their rank in the group, which depends to some extent on size, strength and the possession of horns. However, seniority mainly determines who is to dominate whom among goats and cattle born into the same herd at different times(147). The amount of space available to each animal influences competition and dominance fights. Even animals who live in closely integrated groups and have developed a tendency to move together butt and fight if they are crowded.

Predatory, carnivorous animals who hunt in packs, are friendly towards each other. They usually have a recognizable pattern of dominance established early on in the individual's life. Play-fighting occurs in almost all litters of puppies raised together, and apparently helps to establish dominance. Species vary in how soon and how permanently dominance rank develops. Fox-terriers are too aggressive to raise in litters larger than three, otherwise one will be killed through the others ganging up on him. Beagles, on the other hand, rarely fight even as adults (41: ch. XI). Beagles, basenji, American cocker spaniels, and wire-haired fox terriers were tested at the ages of five, eleven, fifteen and fifty-two weeks for dominance over their litter-mates by showing a bone to two litter-mates, and dropping it between them at an equal distance from each(278). Dominance hierarchies developed differently in the four different breeds. Basenjis, for instance, developed one rank order between the ages of five and eleven weeks, and another between the ages of fifteen and fifty-two weeks. In cocker spaniels, on the other hand, the same dominance order persisted throughout the first year. Males always dominated the females. The experimenters considered that the genetic differences between the breeds affect the threshold at which appropriate stimuli become effective. In addition to genetic differences, the individual's experience of success or defeat is very important (41: ch. XI). An animal who has been repeatedly defeated will make little or no effort to obtain the bone in the tests. Threat gestures, cues such as hair standing on end, or the growls of the other, suffice.

The bodily attitudes through which dominance or submission is expressed may take their form from a number of other patterns of behaviour. A now classic study of expressive postures in wolves(316) showed that some expressions of submission of the young, of females, and of low-ranking males are identical with parts of female sexual behaviour: lying down, and allowing the dominant animal to smell and explore its anal region, for instance. Superiority in dogs may express itself in mounting the other animal regardless of sex. Overtures to friendliness may take the form of 'presenting' – which is the female's invitation to coition – to the other animal or even to humans(320). The angle at which wolves and dogs hold their tails indicates their social standing. The socially confident hold their tails erect and have an imposing gait. The social inferior has a lowered tail and crouching movements. Imposing attitudes may act as threats, initiate fighting, form a part of courtship, or occur when a social superior meets an inferior. Such social gestures often initiate social play with age-mates, or humans. A young badger who became very attached to one of his keepers frequently invited him to fighting-play by 'shaking' his trouser-leg (in the manner of predators). This is a ritualized threat gesture(97). His play with objects also consisted of 'shaking' as well as biting and chewing them, although he rarely tore them apart. If the invitation to play was not accepted, however, the badger occasionally became angry. Badgers become frightened or angry if the game is too rough, but Eibesfeldt, who reported this, commented that a human who has reared the badger from infancy will be allowed a great many liberties.

'Fighting' play usually occurs in the context of friendly social contact. Certain movements or calls act as signals to indicate that the subsequent activity is to be friendly rather than hostile. It has been suggested that signalling devices evolved as a form of 'displacement activity' (see Chapter Two) which has become ritualized and forms part of a different behaviour sequence (105: ch. VIII). If it is correct to assume that, in some cases, situations leading to fighting-play contain elements of conflict – calling out both attack and friendly responses – displacement behaviour could be expected to occur.

It is often suggested that relatively intelligent animals, like dogs, are aware of 'pretence' in play-fighting. A hard push given in play does not have the same effect as a much weaker tap given in reprimand. However, all that needs to be assumed is that the dog has learned to discriminate the many different cues which distinguish friendly from hostile situations.

Exploring Play and Play with Objects in Mammals other than Primates

Mammals spend a good deal of time exploring, investigating and manipulating objects without apparent aim. Much of this has been reported as play. Young animals show greater curiosity than older ones. This may be because younger animals are less familiar with objects. Alternatively, the investigations of older animals may be less easy to detect. Younger animals are more excitable generally, and habituate less quickly to all kinds of situations(228). These alternatives are not necessarily mutually exclusive.

Species differ in the extent to which they explore 'aimlessly'. This seems to be connected to some extent with the animal's feeding habits. The playful mongoose(296), lives mainly on flying and crawling insects, and small animals that have to be sought in holes and chinks. Constant exploring is clearly an asset in this. Dolphins(60) and whales (333) are playful. They chase one another, throw dead fish or balls into the air and catch them. They play with objects floating on the water, bring up stones from the bottom and spit them at bystanders, and turn somersaults. Dolphins and pilot whales have been observed to play for an hour with the feather of one of the pelicans with which they shared the tank. They are carnivorous animals who need to stalk and catch their prey. This involves active search, and a wide range and adaptability of behaviour. The connexion between feeding and play is not direct. Young dolphins catch small fish, let them go again, catch them again, without eating them. There is even a record of a small dolphin who repeatedly threw a tube over the rail of its tank, waited for the attendant to throw it back, only to start all over again. A dolphin newly introduced to the tank quickly learned the game.

Butting, moving water buckets, troughs, and unbolted doors for the clatter this produces has been reported of cattle(54). Elephants dislodge and roll dry clay. Response to novelty and change characterized Eibesfeldt's badger's emptying drawers and waste-paper baskets and general exploring play. Learning was clearly involved in a game he 'invented'. This started as a chance combination of movements when he tried to squeeze into the space between the wall and Eibesfeldt's desk, started scratching his tummy, lost his balance and turned a somersault. After this he turned somersaults repeatedly, first only in the original place, but later in other directions too(97).

The biological advantage to the animal of knowledge acquired in the course of 'aimlessly' exploring the environment and experimenting with objects is obvious. Experimental investigations have shown that animals do learn from spontaneous exploration, although such learning tends to be inferior to learning when they are hungry and get food as a reward (see Chapter Two). Exploring is not the same as general activity, but a reaction to definite characteristics of the environment, especially novelty and change(87). Different kinds, amounts and frequencies of change in relation to the organism's previous state may affect it differently. A sudden loud noise, or flash of light in unfamiliar surroundings will usually send an animal scampering off in fright, while a very slight transient change in illumination may merely alert it briefly to look and listen, if it is otherwise occupied. This is the 'what is it?' or 'orienting response' (277), which puts the animal's sense receptors into the best position for receiving information from the environment. Focusing upon an object gives a clearer picture, for instance. Investigation, exploration and manipulation of objects occur mainly in conditions which are only relatively novel, and to changes that are not so intense as to frighten the animal.

Changes in the environment like a rise or fall in temperature, the movement of other animals or of objects, novel objects and situations are typically reported as conditions for play in mammals.

It is not clear to what extent play which consists in manipulating objects comes into the same category. Manipulating objects does, of course, itself produce changes in how the object looks, sounds, or feels from different angles, and when it splinters or disintegrates. These changes themselves presumably stimulate further exploration. But exploration declines with familiarity(137). Play-objects, on the other hand, are often used repeatedly. Certain objects Eibesfeldt's badger(97) found in the course of his investigations, cloths, slippers, a rubber mat, and a brush, became favourite toys after being 'marked' with excretions from his anal gland. Scent-markings help the badger to find his way about. They serve both as sign-posts, and as flags to mark the object or territory as his own.

Sometimes familiarity with the object is a requisite of a toy. A juvenile panda was known to take his toy-hoop to sleep with him evading all efforts to deprive him of it(181). It has been suggested that such attachment to objects in young animals is due to some need for physical contact, or serves as a substitute for something more satisfying. A juvenile elephant cow who played more excitedly with her rubber-hoop when separated from the old cow has been given as an example(181).

Confined animals whose opportunity for external stimulation is limited have frequently been described as 'bored' (156). Under these conditions play may be a form of seeking stimulation, rather than reducing excitement due to novelty or change. There is a report of a bear at the Berner Zoo who had no playthings but made himself a snowball with which he played.

Nervous Activity, Stimulation, and Feedback

Detecting changes in the environment is clearly important for the animal so that it can adapt and remain alive. The mammalian receptor, nervous system, and brain function to detect, sift, coordinate, and store information about changes in the environment. They do not receive stimulation passively, however, but are continually active themselves(391). This has its own importance in the functioning of the system (140). External stimulation keeps the animal in touch with the environment, but is also necessary to maintain normal functioning. Experiments have shown that animals reared in dull, uniform cages, either in darkness or with little possibility of discriminating objects, are poor at learning mazes, or problems which involve visual discrimination later. Whether deprivation of experience in infancy always has more severe effects than when it occurs during adulthood, and to what extent deficits produced early can be made up by adequate experience later is not yet clear. The problem is complex, and a variety of experimental procedures have been used. Differences in genetic strains, and ages of the animals, the type of deprivation, the length of the experience, the time and length of subsequent training all influence the results. It has been suggested that some experiences may be more effective during a limited 'critical' period, for example before weaning, than at other times(322). This has been connected with the maturation of nervous structures in relevant parts of the brain during this time(315) with the possibility that the nervous system of young animals is more easily injured than that of older ones, or more sensitive to physical and chemical changes or because the homeostatic or steadying mechanisms do not function adequately in infancy. It may also be that a first experience is, in any case, more effective than any subsequent one (41: ch. XVI). However, it is most likely that a variety of factors acting together, rather than one unitary developmental one, contribute to results which have given rise to the concept of 'critical periods'.

Different physiological effects of restricted versus 'enriched' or complex environment (with plenty to do and see) on brain chemistry and weight in rats have been demonstrated(200). It has been argued that stimulation is essential for the development of neural structures (115: ch. III, 158). There is evidence that optimal stimulation does accelerate functioning(199). Different species react differently. Animals reared in darkness from birth for four to twelve months show changes in electrical activity recorded from the brain as compared with normally reared animals, consistent with an increased responsiveness to stimuli of various kinds. This returned to normal after a period in light, which was longer for animals higher up the evolutionary scale than in lower mammals(317).

Return information (feedback) from adjustments which are being made is important in most behaviour. The notion of the central nervous system as a control system of self-regulating units is fairly general(132, 184, 290, 374). The maintenance of a constant internal environment, for instance, requires a concept such as negative feedback, i.e. return information when adjustments go amiss. If the environment gets too hot and body temperature rises, a control system adjusts the internal temperature back to normal(349). If the inflow of sensory information from receptors in the joints is interrupted, posture becomes awkward. Interference with, or distortion of, visual information leads to errors in movements. There is even some evidence that visual changes produced in a cat by means other than its own movements are less effective for correct performance later. For instance, a kitten which was strapped so that it could not move and had all its visual experience provided by moving screens was less efficient than a kitten which got the same visual experience through moving about(159).

The play of young mammals, involving a constant interplay between movement and perception of external and internal stimuli is probably concerned in establishing or speeding this control.

Monkey Play

Monkeys are proverbially playful, and up to 'mischievous' tricks. Climbing, sliding, jumping, turning somersaults are favourite chimpanzee play, but they also have more ingenious games. One chimp(156) attracted the attention of zoo visitors to itself by cries and putting a brick on his back which he carried around. When a sufficient crowd had gathered, he suddenly threw a handful of sand at them so that they had to duck away. This apparently delighted the chimp who repeated the game. The monkey brain is more effective in coordinating and controlling behaviour than that of 'lower' animals. Monkeys are excellent at learning and solving problems. They are active, inquisitive creatures; but humanoid apes, like the chimpanzee, whose brain development is more advanced than that of the lower monkeys, are more discriminating and controlled in their activities.

The central nervous system of monkeys and man(252) may be thought of as hierarchically arranged, upward and outward spiralling systems with an overall integration and control in the newest (in terms of evolution), top-most brain-structure, the cerebral hemisphere. Phylogenetically older, lower parts of the brain, brain-stem and spinal cord serve as relay and control stations. They have, in varying degrees, integrating and boosting and inhibiting functions as does the thalamus(2), and control the organism's basic physiological functions, especially the hypothalamus(349, 374). Older structures, but more particularly a part of the hind- and mid-brain and extending into the fore-brain, known as the reticular formation, are involved in non-specific or diffuse excitement, in being 'aroused' or alerted, and are thought to facilitate attending to specific features of the environment (4, 86, 235, 312) although the cortex, the phylogenetically 'new' brain, is essential to the latter in monkeys and man. Removal or damage to the parts of the cortex known as the temporal lobes produces a number of changes in mature rhesus monkeys. These include attending to and investigating everything within sight indiscriminately, a loss of caution, and inability to understand what an object is by just looking at it(195). With inferotemporal lesions there is an impairment on visual discrimination learning tasks. The damage in the earlier cases involved the hippo-campus which is near the temporal lobes, believed to be important in reactions to novelty(207). Enhanced reaction to novel stimuli as well as difficulty in adapting to changes is typical with lesions in the frontal cortex, the foremost of the new brain structures in mammals which are most prominent in monkeys and man(372).

Play as Incomplete or Irrelevant Behaviour in Monkeys

Infant chimpanzees make nests, although less tidily than older animals. Normally nests are made at twilight to sleep in for the night(390). Young animals, however, build nests in the daytime 'for fun'(196) with anything they get; straw, grass, rags or ropes. They also play with these materials. Captive chimpanzees reared without nesting materials build only crude nests in adulthood, or may fail to build nests altogether. They do play with the materials when these are given to them, but generally less than animals who build nests(35).

Sexually immature monkeys play sexually both with themselves and each other(26). Primates need experience and practice for mating. Sexually inexperienced adult males are often incapable of performing the act adequately even with a receptive female. It is probable that the juvenile sex-play of primates does function as learning. This does not mean that each item of the behaviour is learned, but that certain experiences may be necessary for the normal pattern to appear. For instance, monkeys groom spontaneously even if they have never seen other animals groom. But a socially isolated chimpanzee whose opportunity for touching and scratching himself was restricted by encasing his limbs in cardboard cylinders between the ages of four weeks and thirty-one months, did not groom long after the cylinders had been removed(264). The behaviour of male infant rhesus monkeys differs from that of females even when they have been raised without contact with adult animals (27: ch. XI). Infantile sexual behaviour of animals reared on artificial mothers, but having contact during some part of each day with three other infant monkeys in a playroom, consisted of brief, incomplete reactions, such as rubbing against or thrusting at another infant. From the age of 72 days until 159 days, this became more frequent, especially in male infants. 'Threat', consisting of a stiff posture, staring at the other monkey, with flattened hair on the top of the head, retracted lips and bared teeth, increased with age. Males showed this significantly more than females from the age of two and a half months onwards. Female infants were significantly more passive; sitting quietly and allowing the other animal to approach, or withdrawing from it, or becoming passively rigid and averting their heads. Males hardly ever did this after the age of about five months. The males initiated rough and tumble wrestling, rolling and sham-biting play, far more often with either sex, while the females rarely initiated such games with males. According to Harlow (27: ch. XI) these sex differences in threat, passivity, with-drawal, rigidity and play are important for the gradual development of normal adult sexual postures. Restricted social experience or no experience with other infants prevented the development of normal adult heterosexual behaviour. For some females later favourable experience eventually did allow them to become pregnant.

Irrelevant behaviour may occur among adult chimpan-zees, under conditions of conflict, slight strain or suspense. A difficult point in a puzzle made chimpanzees pause and scratch their heads(390). Rhesus monkeys, especially the more excitable females, grimaced, threatened or smacked their lips when food was presented at the same time as some feared object(238). This can hardly be called play, but it resembles the behaviour reported of chimpanzees im-patiently waiting their turn for an experiment in which they got food as a reward. Some animals rocked themselves, others drank or washed their hands at the drinking fountain, or plucked hairs out of their fur, and one chimpanzee amused himself by spitting on a steel post, watching the saliva run a little way down, and then redepositing it a little higher up again(390). The latter would be labelled 'play' if a child did it. Whether tension, or blocking some other activity are important conditions for it needs investigating. In a group of howler monkeys observed in their natural habitat(68), an animal would approach another, casually eating some fruit until it came within striking distance, then suddenly leap upon the other and begin playing. The 'sham activity' gains advantages of time and position. It seems to have affinities both with displacement feeding during an inhibited moment in a fight, and with 'pretence' in human play. The young chimpanzee who amused himself by throwing sand at his visitors would first threaten them with a brick which was too big to go through the bars. While they were laughing at him, he quickly dropped the brick to throw sand, catching them off guard.

Social Play between Monkey-parents and their Young

It has been said that a chimpanzee kept in solitude is hardly a chimpanzee at all (196). Chimps and rhesus monkeys become frantic when separated from their companions, and the latter respond to the isolated animal's distress, provided they can see or hear it. Animals captured in the wild work harder to release their companions than laboratory-reared animals (27: ch. XI).

Monkey species differ in their reactions to newborns, and individual mothers vary too. Baboon and rhesus mothers (300: ch. X, 41: ch. XX) do not allow other interested females to handle their newborn babies, and limit the infant's freedom of movement and social play when it begins to be able to move about by itself. Langurs (300: ch. IX) are more tolerant. Howlers control their young, but interfere less than baboons with their infants' social contacts. In general, a monkey mother holds, supports, nurses, inspects, grooms and almost constantly attends to her baby. The infant clings to her, and at first appears comfortable only in contact with her. Later he explores her body and actively seeks her attention. If infants are separated from their mothers both become distressed, the more so the more frequent the previous contacts between them. On being reunited, mother and infant cling to each other for a time in the way they did when the infant was much younger. Newborn monkeys, completely isolated from their mother and from all other animals for prolonged periods, showed poor social relationships at maturity. Their sexual responsiveness was low, and they made bad mothers, rejecting and even attacking their young (300: ch. VIII).

Play between monkey mothers and infants is relatively rare, except in so far as the mothers' constant grooming, inspection and physical contact can be called so. But it does occur.

Langur mothers play a sort of teasing game with slightly older infants, or wrestle with an infant trying to escape grooming (300: ch. IX). As the infant grows older, the mother loses interest in it. It is increasingly the monkey child (the juvenile after weaning but before adolescence), who initiates contacts. Adult howler and langur males are indifferent to babies, but respond to some of the older children's play, and retrieve and protect them if they are in danger. Male baboons approach and touch babies with lip-smacking and other signs of good will. They protect mothers with young infants, and tolerate the older child's play long after the females have ceased to care for the weaned young-ster. The young are allowed liberties permitted to no adult. Juvenile males initiate play of a quasi-sexual kind with adult males, embracing, clasping and mounting them. The pro-tection of the powerful adult males is necessary to the young baboon since they live on plains more exposed to predators than the more peaceful and mainly tree-living howlers and langurs. Chimpanzee fathers in captivity also play more with the older children than their mothers. When isolated as a family from other monkeys, chimpanzee mothers protect and supervise their young much longer than in the wild. Under these circumstances the female will occasionally initiate play with the infant by hugging, grasping, tumbling or tickling it(37).

The importance of physical contact to the monkey infant was demonstrated by the well-known experiments of the American psychologist, Harlow. Harlow raised monkey infants on different types of artificial 'mothers'. Comparison of cloth-covered blocks of wood with bare wire contraptions both fitted with a teat from which the infant fed showed that contact with something soft to cling to is more important than obtaining nourishment for establishing the 'bond of affec-tion' between the surrogate and the infant. When frightened, even infants who had been fed on wire mothers would run to the cloth-covered mother rather than to the wire mother for comfort (151). Rag-mops or other objects that can be clung to and clasped are played with by young chimpanzees when they are in the familiar surroundings of their home-cage. When in strange surroundings or when frightened, however, play declines and clinging increases (91 : ch. XV).

The effect of a close relationship between monkey mother and infant on its social relations with peers is not yet clear. Harlow showed that it might hinder rather than help if the infant had no contact with other monkey children. Infants brought up in small cages, with only their mothers for the first seven months of life, showed no interest in other infants when given the opportunity, and were less likely to develop normal adult sexual behaviour than infants brought up on surrogate mothers, but together with age-mates (300 : ch. VIII). On the other hand, there is one report of two infants brought up together without mothers from the age of ninety days, who simply clung to one another without showing normal infant behaviour towards each other, or to other infants (41 : ch. X). A close tie with the mother early on, emancipation from her, and experience with age-mates are probably all important for the cohesion and cooperation of the members of a monkey troupe as adults. The mother's rejection of the older infants, and the infant's tendency to explore further afield, turn the child's interest towards his playmates, according to Harlow. The constantly active, moving young provide more stimuli for investigation and exploring than inanimate objects.

The Social Play of Young Monkeys

Typically, young monkeys of all species spend most of their time playing with each other, mostly 'play-fighting' (91 : ch. XV). Howler young(68) sometimes play on their own with their hands and feet, tail, leaves and twigs, but far more with playmates, chasing each other and wrestling while hanging from branches by their tails. The games of howlers, who rank rather low in the intellectual hierarchy of primates, are relatively simple and repetitive. As they grow older the wrestling becomes more vigorous, and it declines after the age of about two years when it becomes painful to some of the participants. Social play with age-mates familiarizes the young with all the other immature individuals in the clan.

Play-fighting is not merely controlled by the infants' responses to each other but also by the adult males, whose grunts, when a juvenile squeals out in pain, immediately stop the game or at least change its quality. Langur mothers initially chase away older ones who come to invite the infant to play, but interfere less as the baby's coat changes from the initial dark brown to grey, and he becomes more active. The young male's play is almost entirely with his sex- and age-mates, running, jumping, chasing, wrestling and exploring each other. The weaker, smaller female child (i.e. the young after weaning but not yet adolescent), gradually drops out of these groups who play more roughly than she can, and plays with other females and younger children. Infant baboons, too, are initiated into play by older children who entice them from their mothers to play. But any sign of distress from the infant rapidly brings protection from the adult males who only have to stare at the juveniles to make them give up the baby and flee in terror (300: ch. X). The play of weaned baboon children is more varied than that of howlers. They make use of piles of rocks, stream beds and other features of the environment in their running and chasing games. Younger infants' play mainly consists of physical contact with each other.

It has been suggested that for baboons and rhesus monkeys play establishes the dominance hierarchy necessary for a stable social order and peaceful coexistence. The individual's status becomes clear-cut with adolescence, and this is also the time when there is much less social play. However, in free-ranging baboons the mother's own social rank is as important as the monkey child's size and strength in establishing his status. The young of high-ranking females live with them near the dominant adult males. They may learn from them how to quell lesser ranking animals, as well as having their high-ranking mothers' protection. The children of the chronically intimidated subordinate females rank low. Competition for dominance status is, therefore, probably not the only determining factor in social play. Dominance order is not necessarily the same for play as for food(180). The younger and more active of two gorillas observed in captivity dominated play, but the older, larger and lazier animal had precedence for food(70). The play-groups of rhesus juveniles tend to be unstable unless each has a fair chance of dominating. Consequently juveniles of the same age mostly play together. When older more dominant animals play with younger ones they do not use all their strength. We do not yet know whether this 'self-handicapping' in play (41: ch. XX), occurs because the juveniles fear punishment by near-by adults if they are too rough, or for other reasons. In any case, invitations to play are heralded and accompanied by definite signals between the animals. Howler and gibbon infants chirp at each other; chimpanzee infants make a 'play-face'(401), rhesus monkeys look at their play-partners upside down through their legs; baboons of both sexes who 'present' in the female sexual fashion as a token of social submission, entice each other to play in this way. Gibbons use the same sort of relaxed approach, embrace and sounds to initiate play with which they introduce friendly social grooming or copulation. These signals do not precede antagonistic encounters (41: ch. XX, 69). The use of friendly signals to herald play would make little sense if social play were solely the means of establishing dominance, with all its advantages of access to food, females and general precedence. It is more likely that the signals function as they do for the other friendly social encounters they precede: they signal that it is friendly. The usefulness of friendly contact between young monkeys belonging to one troupe is obvious.

Captive young chimpanzees show mutual attraction and strong preferences for individuals. Some individuals associate constantly, and there are struggles between rivals for the privilege of grooming, walking, sitting or playing with a favoured one. A systematic study of pre-adolescent chimpanzees(265) showed that their consistent dominance order was quite independent of an animal's being preferred for the grooming and play which formed most of their social behaviour. The younger, on the whole, preferred those who played and groomed more. Social play in the higher apes, such as the chimpanzee, is by no means confined to chasing, wrestling or play-fighting. They will pull each other about in sacks, perform 'dances' together, and are interested in each other's artistic productions – such as some object smeared with faeces or paint. Some gorillas had a regular game in which they took turns sliding over a tree-stump(70). Various types of games become fashionable for a time, then their popularity wanes again. Intelligence seems to be a preferred characteristic in a playmate. The stupider animals have greater difficulty than others in finding partners(196).

In frightening situations, or on being reunited after separation, young chimpanzees cling to each other; a little later they may groom. It is only after these initial minutes that social play begins and increases to its normal level (91 : ch. XV). Experimental studies have shown that rough-and-tumble play stimulates young chimpanzees and produces greater arousal. In conditions of extreme excitement and fear, however, play is absent or avoided. The animals tend to cling to others or to objects. It has been suggested that clinging, which reduces excitement, and play, which increases it, function between them to maintain an optimal level of arousal for the animal (240: ch. IX). Typically, social play occurs in conditions of moderate arousal, and increases when new or exciting stimuli are introduced.

Exploring and Playing with Objects

Monkeys play with everything. Baboons carry bags, wear baskets on their heads, tinker with watches given to them or with toads they have found. Young chimps show a great variety of play, in acrobatic games, experimenting with new ways of eating and drinking, looking at the world upside down through their legs, punching a hole through a leaf and peering through it, contemplating their reflection in a puddle of water. When no longer hungry they make a mess or pulp out of their food, dip straws and sticks into their drinks and suck them. Any object that can be taken to pieces is soon reduced to fragments. Empty tins or hollow objects that make a noise are banged vigorously. Köhler's(196) famous chimpanzee, Sultan, invented a game of jumping with the aid of a pole although this did not get him anywhere in particular where he could not have got more easily by walking or climbing. Other chimps imitated Sultan, and the game subsequently developed into the regular use of the pole as a tool. When Sultan was given two hollow sticks, neither by itself long enough to reach a banana outside his cage, he failed to fit them together even after having been shown that they were hollow. After a period of apparently idle play with the sticks, however, he solved the problem.

Experimental studies in which one group, but not another comparable one, was given the opportunity to play with the tools necessary for the solution of a problem, have yielded contradictory results about the beneficial effects of play on the solving of problems(39, 318). This is probably because any such effect must depend largely upon the nature of the task as well as of the play-experience. If an animal's attention has been drawn to aspects of a tool, material, or situation which are relevant in a later task, then it is probable that play with the tool or material will facilitate a solution. If there are no such attention-catching clues, the probability of a restricted period of random play yielding information on just those aspects of a tool which are relevant to some task the experimenter has in mind becomes much less. The richer and more varied an animal's past experience of all kinds of situations, materials and events, the more likely that some of it will be relevant to some later task. This applies even more to the higher primates, whose brain is better at coordinating and recording information, than to the lower mammals. Unlike dogs in one study(356) rhesus monkeys who have been deprived of stimulation in infancy become inactive, show less inclination to explore and prefer less complex stimuli to look at and handle(311) than normally reared ones. The extent to which restriction in infancy produces more or less exploring in adulthood probably depends on species differences as well as on the severity and length of time of the restriction. Human infants certainly seem to explore and play less when they have long been accustomed to absence of toys and little contact with adults.

The Development of Play in Monkeys

A systematic study of four infant racoons removed from their mothers at the age of two weeks records that prior to the time of opening their eyes, the infants' behaviour consisted almost entirely of simple reflexes, and reactions associated with hunger, urination, excretion or other discomfort. A day or two after they opened their eyes (at about twenty-four to thirty days), they showed the first signs of interest in objects, gently touching different surfaces with their paws and nose. As they became older this increased in vigour and frequency and they mouthed, bit, chewed, sucked, tugged and trod on the objects. These activities never occurred during periods of hunger or stress(378). It has been suggested that their relatively sudden appearance is associated with the maturation of a new set of functions in the central nervous system. Infant rhesus monkeys(118, pp. 75–88) already liked looking at things at the age of three days. They handled objects with great and increasing intensity by the age of twenty days.

The very young explore everything, the more so the larger, stronger, or more mobile the object is. They are only restrained by the mother. By the age of twenty days there is a gradual development of fear. The characteristics which elicited most approach before are now feared and avoided.

Relative novelty, complexity, and changes of all kinds elicit exploration and play. Experimental studies of young chimpanzees have shown that any object which was relatively new to them was touched and handled more often than relatively old ones. Objects that 'did' something when handled – banged, rang, came apart, moved or caused some other change were preferred to stationary, unchanging objects. The larger, brighter-coloured and more variously shaped the objects were the more they were looked at and handled(375, 376). There were differences in the play of infant, child and pre-adolescent chimpanzees. Infants up to the age of two years were more cautious initially in this situation: looking at rather than handling novel objects, until they became relatively familiar. Chimpanzee children between the ages of three and four were highly curious, and played significantly more than pre-adolescents at the age of seven to eight. Pre-adolescents were as eager to handle novel objects as the children during the initial minute of encountering a novel object, but they got tired of it more quickly. All animals handled the objects less as each session wore on, and less from one session to another, but the older animals showed a faster rate of satiation than the younger ones. Any change, even just changing the colour of an object previously handled, immediately restored interest in it for a time(377).

It has already been mentioned that even adult rhesus monkeys will learn to work mechanical puzzles for no other reward than to be allowed to work another puzzle(149). Exploring visually is also extremely persistent(63). Welker (377) found that young chimpanzees got tired of novel objects the more frequently they were given, and would only continue to touch and handle objects so long as new ones were introduced periodically. Harlow's(150) monkeys on the other hand, went on manipulating mechanical puzzles – hooks and eyes, cotter pins, and so forth, without any sign of getting tired of them. Whether these discrepancies are due to age and species differences, or differences in the task, or in the objects presented to the monkeys, is not as yet clear. Harlow had evidently hit upon particularly interesting play-objects in his mechanical puzzles. But why they were so much more interesting than the novel objects of Welker is not certain. It is possible that Harlow's objects were more suitable for producing further changes when manipulated, i.e. for what has been called 'diversive' as distinct from specific exploration(34). More probably, persistence of manipulation was less a function of further sensory changes than of the continuance of a problem. In the comparable case of children, persistence of play with toys has been shown to vary from three minutes to three-quarters of an hour, depending on the extent to which the toy presented some sort of problem to the child(257). This would be more a form of what Berlyne(34) has called 'epistemic' curiosity.

Novelty and change, when they do not frighten the animal, typically call out various actions which put the animal in touch with the stimulation. Turning the head in its direction, looking and listening, have this effect. So does investigation by touch, biting, sucking, chewing, clawing and sniffing. But lengthy manipulation of objects is probably not always an attempt to bring about further changes, or trying to solve a problem, and may consequently not always be similar to exploring. Animals often play with those objects that elicit clinging rather than avoidance in frightening or unfamiliar surroundings. Familiarity, association with reassuring events, characteristics which innately call out a certain response may, at times, be more important in play-objects than the possibility of change.

Animal Play and the Play Concept

Observations and studies relevant to the conditions determining play, suggest that play is not biologically useless. Animals who are inactive get out of condition. Preventing the exercise of movements even if they are already perfect in infancy may cause inefficiency in the relevant behaviour pattern later. Social play may function to acquaint the members of a social group with one another so that they can recognize each other and act in concert when necessary; or to establish a social-rank order which preserves peace, or gives access to food and mates to the most viable adults; or possibly to provide social experience for mating.

In the higher mammals investigating, exploring and manipulating objects probably serves to gather information for later use. The active exposure of the sense receptors to external stimulation is essential to keep the animal in touch with environmental changes, and is necessary to maintain the development and normal functioning of the central nervous system. It may also be necessary to keep the level of stimulation relatively constant. In whatever way different kinds of play originally became useful to given species in their survival, these functions are not, of course, goals to any individual. An infant racoon is not aiming to stimulate his receptors, improve his muscle tone, or further his social rank when he is playing. But as conscious goals should not be predicated either of the mating badger, or baboon elder staring at an impertinent juvenile, absence of purpose cannot distinguish play. The felt benefits of rushing to and fro may be quite as immediate as those of feeding; their ultimate biological goal is equally remote. The functions of different kinds of play have yet to be established, but if play is defined as biologically useless, it will sooner or later apply to nothing at all.

It is tempting to restrict the term 'play' to one or other category. But social play, general activity, lengthy handling of objects or juvenile exercise of adult patterns, are equally good or bad candidates. Here the word 'play' is retained for everything ordinarily called play, but with the suggestion that different kinds of play are subject to a somewhat different array of conditions. Even within any one category play differs between species. The characteristic movements differ as do the body structures on which they depend, whether used in play or otherwise. Some species rely more on vision, others more on other senses for information about the environment. There are differences in the kind of experience they are likely to encounter, and differences in the cues to which they are most likely to attend. Species with complex central nervous organizations who are good at solving problems are also more varied and intelligent in their play.

Play is often described as 'spontaneous' activity, implying that it is not caused by external factors. If anything, this is probably the reverse of the facts, at any rate in animals. If there is any one characteristic in common between the reported play from birds to monkeys, it is that it is preceded by some change in the environment. Atmospheric differences precede the flight play of birds; novel moving objects and other attention-catching ones are followed by play in mammals. Even social play is probably partly a response to the many changes of stimulation provided by another moving, squealing, prodding infant. The other condition, almost balancing the first, reported as essential for ants play-fighting as well as baby monkeys fiddling with twigs is the absence of anything to make them frightened or uncomfortable. Typically, although he explored everything, the badger played with objects after he had marked them with his own special and familiar scent. Too much should not be made of this. Being curious and comfortable may not characterize play alone, or all kinds of play.

The attempt to classify examples of play into four pigeon-holes leads to a number of questions. Are the conditions said to favour play the same as those for non-specific activity generally? Do sudden spurts of activity, such as the flight antics of some birds, depend on particular stimuli? If so, which? Is the frisking and skittishness of young mammals due to a heightened sensitivity to all external stimuli or to lack of familiarity with them, or to lack of motor control in the immature central nervous system, or all these? Does the 'irrelevant' play of young mammals depend upon not having learned to discriminate appropriate from inappropriate objects, or does it occur because shifts of attention from one stimulus to another happen more rapidly, or because the behaviour cannot be integrated until the organism is fully mature? Is play-fighting not lethal because social factors inhibit it, or because infants lack fighting skills, or because they react indiscriminately with all possible motor patterns to any physical contact? Does continued manipulation of objects occur only under conditions of heightened excitement, or when there is a lack of external stimulation, or both? Is play with familiar objects determined by the changes in perception to which it leads, or is it a result of the object's having been associated with reward in the past, or having some characteristic to which the animal is predisposed to respond – something warm to cling to or shiny to pick up for monkeys, something to gnaw for rats, to bite and shake for badgers? The alternatives do not necessarily exclude each other, but answers must wait on more experimental studies specifically concerned with play conditions.

The examples of play from arthropods to monkeys show that at least four categories are needed to classify play activities, and these require analysis in terms of at least four different sets of conditions. General activity, like skittishness and frisking, seems to be largely a question of the degree of excitement or 'arousal'. Violent excitement or disorganizing arousal issues not in play but in avoidance. But anything that moderately excites an animal tends to lead to general, undirected activity, usually called 'play' in the young.

The occurrence of incomplete or irrelevant behaviour, on the other hand, like chasing inappropriate objects, singing by the young which does not have the adult function, nest-building movements when these cannot result in the building of proper nests, or juvenile sex-play, requires study in the context of the development, integration and control of biologically necessary behaviour sequences. Reactions to characteristics in the environment to which the animal is innately predisposed to respond, but before it has learned to narrow these down to appropriate objects, is one subdivision of this kind of play in the young. The interplay between perception and performance, for instance for vocal and movement control, is another. Special conditions, for example when ongoing behaviour is checked by conflict, satiety, altered by conditions of captivity or domestication, or arrested by other inhibiting factors, is probably more relevant to some forms of play in adult animals.

For some mammals, and especially for primates, exploring the environment and experimenting with objects appears as play when the exploration is generalized, or when the novelty of the experience is not obvious to the observer. Here questions of the detailed functioning of perceptual scanning, attention, discrimination learning, and their relation to the stimulus input are relevant.

The largest category of mammal play is social play, and it mainly occurs between the young of a species. This seems to involve all the other play-forms in varying degrees, and can, consequently, not be very different from these in its causal analysis. At the behavioural level, however, social play, at any rate in some species, differs in some essential respects from solitary play; for instance, in the use of signals to precede play-fights. Not all social play consists of friendly fights although a good deal of it does. The nature of the checks on the degree of aggression shown, however, probably differs with the conditions which determine the social organization of a species, and these have to be taken into account.

The categories of play used here almost certainly conceal other distinctions. To suggest that all these different forms of play are unlikely to be explicable by one particular arrangement of conditions only is not to say that there is no overlap in the conditions at all. The degree of arousal, for instance, must be taken into account in explanations of all kinds of play; but so it would in most other forms of behaviour. The question is what weight should be attached to it in any one instance.

There is little doubt that all forms of play in mammals occur more in the young than in mature animals. The development of different kinds of play in the young of one interesting species – the human – will be discussed in the following chapters.

CHAPTER FOUR

EXPLORING AND MOVEMENT PLAY

The Beginning of Exploring and Practice Play

My little girl, instructed to amuse the eight-week-old baby while I was preparing his feed, exclaimed excitedly: 'Mummy! The baby likes to look at everything! Why?' She was intrigued by the fact that whatever she held up to him, a rattle, a doll, a book and finally bits of paper and cardboard seemed to be effective in making him stop crying, and look and smile. Although she was playing with the baby to please me, she had become interested in the baby's responses for their own sake, and was experimenting to see if she could vary them by showing him as many dissimilar objects as she could think of. She was exploring.

An eight-week-old baby's repertoire of actions is, of course, limited. He cannot, for instance, reach for, or grasp the things he looks at. But he can focus his gaze, follow a moving spot of light, and turn his head in its direction. For the time that he does so, the general movement of arms and legs and body that goes on practically all the time he is awake becomes less or stops altogether. Things to look at or listen to may even stop his crying when hungry, and make him smile, provided he is not too uncomfortable. From signs such as these we infer that he is interested, and 'likes to look'. It is the 'what is it?' response and the beginning of exploring.

Even the newborn baby, whose higher brain centres are almost functionless as yet, has some of the visual and central nervous system organization necessary for reacting to change. He can focus on and follow a moving spot of light and a moving object brought within his line of vision(307), although he does not yet always use both eyes in coordination. His alertness increases and even becomes 'avid'-looking within the first two weeks of life(222). He reacts differently to sudden, intense and abrupt stimulation, than to stimulation which is gentle and continuous. Discontinuous loud noises 'startle' him: a reflex in which he flings out his arms and legs violently and then flexes them in a sort of clasp. But repeated and gentle sounds decrease his movements. His body assumes a reflex posture orientated towards the source of sound as if he were listening(136). Talking, singing, gentle stroking, and rocking, i.e. continued repetitive, gentle stimulation, have always been means of soothing a crying baby.

Individual babies differ in their reaction to different intensities of stimuli within the first four or five days of life(38). (These may be, but are not necessarily, inherited differences. Birth injury, for instance, may alter responsiveness.) Repetition of the same tone, sight or smell decreases all reactions aroused by it initially. The baby gets used to it, and so shows a rudimentary kind of learning at a surprisingly early age(22, 47, 102). Although the range varies among individuals, the characteristics of stimuli which elicit sustained looking and listening are midway between those intensities that produce disturbance, crying or avoidance, and the monotonous repetition of mild stimuli that lead to inattention or sleep. Six-month-olds cry when they first hear a familiar voice coming out of a mask, or a distorted voice from a familiar face. By the third repetition they show some signs of attending without fear, and by the fourth they are interested(58). Some babies, from the age of two weeks onwards, began to show signs of boredom at being repeatedly shown a moving metal disc(222). They started looking away at the white surroundings, then repeatedly had a sneaking look at the object, apparently having some sort of game. Before this, when they fixated it they stared unwaveringly. To look or listen at all, infants must be dry, fed, comfortable and awake in a state of 'alert inactivity'(386).

Presumably to the very young baby, almost every stimulus is equally new. Contrary to what one might suppose, complex patterns like bull's eyes, or black and white chequer-boards, were looked at significantly longer than simple figures, such as outlines of triangles or squares, by babies aged between four days and fifteen weeks(109). In another experiment, the infants were shown three flat objects the size and shape of a head. One was painted with a stylized face in black on a pink background, on the second the features were rearranged in a scrambled pattern, and the third had a solid black patch at one end covering the same amount of space as the total area of black in each of the others. All the infants looked longest at the face, next at the scrambled one, and largely ignored the oblong with the solid black and pink patches when the three were paired in all possible combinations. Whether the face pattern was looked at longest because it was relatively the most familiar pattern even at that age, or because there is an innate preference for either face-like or for complex patterns is not yet conclusively established. Complexity, for example the amount of contour in a pattern, is one of the variables which increases the time of looking at patterns in adults too (131: ch. VI). But there is evidence that even very young children can discriminate between certain shapes and some aspects of depth(109, 371, 104).

When babies are awake and comfortable, they spend their time looking, listening and generally responding in a way which has led people to describe them as 'hungry' for stimuli. This becomes more obvious as they grow older. A five-month-old may find it difficult to go on eating if anything else interesting is going on, and I have known a hungry one-year-old refuse his bottle with screams of indignation because it obscured his view of the pretty pattern on his new pyjamas. The common practice of hanging rattles on babies' cots probably originated as magic to frighten off evil spirits. But brightly coloured rattles hung where the baby can see them, and hear the noise they make, do avert boredom. Swaying branches, pictures and patterned curtains are stared at with unblinking intensity by young infants.

Exploring more usually implies moving towards, touching and handling objects. This cannot occur until the coordination of hand and eye is established about the third to fourth month. A lot of 'practice' waving of fists in front of his eyes goes on before the baby can touch what he is looking at, or take a swipe at hanging rattles, biff the crooning adult's head or arm, or take off his father's glasses if the latter's face is injudiciously close. Something clearly recognizable as play now occurs. Between the ages of four and five months one of my sons developed a game which, for a time, never failed to amuse him. It began when I was changing his nappy and my head happened to be close enough for him to give me an unexpected blow. My start and squeal at this made him chuckle so delightfully that I repeatedly put my head close enough for him to touch whereupon he invariably repeated his blow, and waited for me to make some sound, chuckling happily. Whenever I omitted to make the noise, he looked puzzled and tried again. A great many baby biographers have reported similar games at that age. Touching and pulling the hair of someone bending over them, knocking toys against the side of the cot, apparently to hear the noise, or pulling down a dangling toy, are often involved. Mouthing, licking, and sucking any object, even when the child is not hungry, babbling, repeating sounds he has just become capable of making are so often accompanied by smiles and chuckles that they have been described as due to a 'pleasure in function' when the activity involves the baby's own body, and as 'pleasure in being a cause' when it involves effects on external objects. Although our knowledge is not as yet precise, it seems probable that the familiarization of abrupt and initially frightening or at least 'exciting' and novel stimuli is involved. The stimuli which induce laughter in babies at about four months are frequently those which at first make them blink and catch their breath. One of my children at the age of four months laughed most at a rattle being dropped from above on to her blanket, and at seeing me give an enormous yawn. In both cases, the first occasion of the incidents had startled and mildly frightened her. The surprising and the unexpected are ingredients in adult humour too(34).

Relative novelty may also be involved in the child's play

with his own body and skills. Piaget (see Chapter Two) distinguishes between doing something in order to understand what is happening, or in order to achieve a new skill, and repeatedly doing it 'for fun'. Trying to touch a rattle, or to make it swing is not play. Doing it repeatedly when the skill is already within the child's capacity, when it achieves no new perception, and serves no serious purpose, is play.

The distinction is not easy to make. Chuckling and other signs of pleasure accompany both exciting play and novel perceptions. It is difficult to decide when something becomes absolutely easy to the child. Children need far more repetition and a far greater redundancy of information than adults to achieve the same facility(382). For instance, children even of nursery-school age need more connecting lines in an incomplete drawing of a horse or umbrella to recognize the object than adults do(138). It is probable that the repetitiveness which appears useless because the child has apparently already developed the particular skill, is in fact necessary to test it out fully, or to confirm and 'fix' a novel experience. Moreover, any complex skill or perception has many facets which may claim the child's attention as much as the original object of the performance. A baby may lift his head to be able to keep some interesting object in view, and then start moving his head up and down 'for fun'. Lifting his head may have produced its own rather novel bodily sensation which he is now exploring. Presumably the stage between initial acquaintance and complete familiarity with every facet of any event is longer the younger the child is, because he is more ignorant of more aspects of new objects and effects of a new skill.

Piaget considers that 'practice' play occurs whenever a new skill is acquired, but that the occasions for it become less as fewer skills are totally new for the older person. Even adults tinker inordinately with a new wireless or car. Saturation point is only reached when there is nothing further to learn about the object(283). This does not fit entirely with his definition of play as pure assimilation without further adjustment as distinguished from serious investigation, which is an adjustment to a novel experience. Nevertheless, his distinction is important. In fact, there are probably at least three slightly different phases involved in 'practice' play: exploring play as a reaction to relatively novel stimulus patterns, manipulative play which itself produces whatever changes there may be; and repetition or repetition with variation. The latter may serve to integrate the experience with the rest of the organism's know-how. It could be distinguished from the others by being less a function of the degree of novelty, than of the complexity and number of skills the individual has already. Only experiments in which some of these variables are controlled can tell us the answer. A recent experimental study has teased out some of the differences between directed exploring of a new object, and the diversification of manipulative play in nursery-school children(176).

Age changes in play may be expected to work roughly in three directions. An increase of play with age as the child becomes capable of more varied activities and so can impose more changes on the environment; a decrease of play with age as fewer events and skills are novel and are absorbed more quickly; and the waxing and waning of specific activities as they develop, become mastered, and are finally fully exploited.

Play-Activities in the First Eighteen Months

Observations collected in baby biographies and longitudinal studies which record data on groups of children over a number of years show that play in the first eighteen months of life increases as the child's capacities increase. It is, indeed, almost identical with these(133). Between the ages of four and seven months, the baby can handle at first only one object at a time; he shakes and bangs that. Given two, he will drop one of them. Later on he can manage two toys. He shakes and bangs those, and this is followed in sequence by rubbing them together, and hitting them against each other. Placing an object down carefully, and actually being able to let go so that it stays, follows throwing down everything possible, but precedes being able to fit forms, hollow sticks and cubes into one another between the ages of twelve and fifteen months. The movements leading to sitting, standing and walking become the object of games. As soon as the infant can crawl, he will crawl most of the time. From the moment he can walk, there will be endless exercise of walking (133).

The ages at which different capacities develop vary widely among individuals, but the order in which they appear remains relatively constant. Charlotte Bühler's(56) group of infants treated all materials alike before the age of ten months. Apparently it was not until about eighteen months or two years that they 'noticed' the change in materials which their own actions produced, and so became interested in varying the results. This does not mean that even much younger children than this are unable to discriminate between a blank piece of paper and one on which they have made a mark. The development refers to their becoming aware of a connexion between their actions and the changes in the object these produce. In a recent experiment it was found that two-year-olds, placed in a playpen that could be made to revolve by shouting or making a noise, quickly learned the connexion between making sounds and the movement of the pen. They made much less noise when the pen revolved continually. Children below the age of a year did not behave significantly differently in the two situations. Between the ages of twelve months and eighteen months some children showed active control of the pen by vocal means (338: ch. XIV).

On Piaget's analysis, the child's perception of the relation between his own actions and their results is a complex achievement which presupposes a number of simpler ones(284). For instance, the very young infant behaves as if objects he has seen someone hide under a screen were irrecoverable. Before he can search behind screens, he must first master a number of other skills: follow rapidly moving objects with his eyes, anticipate the final position of a falling toy, recognize an object from merely seeing a small part of it sticking out from under a cover, see an object 'disappear' while still holding on to it, be able to delay his actions and so on. These are involved in the child's perception of objects as spatially independent of his own actions; and consequently in his appreciation of the relation between his actions and the material. Each of the subsidiary achievements becomes, in turn, the object of play. Dropping toys from a height is greeted with delight by the baby until he can sit up. Later he tirelessly drops cups, spoons, dolls or plates from his highchair or out of his cot, watches them disappear, tries dropping them from different positions, and waits for the noise they make. Judging distances and depth, or anticipating the position of a moving object is not a simple matter even if some aspects of depth are recognized innately(371). Catching balls may retain its challenge for years. Hide-and-seek games, from the first peep-bo initiated by the parent until the infant spontaneously hides and recovers his teddies, bits of old tape, or pennies, become elaborated by ever more ingenious ways of hiding and finding. Spatial arrangements often become the object of play at about eighteen months. At that age, one of my children, after an ominous period of quiet, proudly drew my attention to a beautiful arrangement she had produced: all available tomatoes carefully lined up on the doorstep, with a little bite taken out of each to make them stand up better.

From the time that hand-eye coordination is established the infant's tendency to touch everything seems almost compulsive. It is difficult for the older infant or toddler not to touch and handle everything in spite of being told not to 'fiddle'. After he is able to move around, the contents of drawers, shelves and especially assemblies of miscellaneous small objects like buttons or coins, heaps of useless fragments attract his attention and keep him amused for relatively long periods. As Fröbel realized long ago, any game which makes use of recently acquired skills, or involves changes of touch, sound and sight, will amuse him.

The Elaboration of Skills and the Use of Materials

The coordination of perceiving and moving and progressive refinements in adapting to the way in which the world is arranged is one of the main developments of the first eighteen months of life. Piaget calls it the 'sensory-motor' period, characterized by sensory-motor play. After this age, the child's activities are more varied, and there are greater differences between the play of individual children. Nevertheless, children's growing skills, finer discriminations, and newly discovered sensations continue to occupy a good deal of their attention after this period. Groos already gave examples of this. At the age of twenty months, two of my children spontaneously played at turning rapidly in a circle, laughing at the sensation of slight giddiness they evidently experienced at the end. This was repeated even after the child had lost his balance on the previous occasion. As far as it was possible to tell, each child had 'discovered' this game by himself. Staring at a light through half-closed eyelids, trying to keep one eye closed while looking with the other, playing with the double vision produced by squinting, pressing on eyeballs for the brilliant patterns this produces, cupping hands over the ears to listen to the circulating blood, and attending to a host of other perceptions adults have long learned to ignore, provide amusement for children of nursery-school age and well beyond. Practising skills like running, jumping, skipping, riding tricycles and scooters, throwing and catching balls, rolling hoops and spinning tops, become, if anything, more important during the early school years. Simple skills are either incorporated or superseded by more elaborate ones.

The tendency to elaborate, to make something more difficult, has been described by a number of observers of quite young children. One of Valentine's children(368), after he had just learned to stand, tried to stand while holding a big ball with his mouth, and repeated this until he succeeded. Looking at the world upside down through one's legs is another favourite occupation at that time. So is carrying enormous bags while walking. Innumerable examples of such elaboration could be given throughout childhood and even, or even more, in adolescence and adulthood: walking on stilts, riding bicycles without using hands, or putting the feet on the handlebars, and so forth. Nor does this merely apply to movement games, but to all behaviour indulged in 'for fun', from solving *The Times* crossword puzzle to playing chess blindfold.

The simplest way to explain setting oneself unnecessary, difficult tasks is to classify it with social facts, such as competition with others, perhaps derivatively with oneself, in which learned rewards are involved. The child whose mother has cooed at him for walking forwards, may generalize, and walk backwards, zigzag, do goosestep or balance on a narrow plank for a further supply of praise. Rewards of this kind are clearly important, but this is not the whole explanation. Perceiving the effects an action has, and attending to some things more than to others, are involved.

Many games start from effects obtained by chance being repeated. Groos pointed out the dramatic effects of splashing in puddles. Once the child becomes capable of appreciating the effects of his own actions on different materials, trying these out seems to follow 'automatically', limited only by his skill and the nature of the material. Splashing in water, pouring it out, running sand through one's hands, or displacing it from one heap to another, do not make great demands on skill, but do produce immediate and continued ripples and visible changes. Not surprisingly, sand and water-play are the earliest nursery favourites. It is also one of the first games to decline although nine-year-olds still occasionally enjoy it, according to an American survey in the 1920s (211). Building often starts with an accidental push which happens to succeed. Building with bricks and other materials, making increasingly elaborate constructions, remains an activity on which children, especially boys, spend a large amount of time until the age of about ten years(110). Building with harder materials, which retain their own shape, offers more possibility of novel effects and for elaboration, although probably less than modelling, drawing and painting. Drawing has its peak popularity somewhat later than building, and goes on until the age of about sixteen, according to the survey. Several studies in the early 1930s show that when children first draw they are almost exclusively concerned with getting some recognizable shape on paper, usually a person or house and occasionally trees. It is not until these are mastered that compositions appear: several people in the family; or the house, family and a tree. Using colour as part of the composition comes later. Younger children recognize and like colours, but are unable as yet to 'spare enough attention' to isolate this dimension when drawing(56). The degree of detail, elaboration, perspective and coherence of children's drawings is correlated both with age and intelligence(139).

How good one is at a given skill clearly makes a difference. Simple bodily activities such as jumping, skipping, swinging on swings are not much in vogue after the age of twelve. On the other hand, games which demand a great deal of skill continue, or are taken up in early manhood, and will be given up only when bodily strength and agility decline. Not many adults climb trees, but rock and mountain climbing which present difficulties are the object of serious expeditions. One of the most interesting findings of the American survey in the 1920s is that between the ages of twelve and sixteen there was a marked drop, not in the frequency of leisure activities, but in their variety. For instance, drawing, painting and music dropped out as active leisure occupations for the majority of people at this age. Whether this is because these pursuits become boring at this stage unless the individual's skill is above the average, or specialization in a few activities offers more novelty and variety than a low level of skill in a larger number is not clear. Common observation would not lead one to suppose that variety or novelty lose their attraction in adolescence. In some respects there just is less that is novel for the older than for the younger, for the adolescent than for the child, especially as far as simple perceptions and skills are concerned. On the other hand, the adult's greater capacity for complex skills, and for digesting greater amounts of information also provide greater possibility of variety than before. Boredom in adolescence is likely if simple skills and experiences have become over-familiar, and the wherewithal for more complex ones has not been acquired. This does not mean that the social rewards of approval, prestige and all they involve are unimportant, or minimize the fact that in adolescence sexual and social interests are likely to predominate, and so restrict or exclude others. But it is probably true to say that the extent to which a child engages in an activity for its own sake depends, in part, on the possibility of variety and change it offers. This will depend on his skill, the nature of the material, and the amount of stimulation offered by the rest of the environment. The experimental evidence bearing on this involves at least five questions: Are changes or elaborations of an activity undertaken because the child has become 'tired' of it, or because some new aspect is perceived which has not yet been exhausted? Are there any systematic changes with age in the child's reaction to novelty, change and variety? Is there a given degree of skill or difficulty of a task which leads to persistence in it? What characteristics or stimulation are effective in maintaining interest? Does it matter whether this results from the child's own activity or not?

Boredom and Novelty

The evidence from animals and humans is that, by and large, continual repetition of the same pattern of sights, sounds, etc., leads to poorer performance on tasks involving attending to these. For the healthy, a monotonous environment eventually produces discomfort, irritation and attempts to vary it. When at ease, animals and humans choose relatively new rather than familiar sights and sounds. Whether boredom and the choice of change must be interpreted in terms of a previous fatigue-like process or whether novelty and change are literally attractive is still somewhat controversial(266).

Questions about what is looked at and listened to have

been classed with the selection of information in analogy with communication systems. This has many advantages, including a common language with other sciences. More importantly, it provides a mathematic for comparing a number of different behavioural functions quantitatively. The basic measurement is that of 'information', i.e. the amount by which uncertainty is reduced (using a binary rather than decimal system for convenience). For instance, if of two events both are equally probable, uncertainty is maximal. If one of the alternatives is knocked out, uncertainty is zero. Eight alternatives represent three 'bits' of uncertainty. The mathematic can deal with conditions where the alternatives are not equally likely, and is essentially concerned with the probabilities of sequences and chains of events. To the extent to which sequences are 'lawful' or patterned, and so predictable, they contain redundant information. For instance, ordinary English, and geometric shapes generated from one matrix, contain redundancies. Some words are more likely to follow others in a sentence, and some lines or angles follow others more predictably in a patterned sequence, than words or lines do in random arrangements. The components of any patterned sequence are restricted by the patterns or rules governing it. 'Information', in this sense, is a measure of the change from what is predictable. It is now generally accepted that psychological processes can be described as processes for handling information(9).

Selection of information becomes necessary when there is a limit on how much of what is received can be passed on. Humans have limited capacities. They cannot notice and respond to all the separate stimuli which are present at any one time in the environment(245). One of the results of experiments on vigilance tasks in which the subject is required to respond to faint stimuli appearing infrequently and irregularly on a screen, as in radar detection, and on listening to different messages fed separately to each ear by earphones, is that the stimuli which are noticed and effective in competition with others are not a random selection. For instance, high-pitched noise, intense stimuli, and novel ones are much more likely to be perceived. Broadbent(49) assumed that incoming stimuli are filtered before entering the limited capacity channel by mechanisms which are biased in favour of certain classes of stimuli. One of these biases is towards novel stimuli, and depends upon the time which has elapsed since one of a given class of events got past the filter last. The analysis necessary for this selection takes place in the central nervous system, and some of the questions involved are at what level there the stimulus input is fully analysed(50, 81, 339, 364). Other questions concern the nature of the 'limit' upon the amount of information that can be handled, and whether this is mainly on the 'input' or on the 'output' side, i.e. mainly on what is perceived or on responding. The effectiveness of information given before an observer starts on his task, and its negligible effect when given merely prior to the response he is to make, suggests that the selection tends to be in terms of what is perceived rather than how it is responded to (348: ch. XX). For adults on tasks like repeating sentences as they are being heard, or tapping to particular words in a message, the limit seems to be on the 'intake'(365).

What is listened to, or looked at, and can be repeated back when competing messages are given simultaneously is by no means merely a question of novelty. On the contrary, in the case of faint signals, or when extraneous noise interferes with listening, correct detection and identification depends on the extent to which the signal has been specified and expected, and the level of errors risked. The chances of detection vary with background noise, i.e. interferences from the sensory processes themselves and from outside. This has been described by the mathematics of statistical decision theory, that is, the sort of mathematics on which it is possible to calculate the pay-off in games of chance. The greater the uncertainty (in the informational sense) about the stimuli, the less likely they are to be detected (348, 351). The rules governing ordinary English allow those who know the language to expect some words rather than others to follow an initial phrase or in a given context. This affects the ease with which words are perceived (see above). Nevertheless, new events which would seem to be most uncertain and informative, are attention-catching. When you expect a mumbling man to say 'should' since the previous part of his sentence contained an 'if' – you are likely to think that he has said it even when he has not, and to miss an idiosyncratic innovation. But a sudden noise, or someone shouting 'fire' will gain your attention when you least expect such a thing. In general, the time it takes to react to a signal is longer the more information (in the technical sense) it contains. But reaction times to unusual events are faster(49).

This is true of children also. In one study, the fastest reactions were to that one of two coloured lights which had not been used in the period just before the test, especially if it immediately followed one that had. Although long-term familiarization led to slower responses, explained in terms of 'boredom', it was also found that any changed stimulus, whether or not it had been previously familiarized, was reacted to faster than an unchanged one(65, 66). Nursery school children looked at novel stimuli longer, more frequently, and produced more responses to them than to stimuli to which they had been exposed prior to this, whether they were geometric designs, patches of colour or toys(64). Preference for new stimuli and improved discrimination between objects when accentuated by novelty has been shown for mentally retarded children between the ages of eight and seventeen(170, 395). On the other hand, when they are irrelevant to the task in hand, extraneous changes interfere with an ongoing activity in children, and do so more for retarded than for normal children. Adults are less liable than children to be distracted from a given task. But even for them some irrelevant novel stimuli get through in conditions when most other irrelevant ones are ignored(168). Adaptation of the sense organs is unlikely to account for the results(168). Detection of regularity and change, as well as ability to inhibit reactions to extraneous stimuli, is basically involved. Young children have learned fewer rules about what to expect, and they are less able to inhibit reactions to novel stimuli (see below). They certainly concentrate on tasks less well than older children (230).

Changes attract attention even if there is no previous specifically 'boring' event. For instance, when a series of pictures and music followed a child's pressing a rubber ball, the child pressed the ball considerably more often (301). Some 'bias towards novelty' there seems to be, and a good deal of exploratory play must be thought of in these terms. It might also account, at least in part, for the tendency to elaborate activities which is characteristic of some play. Novel effects obtained by chance will be repeated. In the young, one might expect 'useless' elaborations to occur most when a skill is at that level of proficiency where chance effects are still frequent if it is combined with some other activity, but the component skills have become sufficiently familiar for the novelty to be exploited. A baby who can stand, but occasionally still topples over when reaching for a toy may start doing a sort of head-over-heels 'for fun' if the mattress is not too hard.

Competence and Variety

Making the first deliberate dent in a piece of plasticine, and appreciating the effect of flicking a full paintbrush may be quite as exciting to the infant as experiments in art are to the student. When the artist is sufficiently skilful for the results to be interesting to other adults it is taken 'seriously' by them. It has even been suggested that what people consider beautiful is largely a question of patterns which contain the unexpected (115: ch. XIV); regularity plus change, or a degree of uncertainty which is slightly in advance of comprehension. The impact of what is relatively novel, or mildly stimulating varies with the level of excitement. It is also likely that this 'optimum' varies with skill, or the extent to which the individual is able to classify, code or otherwise intellectually digest the new material. To listen to what we know already becomes boring. Something too complicated to make any sense to the uninitiated is equally tiresome. But a familiar argument given a new twist, a common experience presented in a new light, unexpected variations on a theme, attract.

Human ability to 'take in' all the changes going on around is limited. Nevertheless, humans can deal with a great deal of complexity in their environment. The ability to group, classify and docket events into manageable chunks is one way whereby limitations to taking in information may be by-passed (245, 246). The average adult finds it difficult to repeat a long row of digits in the right order immediately after hearing it. Grouping the digits makes it possible. A string of nonsense syllables is more difficult to repeat than a meaningful sentence containing the same number of syllables. Having rules for pigeonholing the material makes it easier to take it in. Children's immediate memory, their ability to repeat digits, words or sentences is inferior to that of adults and improves with age (67: ch. VII). They need more time to pigeonhole experiences, or may even have to construct the pigeonholes as they go along(284). In general, adults know more, and have more means at their disposal whereby they can organize and intellectually digest information. On this basis, one would expect that children, given the choice, would prefer simple, repetitive material which needs less skill of any kind. Young children's demand for the same story as before, the appeal for the same game, is well-known, if not exaggerated.

A recent series of studies probed the assumption that children's preference for variability is related to their ability to deal with, classify, code or otherwise intellectually digest material. Letter and word sequences varying in the degrees to which they approximated to ordinary English, and in the amount of repetition, were projected on to a screen. The subjects, children between six and fifteen years of age and young adults, were to mark the preferred one on a prepared sheet of paper. As expected, the younger children preferred more repetitions, and language sequences containing greater amounts of redundancy, than older children. Adults showed the greatest preference for random sequences, i.e. those varying most(259). On the other hand, when the stimuli were random geometric shapes, differing in the number of turns or corners in the contour from 4 to 40, all chose a figure with 10 turns most often, but the younger children preferred more shapes with a large number of turns than older children or adults, in spite of the fact that the younger children were just as inferior to the older and to adults in classifying the shapes and estimating the number of corners as they were linguistically(260). If what is 'preferred' is some variability slightly in advance of what is easily digested intellectually, the young ones' greater preference for figures of many turns needs additional explanation. The author found one in the known tendency for young children to attend to parts of a pattern rather than to the whole. In that sense, the figures may have seemed 'easier' to them. However, the 'complexity' of a pattern is not necessarily to be equated with difficulty. An ashtray, a soap-dish and a boot differ in a large number of ways, but are more easily distinguished from each other than a circle and a triangle which differ in shape only and are consequently 'simpler'. A shape may be both more complex and easier if it has a large number of features which help to distinguish it from others although only one such distinguishing mark would strictly be necessary. The redundancy of the cues makes the figure complex, but easier to discriminate given sufficient time (131: ch. VI). The vote for the complex figures in the above experiments may have been merely a vote for more time.

Age and the Preference for Repetition and Novelty

There is a puzzle about children's preference for repetition and change. Children like repetitions, but they also appear to respond more to novelty and variety than adults do. Whether this is merely because more objects and aspects of events are new to them is the question. Children are known to change frequently from one occupation to another in free play. Individuals vary considerably, and with different activities, and different toys(160, 257), but, on the average, six-year-olds spend more time doing any one thing than three-year-olds(56). The fact that young monkeys tire less quickly of novel objects than older monkeys(375, 377), and children bring complex figures back into view more frequently than adults do(34) is also cited as evidence for the preference of the young for novelty and complexity. But these measures may merely indicate the need to repeat, to look, or handle longer; to get more of the same information. The length of time a pattern is looked at, the speed of responses to it, the frequency with which it is brought back into view, the number of times it is marked as preferred, and the length of time taken until the individual is 'tired of it' have all been measures of 'preferences', but they are not necessarily interchangeable.

Nevertheless, it is well known that young children are far more easily distracted than older ones. In the somewhat comparable case of intellectually subnormal children who have also been described as easily distracted, it has been found that they differ from those with higher mental ages, not in the rate at which they learn to respond with a given movement to a given cue, but in the time they take to cotton on to which is the relevant cue. They appear to distribute their attention more evenly(396). It is possible that this applies also to normal children at different age levels. Older children will have learned to discriminate more aspects of the environment, but will also have learned to attend to some of these more than to others. They will, therefore, be more selective. Young children and retarded individuals may actually discriminate fewer dimensions of an object, or aspects of an event, but will attend to those in a more random fashion and so appear to be more easily distracted(396). In this situation novel stimuli may be privileged.

Russian investigators also consider attentional defects (in terms of orienting reflexes) to account for the fact that mentally defective and very young children are easily distracted. Sokholov(339) distinguishes two main aspects of the orienting reflex: general arousal, and attention to specific stimuli.

Incoming stimuli (e.g. a light or a sound), produce two types of electrically measureable currents. One which starts in the sensory nerve concerned (e.g. optic or auditory), and goes to those areas of the brain concerned with the particular sense (vision or hearing). This gives rise to specific visual or auditory reactions. The other current is due to visual or auditory excitation arriving at subcortical centres, particularly the reticular formation (see Chapter Three and below). From here the excitation spreads to the whole cortex, alerting it and putting the organism 'at the ready'. This reaction is longer but habituates more quickly than the cortical orienting reaction which lasts only a short time but resist repeated stimulation longer(339). Concentrating on a task depends upon continued cortical orienting reactions when the stimuli are analysed as new or otherwise significant by the cortex. Unlike Broadbent's theory (see above), Sokholov's theory assumes that incoming information is analysed fully by the cortex before 'gating' takes place). These inhibit reactions to irrelevant and incidental stimuli via the reticular formation. In the young and in the retarded this inhibition cannot take place(227) since the cortical orienting reactions are weak or absent. Consequently they react to all sorts of irrelevent stimuli in the environment.

The problem has many facets including questions about the behaviour of monkeys and men with lesions in the frontal lobe of the brain (372: ch. III). Lesions or stimulation of the frontal lobes impair efficiency on tasks involving immediate memory(374). Individuals with such lesions tend to persist in behaving in ways which were at one time, but are no longer, successful. They fail to adapt their actions. They seem to be unable to use their short-term memory 'store' (372: ch. 5). At the same time, they are more responsive to any slightly novel event. This has been explained by supposing an impairment in the frontal lobes' functioning to suppress whatever has been the animals' preferred mode of acting, including a bias to respond to the novel(55, 249). Another suggestion is that animals with frontal-lobe lesions fall back on established or familiar ways of behaving when they cannot cope with a task, and that the defect is in noticing and using the order in which events occur (372: ch. III).

Normal young children too have difficulty in using sequences. When asked to copy a bead chain or the way in which a doll's clothes were hung on a washing line, a four-year-old may remember all the shapes of beads or items of clothes quite correctly, but may have difficulty in stringing them up in the same order(179). Children of kindergarten age do well in guessing games where the chances are 75 per cent to 25 per cent, by sticking to whatever brings the higher number of rewards(343). But they are poorer at these games than older children if the pattern or sequence of previous events has to be taken into account(78, 141). Ability to perform sequential tasks improves with age. This could mean either that they do not attend to the sequence of events in the first place, or that they are less able to organize or re-code immediately preceding events, or are more easily distracted by irrelevant but to them more salient cues, or use a different 'strategy' from that of older children (e.g. to repeat whatever has been successful rather than to look for a recurring pattern), or discriminate less well between numbers of events when the proportions are closer to a 50/50 distribution.

How the developmental changes tie up with results from adult brain damage is as yet unclear. For one thing, damage to the same site in the brain has slightly different effects on younger than on older subjects (372: ch. VII). Increased attention to whatever has *not* just been seen or heard, and inability to shift one's reactions when they are no longer appropriate are probably not explicable by the same mechanisms (372: ch. V).

The question whether there are consistent changes with age in the reaction to novelty and change is complex. It is by no means established that younger children are less capable of concentrating than older ones under all conditions, for instance, if the events are relatively equally novel for the older as for the younger, or demand proportionately equal skill. Harlow's young monkeys(150) persisted for many sessions without reward or signs of boredom in playing with puzzles of hasps and clasps, cotter pins and the like. Human children are able to concentrate for long periods on, to them, interesting occupations. The experimental results of a number of studies of the length of time children spontaneously play with toys strongly suggests that 'complexity' of the toys, in the sense of their presenting some problem to the child, was an important factor in the length of time children would play with a given toy. As an example, a simply designed small red car was lowest in the average amount of time children between the ages of three and five played with it. A toy which involved problems of assembly and simple mechanical principles ranked high(257). As Berlyne pointed out, the novelty presented by sensory changes must be distinguished from the novelty presented by an intellectual 'puzzle'. It is not as yet clear whether there is a systematic age-relation between these.

There are thus a number of factors involved in the responses to novelty and change which make up a good deal of 'play' activities. The young organism's physiological mechanisms for keeping a steady internal state are less well organized. They are more easily excited by changes and habituate less quickly to new and abrupt stimuli. They are more easily 'distracted', either because they are unable to inhibit attending to irrelevant sensory changes, or because fewer events are of any significance to them, or they have not yet learned what can be ignored. They have shorter spans of immediate memory, and are less able to delay their reactions. A great deal more research is needed before we know the exact tie-up of all this with the rates of development of specific brain structures, although the general immaturity of the cortex is, no doubt, involved. Some essential behavioural facts are still unclear. For instance, whether there are differences with age in the number of shifts per unit of time in attending to any one aspect of a perception, as well as differences in the amount that can be handled sequentially. There are also the effects of experience. Not only has the young child developed fewer biases other than towards the novel, and less experience in discriminating various aspects of events; the older child has more information available to him to pigeonhole and classify new events, which makes it easier for him to react quickly and dismiss the problem earlier.

These aspects are all involved in the response to change, but it is unlikely that they are all explicable by a single process, and they may not change in the same way with age and experience. In the meantime, their combined effect on behaviour does not allow definite generalization about age changes. However, since there simply are more novel events and fewer and less varied reactions available for the young child, one might expect that to keep a child going on a given occupation would, generally speaking, require more changes going on externally than for the adult who may contribute more variety by his own activity. A child could not be kept long interested with one sheet of paper and a pencil. A mathematician, or a painter should have little difficulty. A child requires greater contribution from outside. 'What shall I do, Mummy?' is the constant refrain of children after they have passed the stage where every fluttering leaf is run after, and every speck of dust or shiny pebble is picked up. An artist is likely to spend more time with a piece of modelling clay than a child, although an unskilled adult might get bored more quickly than either.

Characteristics that Attract Children's Attention

For children as for most mammals novelty and changes of all kinds attract attention. The newer, the larger, the brighter, the louder, what moves, flies, rings a bell, flashes a light, is coloured, makes a sudden smell, or is uneven to the touch, will make them stop, look and listen, at any rate, initially. Continued changes will sustain attention, but there are, as far as I know, no experimental studies comparing children's reaction to novel objects with their response to familiar objects in which changes can be produced by handling them, and to those which can be stacked, taken to pieces, fitted and generally present some problem. But other findings suggest that objects which present some sort of puzzle, like cotter pins and hasps and clasps, for monkeys, assembly tasks, and tasks involving rules for children, are better at sustaining attention than novel objects which produce a limited number of effects, but have fewer 'uses', although such objects might attract more interest initially. This would fit in well with the common observation that elaborate new toys frequently monopolize children's interest for the first day or two, and are then thrown aside and the child returns to more engrossing occupations.

The surprising, the incongruous, events which arouse incompatible expectations or responses(34) alert children as well as adults, but reactions to these aspects of change must depend greatly on the children's previous knowledge and familiarity with the material. Complexity is another variable which compels attention, but is itself a 'complex' term. Complexity may refer to the number of aspects of an object, to the number of 'turns' in a design, or to the difficulty of a prose passage for someone who has not fully grasped the language. While the latter is 'difficult' by definition, complexity of shape may make discrimination easier. Even children of low intelligence learn to discriminate common objects which have many distinguishing marks but have greater difficulty with apparently simple designs such as squares and triangles which differ from each other in shape only (396). Complex objects may be liked because they make discrimination easier, or because there is more to look at. So far it is not clear which. There is plenty of evidence, however, that any task which is 'too complex', when this means so difficult for the individual that it leads to consistent failure, will generally speaking be avoided. A game must be within a child's capacity to be played at all.

The largest category of characteristics which attract children's attention is learned. Whatever is significant, i.e. has previously led to goodies or smiles, or is associated with important events, or is familiar, or probable in the context, has a better chance of being noticed than other cues. People hear their own name when little else gets through to them

(363). Characteristics of objects close to a 'goody' are more likely to be noticed than those further away.

What is noticed must depend on the maturity of the whole perceptual apparatus (including attentional and memory factors), previous discriminations and the mental pigeon-holes available to the child. A few examples must suffice. Infants look at objects near them. What is further away is noticed more with age. Children of nursery and school age overestimate the size of whatever object they are looking at. They are more affected by the effects of what immediately surrounds a figure than adults are(286). At the same time, they are less influenced than adults by the remoter frame-work, such as the walls of a room, or the edge of the paper, in judging whether a shape is horizontal. Children are less aware of exact differences between shapes. When confronted with a complex shape they tend to see an undifferentiated mass plus some outstanding detail(369), and to respond in terms of that one variable only(88). Children require a greater variety of cues than adults to maintain a stable perception when the object moves(382). Although children between the ages of eighteen months and five years can discriminate shapes, shape is not the most potent aspect for them. For mentally defective as well as for very young children solidity, contour or size of a figure rather than whether it is pointed or round are the important cues. The amount of attention an object receives is related to the degree of uncertainty (in the informational sense) about it(33). Generally speaking, the greater the lack of information, the poorer the perform-ance, and within limits, the greater the curiosity or time spent on something. Children's performance on perceptual tasks is poorer, they need a greater amount of redundancy of information, and they possibly operate in a 'noisier' system than adults. If so, they must be expected to show greater perceptual curiosity.

Although there are, to my knowledge, no studies on this, it seems likely that human infants, like young chimpanzees, are attracted by very small objects, especially if they are shiny irregularities on a surface. Bits of fluff on a dress, crumbs on their plate, small shiny stones, spots on their skin, and so forth, are almost invariably picked at or picked up.

There is also some evidence that different senses may be more important at one age than another. For instance, younger children explore objects by feeling and handling them, while from the age of five or six this declines and examining by looking only becomes more frequent, except when the object is completely unknown. In this case, older children too manipulate the object(394). This may mean either that different senses are more important at one age than another, or that when there are fewer means of classifying a new object, more responses are tried out.

Movement and Repetition

A girl of four when told not to fidget with the crockery on the table replied that her arm would get bored if she stopped. The constant movements of arms and legs, not being able to sit still for any length of time, sudden spurts of 'mad' activity – rushing about 'aimlessly' and useless repetition of movement patterns – are major differences in the behaviour of adults and children.

Individual babies vary considerably even at birth in how active they are. There is probably a genetic basis for this, although a good many other factors contribute to the general level of activity (see Chapter Three). The possibility of moving after having been deprived of movement has been shown to act like other rewards in the learning of animals. Variations in temperature, especially in young animals whose body temperature is as yet imperfectly controlled, affect activity. So does abrupt and intense external stimulation which arouses the organism's mechanisms for emergency action, and milder changes which lead to exploration and manipulation. Separate 'drives' for muscular, sensory, exploratory and manipulative activity have been proposed at various times, but the very multiplicity of drives makes them useless as explanations. This is no reason, however, for blurring the distinction between different types of activity.

Squirming

The unceasing movements of the young, the gratuitous flexing of feet, hands, arms, and shifts in bodily position, which distinguishes them from the more or less measured and deliberate actions of adults demand explanation in terms of immaturity of control, i.e. the inhibition of random activity and its integration with developing voluntary action. The development of the voluntary control needed for sitting, standing and walking occurs in definite sequences. This is true also for handling objects. The initial undifferentiated push eventually comes under the fine control required for picking up objects, for writing or sewing(148, 233). These sequences are paralleled by the growing differentiation and maturation of the relevant areas in the brain. Among other things, the neurons conducting nervous activity must acquire insulating sheaths (myelination) to function properly, although sometimes function can precede myelination(293, 315). Broadly speaking, the stability, smoothness and efficiency of movements increase with age. One of the effects of a maturing brain is better organization and integration. The 'squirming' of infant mammals is a by-product of their immaturity itself functional in maintaining or developing control(140).

Inaccurate, undifferentiated, gross rather than fine, movements are not themselves a necessary characteristic of play, but they probably add to the impression of lack of direction and purpose of children's activities and consequently to the impression of 'playful' activity.

Arousal

The apparently causeless sudden spurts of activity; the necessity to rush around, shriek and violently 'let off steam' which occurs more often in the young is often taken as a hallmark of play. As such it has not, to my knowledge, received specific investigation. However, a good deal is known about the mechanisms concerned in alerting,

arousing and mobilizing mammals and man to action. Of
particular importance in this is a part of the hind-, mid- and
fore-brain known as the reticular formation (see above and
Chapter Three). This may be thought of as a sort of indirect
relay and amplifying system for sensory impulses. It has
reciprocal connexions to the higher centres and downward
executive fibres. Together with portions of the adjacent
hypothalamus by which sensory impulses are directly relayed
to the higher centres (cortex), it is essential for alerting the
organism. The connexions both to and from the cortex to the
reticular formation form relay loops. Direct electrical stimulation of the reticular formation excites the animal; lesions in
it interfere with the animal's being aroused except briefly(4,
86, 235). Immature brains differ from mature ones in a number of ways especially the higher cortical centres(101, 293).
It has been suggested that the arousal pattern of newborn
children resembles that of animals without a cortex, and
that the adult pattern only develops when the cortex is
mature. At any rate, young children are less selective in their
reaction to stimuli. As a corollary, the frequent, brief and
apparently causeless spurts of general activity in the young
may occur because indifferent, non-significant, incidental
and irrelevant stimuli have a more equal chance of setting
off a brief general reaction. Stimulation which arouses the
young organism without exhausting it accelerates matura-
tion(199).

Self-Regulating Devices

In another sense of play, it is essentially repetitive. It has
long been known that infants and children spontaneously
'practise' each new skill as it arises. Babies suck when there
is nothing to suck, babble when no one is listening, wave their
fists while staring at them, reach up to try to stand, or move
from chair to chair when no one is rewarding them for doing
so. This and similar play occurs too early, is too universal, to
be explained by learning through rewards. A psychologist
called Baldwin in the late 1890s called these 'circular reactions' and supposed that they arose in a reflex fashion by an

automatic re-initiation of the action by the stimuli it produces. A child cries, hears its own cry, and this stimulates him
to go on. Piaget accepted this description and extended it to
include similar stimuli from the environment setting off these
reactions, gradually becoming incorporated in them, and
so giving rise to more elaborate secondary circular reactions.
Novel effects produced by chance actions are particularly
important in the repetition of these actions. For instance,
accidentally pushing a rattle makes it swing or make a noise.
The movement is then repeated for the sake of the new
effects. In turn, the action and perception become part of the
baby's repertoire and are tried out on other similar objects.
Repetition and further accidental changes will produce
further novel experiences which are then reproduced. Finally
the child becomes capable of varying his actions and tries
them out systematically for the sake of the different results
(see Chapter Two). He drops objects from different places,
knocks his spoon on cups, tables, bottles and anything else
which will give him more information than a simple repetition would have done. The process can also be described in
terms of conditioning, as the association of a movement with
a sensory event followed (reinforced) by reward which in this
case is some environmental change(34).

There are advantages in classing circular reactions with
other devices of the organism for regulating its actions according to their effects. In analogy with automatic self-regulating
devices, the organism will need built-in loops between
centres controlling a movement, and signal-receiving stations
which can flash back whether or not the movement hits the
target, or picks up discrepancies between points looked at
and reached. In the case of birds (see Chapter Three), a
young bird's hearing of the song as sung by himself is essential in establishing the normal song. In the case of children,
babbling and other forms of 'practice' are equally important for the development of normal speech(393).

Distorting, delaying, or displacing the signals that normally come back, disrupts behaviour. If you trace over a
star-shape, but are only allowed to see the movements of

your hand in a mirror, or on a television screen that distorts the angle at which you would normally see them, the quick smooth tracing movements become slow, jerky and faulty. The greater the distortions, and the less systematic they are, the more they will affect the movements(337, 338). Fixing earphones so that a person is prevented from hearing himself speak, except after a period of delay, slows down his performance, and can produce serious disturbances of articulation rather like a stutter. Neurophysiological as well as behavioural evidence requires a concept such as 'feedback' (140, 290). Visual signals and sensation from muscles are important aspects of the information that is returned, and which controls further action through central nervous integration.

Whether there is a particular form of return information which is more essential than others is as yet controversial. It has been held that sensations arising from an individual's own movements, correlated with what is seen, are a *sine qua non* for normal development(158, 159). It has also been argued that any perception of a mismatch between two external sources of information, or indeed any information to the agent of the results of his actions, is sufficient(171). There is a related doubt whether children come to see the connexion between their actions and the results these achieve as the result of a maturational process, or whether this is a complex, learned achievement (see above). Children certainly exhibit signs of pleasure and glee when they produce effects upon objects or people by their own actions, quite apart from whether such results are good, bad or indifferent in terms of getting goodies or praise. This is the behaviour referred to in descriptions of play as 'pleasure in being a cause', 'mastering experiences' (Freud, see Chapter Two), or 'effectance motivation'(380). Whether or not different mechanisms must be postulated for the perception of effects and changes produced by oneself, and perception of changes and effects which do not depend upon additional information from muscle endings, still needs clarification. But it seems reasonable to assume that some form of feedback mechanism underlies this kind of play.

On Piaget's theory circular reactions have two functions: that of matching actions progressively to incoming information (accommodation), and of incorporating this with existing know-how and means of classification (assimilation). The latter corresponds roughly to the encoding and storing in the memory-stores of cybernetic models. On these models, the repetition and repetition with variations of actions are due to 'feed-back' processes. We would need to assume that some forms of sensory-motor play are the overt manifestations of these regulatory processes before they have become automatic, covert and short-circuited in the adult.

Some Comments on Sensory-motor Play

Play which consists of movements in space, handling objects and the perceptual control this involves, is characteristic of the first eighteen months of life when it first develops. It is not confined to this period. Play with more complex skills embodying simpler ones is quite as frequent in childhood and later although differences between individuals increase.

Sensory-motor play as movement may be divided into (a) 'squirming', i.e. movements prior to full voluntary control; (b) 'aimless' sudden spurts of activity apparently without or with only insufficient cause; and (c) 'repetitive activity', i.e. the spontaneous exercise of movements from the compulsive-looking repetitiveness of early infancy, to the endless walking and climbing exercises of toddlers, and to planned practice of sports. Although we know far too little about it as yet, it is probably true to say that the conditions for the three aspects of play are somewhat different. Immaturity of cortical integration is more important in explaining squirming. Aimless sudden spurts of activity probably depend more on level of excitement and lack of discrimination between stimuli. Repetition, on the other hand, from the seemingly compulsive repetition of early movements to the deliberately planned exercise of elaborate skills, may be an aspect of the kind of return regulation there is, and its level of integration in the cortex and below. Deliberately planned exercise is likely to be organized at the highest cerebral level while 'compulsive'-looking exercise like early autogenous practice may occur only before the cortex is fully mature.

Sensory-motor play as a response to the external world may be subdivided into exploring, manipulating and practice play. Not all exploring which is not for some goody or to avoid pain can be called play. The least inquisitive response is probably the 'orienting reflex'; the cocking of ears, looking, the changes in breathing, heart-rate, size of pupil, and all the other physiological accompaniments of being on the alert. This is not play. During the period of familiarization there comes a point of interest between fear and familiarity which leads to exploring. There is another point somewhere between familiarity and boredom which may be called playful. Tentative approach is not play. Prolonged or repeated contact without fear is. Such contact – provided it is not merely en route to a goody – could be divided into 'exploring play' when the object or the experience is relatively new, 'manipulative play' when the object itself yields little further information but doing something to it does, 'practice play' when there are further changes in the activity rather than in the object, and 'repetitive play' when the repetition, with or without variations, places, dockets, or codes the experience in some way.

There are a number of conditions when exploring is likely to be called playful. Younger organisms are more easily aroused or excited by environmental changes than older ones since their control mechanisms are less well integrated. Consequently there will be greater response to novelty. Incidental and 'irrelevant' stimuli will arouse responses in the young which might be inhibited by more mature cortical processes. Lack of experience is another important condition for playful or diversive exploring. Although often overlooked by an observer, a great many more stimuli and events are genuinely new to the young and so equally as attractive as one another. There is also less possibility of selecting stimuli on the basis of the significance they have acquired by previous learning.

'Manipulative play' will to a certain extent also be determined by response to novelty – especially in the form of changes produced accidentally. This seems to be the starting point of many games and elaborations. Nevertheless, the process is probably not accurately described in terms of quasi-passive responses, but involves active 'search', i.e. scanning of the environment. 'Practice play' – whether regarded from the point of view of the movements involved, or from the stimuli which affect these – needs investigation within the context of regulatory and control processes involved in the development of skilled movement. Finally, continued repetition with or without variation is more likely in the young since more tasks (whether or not they are self-imposed) present difficulties to the young because they have less facility or means of coding in-coming information. It is probable that young children's shorter span of immediate memory plays an important role in this.

These categories of movement and exploring play and the conditions for them are more in the nature of a plan for research than an account of results. But it should be possible to isolate the various forms of play experimentally, and to test whether the conditions which seem to underly them, in fact do.

CHAPTER FIVE

PHANTASY, FEELING AND MAKE-BELIEVE PLAY

My five-year-old and her three-year-old brother rushed into the kitchen, demanded 'real' cloths and 'real' water and Ajax in order to clean the doll's pram and toy car. After rubbing away for some time, my daughter said 'Now we will play'. Somewhat surprised, I asked whether they had not been playing all along. No, according to her, they had been working. 'Play is only when you pretend'. They placed some upturned stools in the hall and pretended they were in an aeroplane going to Italy. My little girl dressed up in a large scarf and held a basket and one of her dolls. My son put on a peaked cap and became alternatively daddy and the pilot.

Pretence and phantasy develop from the time when the child will take a sip out of an empty toy cup with apparent satisfaction, catch imaginary balloons, bath and feed her dolls, pretend to be a cat or the milkman, to buying cardboard sweets with marbles for money at a shop consisting of an upturned clothes-basket. It moves from fragmentary, disjointed bits of pretence to integrated and internally consistent sequences of make-believe.

Pretence and Phantasy as Aspects of Intellectual Development

Make-believe play is at its height between the ages of about eighteen months to seven or eight years. This coincides with learning to refer to objects in their absence, and to communicate by means of language or symbolic gestures. A number of child psychologists have taken the view that make-believe or symbolic play is an aspect of this development, but we are indebted to Piaget for detailed observations on the changes of imaginative play with age(283).

Piaget assumes that symbolization develops out of what the child does with, or in relation to, objects. Actions which have followed each other by chance, perhaps because this produced unexpected effects, are repeated in an almost ritual fashion. One of Piaget's daughters happened to hold a strand of her hair when being placed in the bath on one occasion, at the age of fifteen months. Her hand slipped and struck the water, whereupon she immediately repeated the sequence, and subsequently played this 'game' whenever she was put into the bath. Make-believe begins when such rituals are used on new objects, or out of their original contexts. For example, Piaget's daughter had a going-to-bed ritual. She held on to her pillow, lay down on her side, and sucked her thumb. She then followed this sequence with a cloth resembling her pillow, the collar of her mother's coat, and with the tail of a rubber donkey. The same sequence of actions is used on different 'substitute' objects. A brick or twig is pushed along as if it were a toy-car, because it can be pushed. The repeated action sequences become progressively more elliptical, acting as symbolic allusions to the object which evoked them originally. Finally, they are no longer executed overtly. These generalized, covert actions, assimilated into the child's know-how, literally stand for or symbolize the object, and form the basis of the child's thinking even before the child can speak, according to Piaget. The actions are equivalent for the child. He ascribes his own actions to other people or to objects. Teddies and matchboxes sit on pottie, and dolls are treated as if crying. Other peoples' actions are used similarly. The child holds up the newspaper, scanning the page like his father, or puts a spoon to his ear as a telephone receiver and talks gibberish into it.

Later, real substitutes are no longer necessary. The child will rock an imaginary baby, or throw a non-existent ball. Elliptical, covert, generalized actions, no longer confined to the original object, make more elaborate make-believe sequences possible. Whole scenes instead of single events can now be played. At first, these consist of some real event. The teddy is taken for a ride in the armchair after the child has been out in his pushchair. Then more elaborate series of daily events are re-enacted. Playing 'mothers and fathers', or 'shops' are favourites. Imaginary objects are not merely absent real objects. They may be 'inventions'. The child has experienced no real object like it, but arbitrarily combines several features of different real objects. Many children, for instance, have imaginary playmates. At the age of two my daughter often saw the child of a neighbour's home-help; a fair-haired three-year-old whom she considered naughty because she hogged all the toys. After the home-help left and my daughter no longer met the child, an imaginary fair-haired naughty girl with a similar name made her appearance. Gradually, my child insisted that her 'Kathy' was quite different from the original. She was much older, was given a different name, and had a medley of attributes of different people she had met. My son invented 'Mr Doory', a deliberate variation of 'door'. After his father had told him that he knew a real man of this name, the imaginary Mr Doory retained his name for years. Everything impressive that happened was attributed to him in turn: a funny face in a cartoon, an enormous car, and anything naughty or outstandingly praised.

The function of names is an interesting aspect of this. A four-year-old, hearing that our new baby was called 'Andrew', said that this could not be true because 'Andrew' was a big boy's name. (It was his elder brother's.) It comes as a slight shock to older English children to realize that a Frenchman refers to a window as *fenêtre* even in the privacy of his own thoughts. The name belongs to the object. On the other hand, dolls are rarely given names before the age of three. Our first doll was called 'Julief', presumably culled from a mishearing of the name 'Juliette' which our child met at the time. The child insisted on the invented name, and it was carried by each favourite doll in turn for more than two years. It was not until the age of about four that each doll received its own permanent name.

Make-believe play in the third year is a more elaborate medley of events actually experienced plus imaginary ones produced by combining features out of their context. According to Piaget, 'The child has no imagination, and what we attribute to him as such is no more than a lack of coherence' (283, p. 131). An example is a song, taken down verbatim at the time, which my three-year-old told me she was going to make up about our expecting a new baby. I told her that I would write it down: 'She invited her to our house. The lovely baby to be born. Once in the fields the baby of a little girl was born. Each rose is a briar rose, but the dear little baby celebrate. Will it be strong? The doors are shut, but one is going out with a paintbrush to paint.'

When I stopped writing at this point, she came to me and said, 'You've still got to write. I haven't finished', and went on: 'Happy news the baby is born, dear baby cannot contrary. We cannot play as rain. Some rain melts. Each rain sows a plain of lessons Rome.'

My daughter insisted that this was not nonsense because we were going to Rome. The items of the 'song' consisted of an assembly of expressions she had heard such as 'happy news', 'lovely baby', 'contrary'; current facts like the door being shut, that it was raining and she could not go out into the garden to paint; a fragment of 'Rain, Rain, Go to Spain', an alliteration to rain, and an association with it of a piece of misconstrued information about snow melting, all strung together. The earliest, spontaneously made-up 'stories' and songs of both my older children consisted of fragments of actual nursery rhymes, strung together out of context. They believed these to be their own inventions. Another example is that of a made-up name. My three-and-a-half-year-old brought in some bindweed and said that the flowers were called 'Lingans' because, 'they live on the fence [cling on?], because they have tiny doors inside, because they live out of the door [outdoors?].' According to Piaget, the three-year-old cannot order events sequentially, and juxtaposes ideas instead of forming coherent concepts because of his 'egocentrism' (a notion more related to difficulties in switching attention than to egotism, see Chapter Two).

After the age of four, the child becomes progressively more capable of orderly sequences in recalling events and telling stories. Make-believe games similarly become more coherent and consistent. Adult intrusions, even by kisses, are resented furiously, not so much because of the interruption but because they do not fit in with the child's role. If the adult makes his request within the framework of the make-believe, he is usually more than welcome. This is not a confusion of reality and imagination by the child. On the contrary, it shows a growing awareness that real objects have characteristics accepted by all, requiring appropriate actions. Children do discriminate between substitutes and the real thing, and usually signify this by giggling when pretending (if they are challenged). It has frequently been pointed out that, however absorbed a child may be in his game, if the rag he uses as a baby really started to cry, he would be frightened. But an eighteen-months-old baby may well try to pick up a realistically painted toothbrush from the page of his book.

Experiments within the framework of field theory (see Chapter Two) have shown that whether children accept substitute objects depends on the context, the nature of the substitute, and their current activity(334). No child between the ages of three and seven accepted cardboard sweets or cardboard scissors after being given real ones, although some of the youngest children tried them out before rejecting them, or used them as shapes to make paths. Merely being told first that they were to have sweets and scissors produced fewer rejections than first being given the real objects. A cardboard ball, on the other hand, was accepted as a substitute for a rubber ball by the majority. How the substitutes function, and the extent to which their function is defined affects their being accepted as substitutes. The majority of children accepted pieces of hard clay and pebbles in lieu of the building bricks they had used just previously. Wooden animals were refused, but the same shapes sawn in half were accepted by all for building.

Changing the context, drastically altered the acceptance of substitutes. When offered as part of a game during play with dolls, cardboard sweets and paper scissors were accepted readily, even more so by older than by younger children. If offered during doll play, without making them explicitly part of the game, especially if the child's attention was drawn to real scissors first, most children refused the substitutes. The length of time an object has just been played with was another factor. Cardboard scissors were accepted in lieu of real ones if the child had previously shown signs of being tired of playing with the real scissors. This is somewhat surprising and suggests that the children did not use the cardboard scissors as substitutes for actual scissors at all, but as different objects appropriate to a different activity.

Attention and Coding

There seems to be no reason to question the assumption that children get better at distinguishing between reality and pretence and phantasy as they grow older. The basis of this development is not so clear.

Ignorance about objects, events and their connexions is one source of confusion. If adults, who are his touchstones about what to believe, 'kiss him better' when he has hurt himself, how is he to know that the kiss does not act like a plaster? If unaware that a placebo instead of a 'real' pill has been given to them, adults will equally ascribe a fortuitous feeling of being better to the pretend pill rather than to chance, or to the relief that comes from having someone attend to them. When dealing with difficult subject matter adults too make mistakes which look like logical errors[1]. It is hardly surprising that a child who is told that the sun will be sad if he does not go out to play, and who hears the stories of talking trains, elephants' fancy-dress parties, and naughty winds who blow when they ought not to, in which our child literature abounds, should have some difficulty in stating criteria for the concept 'alive', or should be uncertain whether intentions can be ascribed to wind and water.

Piaget described children's thinking as 'animistic'(282). They tend to treat inanimate toys as if they were alive, and to believe that causal connexions are invariably due to some-one's volition. The question is whether this 'animism' is merely the result of lack of knowledge and experience, or even of well-intentioned mis-information by adults, or whether such mistakes are due to the inadequacies of the child's logical tools, his unawareness of logical inconsis-tencies and impossibilities. The question is still open. By and large, studies replicating Piaget's investigations with varying degrees of methodological improvements, have found that the sequences in which logical concepts are attained by children as they grow older are fairly consistent (100, 225, 335, 383).

However, the way in which tasks are presented to the child, the number of items with which he has to cope simul-taneously or successively, the sequence in which relevant information is given, the redundancies and irrelevancies present, the fact that some problems and some concepts involve more logical steps than others, or involve non-logical operations the child has not yet learned (e.g. measuring), have all been shown to affect young children's performance on reasoning tasks(45, 112, 189, 191, 336, 383, 384). In addition, younger children are more likely to misconstrue or forget the initial instructions about what they are to do, and to shift their attention to irrelevancies in the middle. Whether this adds up to a different logical status for child-ren's reasoning is a moot point. It is unlikely that even the best-thought-out programme of instruction could get the average two-year-old to solve quadratic equations. At the same time, some of the difficulties children have in under-standing concepts are due to the adult's failure to convey ideas in terms adapted to their limited experience and knowledge. When they were four- and two-years-old re-spectively, two of my children played at 'being in the army' – an expression they had just heard. The game consisted in getting into the wardrobe and shutting the door. On being asked to explain the game, the elder one said that the wardrobe was 'the army', because she thought that 'being in the army' was like being in a hotel.

It is probable that the game of 'being in the army' was due to verbal confusion rather than a logical failure to appreciate a given level of abstraction. Some psychologists have argued that lack of verbal facility more than other learned mediating responses (see Chapter Two) accounts for young children's failure to use implicit rules and generalities and to respond instead to the concrete perceptual aspects of a task(76, 189a, 190, 191). The rule for spotting the odd one out is the same for pictures of cars as for types of fruit, but neither colour, shape nor other perceived dimensions are relevant in switching from one to the other. Some kind of symbolic coding device seems to be needed for problems such as going 'twice right, twice left, twice right'. Language has been an obvious candidate for this. Discriminating between two sets of meaningless shapes is easier if the sets are labelled differently(92). Dissimilar objects of the same name are treated as equivalent. It has also been suggested that linguistic proficiency is responsible for the shift necessary when a new task involves doing the opposite of what was done before(188, 190, 201). For instance, two series of large and small black and white squares are shown. The child is to learn that the large one (regardless of colour) is correct. The task is then switched so that the small square becomes correct instead. The response is the reverse of what was done before, but the tasks are equivalent if size is used as the relevant dimension. Adults and older children find this easier(61) than the logically more complex task of switching from one dimension to another, e.g. size to colour, as the basis of discriminating between the shapes. Young children, on the contrary, have greater difficulty in the first situation(188, 189a). They do better if the response remains correct even if colour rather than size now becomes the dimension which differentiates the correct shape. The problem belongs to questions mentioned in Chapter Four. By no means all the evidence is accounted for by assuming a lack of verbal mediating responses(234, 310, 396). The dimensions (size, shape, colour, direction, etc.) which are used to identify important cues may determine whether a subsequent task is treated as equivalent. The switch from one task to the next involves the probability with which the child attends to some dimensions, or aspects of a problem, rather than to others. This, in turn, depends upon a number of variables: for instance, the amount of pre-training on a relevant dimension, the number of relevant and irrelevant cues available at the time of training, and the extent to which a task has been 'over'-learned(400).

Attentional factors as well as linguistic confusions account for a good deal of make-believe play. Several months after we had returned from Italy my five-year-old found a large deflated beach ball with which they had played at the sea-side. Greatly excited she put it on her head, and calling her brother, marched solemnly around the garden with him, saying that she was 'the Italian lady with the hat'. I then recalled a lady at the seaside whose enormous black beach hat had greatly impressed the children at the time. The deflated ball resembled it very closely in shape and size.

Modern Russian investigators stress attention (in terms of orienting reactions), language learning, and feedback – the processes whereby results of actions are signalled back and affect subsequent behaviour – in the development of thinking(5, 213). At one level, conditioning merely consists of forming temporary connexions; at another, behaviour involves rules and conscious planning. The development of thinking depends on the generalization, abbreviation and internalization of motor actions, and the orienting responses aroused when some signal of inadequacy of action is analysed by the brain. But in man, according to Russian theorists, the ability to learn to speak changes the process qualitatively so that conscious planning becomes possible. Learning to speak is a social process. Through conditioning, objects and stimuli come to signal biologically important events. But words also represent society's stock of acquired knowledge of objects and events that the child has not himself experienced. Initially the word signals that actual object to the child which the adult has linked with it. Hearing people apply the word to other objects which the word signifies, directs the child's attention to characteristics these objects have in common and to differentiating them from other, outwardly similar, ones. By speech the adult draws the child's attention to connexions and rules he could not have made unaided(213). Learning any branch of knowledge at the same time forms an individual's logical ability.

In addition to conditional reflexes and conscious planning, modern Russian investigators also speak of 'image-driven' behaviour(32), common to the higher vertebrates, including children. It depends on feedback processes which match information returned from the accomplished action with previous information about the situation. Anokhin, a follower of Pavlov, extended his notion of chain-reflexes to include 'return impulses' at every stage of this process. He postulated that the complex of central-nervous processes aroused by an event in the past will be re-excited by the learned cue which signals it. The returned impulses from actions must correspond to this complex to be 'accepted' or 'sanctioned'(5). If they differ, the reorganization of the action to adapt it to the event continues. These complexes of excitation, against which incoming information is matched, are the bases of concrete images of objects and events which steer subsequent behaviour. Voluntary movements depend on these images. Indeed, the slightly unorthodox Beritoff(32) considers that, in animals with 'new' brains (neocortex), 'image-driven' rather than conditioned sequences may be primary. Actions which are frequently repeated without check or impediment become automatic sequences. The adult buttons his coat automatically without thinking about it. But during initial learning in childhood, the actions depend on the progressive perfecting of images, i.e. of the re-aroused complex of sensations, from external and internal receptor organs, stored in the central nervous system. The voluntary behaviour of higher vertebrates like cats, dogs and children up to the age of about two is regulated by individually learned concrete images. In humans this is gradually replaced by planned behaviour from the age of two onwards, depending upon the ontogenetic (i.e. individual) development of the new brain and on language learning(32). Images can be spatially related to each other and to the individual, and can be projected into space. A dog can beg for meat he has seen put behind closed doors, and will run straight into the room to it when the door is opened. Macbeth 'saw' the dagger 'before' him. People can see the broken vase still standing on the table if they try, although the clarity with which they are able to do this varies.

The notion of 'image-driven' in contrast to planned behaviour is in many respects similar to Piaget's assumption of concrete individual schemata which precede logical thinking. Make-believe and imaginative play would then be, literally, the manipulation or acting of images. I am not aware of any systematic experimental investigation of the relation between make-believe play and the development of images. Images have only just become scientifically respectable again. A number of investigations in the 1930s focused on 'eidetic' imagery: images so vivid that the child is able to 'read off' unfamiliar items from a picture shown just previously, and can point to small details located in specific directions as if the picture were still present. In fact, these are not more accurate than other people's recollections (274: ch. VI). Some 50 per cent of schoolchildren, but few adults are said to have it (258: ch. XI). Vivid imagery tends to occur during the initial period of falling asleep, or when attention 'wanders'. It has been suggested that images are constructed from past sensory information when some difficulty is encountered in a task for which this information is needed (274: ch. VI).

Neither Piaget, nor the Russian investigators assume that image-driven behaviour and schemata consist of visual representations alone or even primarily. They stress the individual's action schema with regard to the object as an important basis of mental representation, or schematization.

Certainly, young children frequently represent an event or object by miming it. 'I am a windscreen-wiper' said my three-year-old on one occasion, swinging both legs rhythmically to the right and left at right angles to his body. Pulling faces, a distorted voice, a contorted posture, or putting on some rags makes the child himself into the symbol of some object or person. The action is, as it were, a classifier.

Modern British and American cognitive psychologists tend to stress the importance of grouping, classifying – 'chunking' – information(246) in the development of planning and speech rather than vice versa (see also next chapter). To use what we know quickly and effectively, the originally experienced events must be resorted, rearranged and realigned. There is good evidence that adults (there are no comparable studies on children so far) can see a great deal more of, say, a visual display of letters than they can immediately report(340). One hypothesis as to what limits this is that it is a question of how much can be translated into a different, e.g. auditory, code, and rehearsed before an answer is given. Recall is poorer when people are prevented from internally rehearsing the material(52). (Although not necessarily under all conditions (402).) The rehearsal also depends upon the length of time the image (i.e. the continued sensory functioning just after the actual presentation is switched off) is available. This can be influenced in various ways by manipulating the intensity and contrast of the original display. The rapidly fading image is quickly scanned, and recoded so that rehearsal becomes possible (hearing oneself saying the letters over and over again). This process is slower, and one which improves the accuracy of recall(340).

Coding visual events in terms of speech is likely to be more difficult for young children(230). It is also possible that for them, re-coding or re-classification occurs by preference in terms of movement or action schemata. This would presuppose a 'rehearsal loop' between what is (or reconstructions from what was) seen and feeling oneself act it, rather than between what is seen and hearing oneself say it. If it is further assumed that in the case of any difficulty the rehearsal would become overt, miming or 'imaginative' play, like being a windscreen-wiper, becomes comprehensible as part of the process of assimilating information. Although speculative, this is open to experimental test. Reclassifying in terms of action schemas rather than in words is less economical, but useful when verbal labels are less readily available.

Phantasy, Make-believe Play and the Expression of Feelings

The view that make-believe play and phantasy express the individual's feelings and private wishes mainly stems from Freud's distinction between wishful and rational thinking (125). According to this, thinking is primarily organized in terms of instinctive tendencies, and uses symbols which derive their significance from their association with instincts. Rational thinking is split off from this when imagined satisfaction becomes insufficient. But unacknowledged, not yet achieved, or impossible wishes continue to find expression in play, and later in day-dreams (see Chapter Two).

Some forms of personality tests, known as 'projective' tests, make use of phantasy and play. The individual is given inkblots, indistinct pictures or sets of dolls and told to interpret or make up a story about them in whatever way he wants. Since such vague and ambiguous material provides only a minimum of objective information, it is assumed that an individual's production will necessarily reflect his own emotional preoccupations. Projective tests, including make-believe in which the child is encouraged to play with miniature dolls and toys as he chooses, have also been used by psychologists of the learning theory school. Play and phantasy are assumed by them to be samples of behaviour which reflect an individual's general learned responses more accurately because he is under no compulsion to behave in socially accepted ways(216, 323).

Feelings such as anger or frustration affect phantasy and make-believe play. The stories of students who had been deliberately annoyed previously, had significantly more aggressive content than the stories of those who had not been subjected to annoyance before(114). Young children's make-believe play became less constructive and coherent during a frustrating experience, such as seeing attractive toys they were not allowed to handle, than it had been in a previous session (21). However, the relation between overt behaviour, phantasy and the ambiguity of the test material is complex. The assumption that the vaguer and more ambiguous the material is, the more it will differentiate between individuals seems fair enough. The responses of a man who sees a skeleton in every inkblot are more likely to indicate something about the man than about the inkblots. At the same time, it is difficult to show such tests to be valid. It may be the timid man who shouts most loudly in phantasy. On the whole, the more ambiguous the test material is, the less the answers correspond to ratings of a group's overt behaviour, and vice versa (262: ch. XVII). This would be expected on Freud's hypothesis, or indeed on any assumption that the conditions for the covert symbolic behaviour of adults differ from those for their overt social behaviour (221).

On the other hand, children's make-believe play with small, standard sets of miniature dolls and appropriate furniture does correspond with some reservations, to their overt behaviour elsewhere (262: ch. XVII). Experiments under controlled conditions with careful coding and checking of methods of scoring, have shown that make-believe play varies with a number of conditions. The reliability of these methods, i.e. the degree of agreement between independent judges on coding and scoring items of children's behaviour, correlations between items of behaviour in the same and in different sessions, is relatively high (216, 262: ch. XVIII, 323) so that the results can be accepted with some confidence. Aggression has been much investigated. Items of behaviour such as hitting, making one doll hit another, scolding, or punishing toys when the child is told to play or tell a story about them as he chooses, are scored.

One of the first factors to emerge is that the material itself influences the amount of aggression shown. For instance, if children are given a doll's house with dolls and furniture arranged in an orderly fashion, their play is more aggressive than when they are allowed to construct and arrange the setting themselves from heaps of wall pieces, furniture and dolls(287). The more realistic and elaborately made the dolls are, the less useful they are for make-believe play(280). The children spend more time investigating them than constructing scenes or stories. Dolls arranged in sets like the child's own family (father, mother and an appropriate number of brothers and sisters), produce more aggression than less explicit figures(306). The presence of adults, who they are, the extent to which they participate, or remain aloof, is important. In the relatively strange laboratory setting at least, normal nursery-school children play less aggressively when there is no supporting adult present. When there is a consistently friendly, encouraging and reassuring adult, the overall score of aggressive acts increases from session to session, and play becomes less stereotyped(328).

Quite short training sessions, encouraging the children to act aggressively, or cooperatively affected the play of seven-to nine-year-olds. One group of children was initially encouraged to play aggressive games such as competing with each other to stand on the same small spot on a mat, getting most 'strips' from other children while protecting their own, or protecting their toys from attack while destroying as many of the others as possible. A control group, by contrast, was helped to perform constructive, cooperative tasks. Frustration is one of the main instigators for aggression. So the two groups were 'frustrated' by a much curtailed film show, and having to give back some of their sweets. The aggressively trained group thereupon played more aggressively than the constructively trained group, and vice versa(85).

Some longer-term individual differences were also reflected in make-believe play. For instance, boys were more aggressive than girls in play as in everyday behaviour. The total amount of aggressive acts varied from session to session, but the position of normal children relative to each other on the number of aggressive acts or talk, did not change greatly, and was similar to their relative ratings in ordinary situations. However, extreme groups – excessively timid or abnormally aggressive children – do not necessarily show the same traits in their make-believe play and made-up stories as in overt behaviour. Some of the most timid children were extremely aggressive in their doll-play, while others were as timid as in real life(14). Anxiety over expressing what is normally disapproved may also have to be taken into account in assessing the play of younger children(323).

Being given a chance to make up aggressive stories after being deliberately annoyed does seem to lessen the amount of annoyance expressed subsequently(114). While this would be consistent with theories of the 'overspill of energy' kind, other interpretations are possible(30). Guilt feelings or anxiety may be aroused by having expressed anger, and so inhibit subsequent exhibitions of it. Once a particular response has been started off, it may go on to its completion to the extent it can, and then stop. In any case, the fact that the same checks work in phantasy productions as in overt behaviour, that it is influenced by training, by opportunity, and by the social context, make it unlikely that make-believe functions solely as compensation. The very fact that our society allows some otherwise disapproved behaviour in the context of play may account, in part, for the greater amount of aggressiveness generally reported in experiments with make-believe play. For instance, a four-year-old when told not to use certain expressions to adults said: 'But I can talk like that to my dolls, can't I?' A child of two and a half, reprimanded for hitting, said: 'It was only pretend hitting. I am playing now.' Most children learn that what is forbidden in one situation may pass when it is labelled play or pretence.

Nevertheless, the content of ordinary children's make-believe play is often weird and wild. The girl-doll may be said to fry mother on the stove, the baby be drowned, demons, wolves and bogey-men appear, and catastrophes are common(14, 216). There has been little or no attempt as yet at a systematic, experimental study of the conditions under which evil symbolic figures and drastic events occur most frequently in play. The psychoanalytic explanation of such phantasies is that they symbolize the child's feelings.

What the child resents and fears in his mother becomes embodied as 'the witch'; his brothers and sisters who are his
rivals in parental affection may be felt as small, ever-present
pests; his fears and guilt about forbidden wishes become
projected as bogey-men, and so forth. The child is not aware
of his feelings or the significance of the symbolic figures,
because they are taboo. Piaget, on the other hand, considers
that symbols of this kind have emotional significance for the
child because the child's thinking during the make-believe
period is pre-logical, based upon affective rather than logical
links between aspects of objects and events. It is 'unconscious' anyway, because the child is not clearly aware of
how he feels and thinks, and may never become so if there
is a social taboo which prevents him from testing and adapting a given pre-logical schema.

According to Piaget, make-believe play declines in the
seventh or eighth year, because pre-logical thinking declines and because the child is better adapted socially than
earlier. Make-believe play is assimilation *par excellence*. It
bends reality to the child's intellectual and emotional re-
quirements(285). As he becomes capable of thinking logically on concrete matters, and at the same time more capable
of coping socially and emotionally, make-believe becomes
irrelevant.

The eight-year-old is certainly rather sturdier, less dependent and less easily aroused emotionally than younger
children(135). But phantasy does not disappear or become
less horrific at times then, and continues into adulthood.
What does disappear at the age of seven or eight is its overt
expression in action. In fact, not only make-believe play,
but also the steady stream of talk, addressed to no one in
particular, which characteristically accompanies young
children's actions also disappears. Piaget accounts for this
by supposing talk, like thinking, to be personal and idiosyncratic first. As speech becomes social, adapted to inform-
ing others, egocentric comments disappear(281). The
Russian psychologist, Vigotsky, on the other hand, assumed
that speech is undifferentiated rather than asocial in young

children. The difference between speech for others which is vocal and grammatical, and speech for oneself which is unvoiced and progressively more elliptical in form, does not yet exist for the young child(370). As this differentiation occurs, the constant talk accompanying actions becomes unvoiced, elliptical inner speech. The process coincides with greater linguistic facility. It could be explained by supposing regulatory and feedback processes to become automatic with practice, and so short-circuiting the route via overt action.

The disappearance of make-believe play may, similarly, merely mark the fact that the child's thinking about objects, people and events has become sufficiently skilled to dispense with the props of concrete action – whatever the state of his emotional adjustment.

This does not mean that feelings are irrelevant to make-believe and phantasy. The hungry man tends to think of food, the angry man of violence and the sex-starved man of sex. Children's feelings are more violent, variable, briefer and less organized but they are not always suffering from disturbance, and least of all when they play. If it is correct to describe make-believe play as thinking in action with few constraints, it is almost a truism that its content is dictated by whatever is of current interest to the child. Whatever is new, impressive, connected with something important in his life, or part of a rule or recurring pattern, or otherwise emphasized, is likely to have some priority of being selected.

The Functions of Make-believe Play

The question that interests is whether make-believe play and phantasy is a 'good thing' or not. Does the vicarious experience of fear and anger 'arouse and purge' the emotions as Aristotle supposed, or does it merely encourage aggressive habits and irrational behaviour? Should we give children toy guns so that they can pretend to play at war and killing and so get it 'out of their systems', or are we merely encouraging aggression? Do Grimm's fairy-tales, with their horrific scenes of stuffing bad stepmothers into barrels full of nails and rolling them to death, express secret longings which had better be satisfied in imagination than in reality, or do they merely encourage sadistic tendencies in the young, or frighten them unnecessarily? The answer is not likely to be a simple yes or no. The alternatives do not exclude each other. What is good for an aggressive child who has not yet learned to feel anxiety about harm to himself and to others, will not do for one who is imitating his elders, or a boy who feels wretched about his destructiveness but does not know how to stop it, and is different again for one whose timidity is injurious to himself. The possibility of aggression and defence is innately given in man as in other animals. Aggressive habits can be learned. There is no point in fabricating a panacea for the world's ills out of what any good mother or nanny might do when she knows the child and his situation.

The interesting question – what we ought to do – must be unpacked before it can receive any sort of sensible answer. From ordinary observation there is no reason to suppose that make-believe play is all of one kind. It may be a form of exploring. The child may rush in with pretended terror of bears or giants chasing him outside ('It's alright, Mummy, we're just playing bears'); or he may pretend to fall off a tree just climbed when he is sure to be able to save himself. A number of child psychologists, including Valentine(368), have given examples which suggest that the child explores his feelings and emotions in much the same way as he explores perceptions arising in the external world. Playing tigers may not be very different from the exploratory play discussed in the last chapter, except that it necessarily involves pretence and symbols. The child could hardly be in a position to explore his feelings or enjoy the increased excitement if a real tiger were chasing him.

Other examples of make-believe play involve events that have genuinely frightened or excited the child. A four-year-old, who had been exceedingly frightened by finding his house full of smoke after his mother had inadvertently left the milk saucepan to boil dry, subsequently played at having imaginary houses on fire and escaping from them. Although the worst fear of boiling saucepans was already over when these games began, repeatedly playing at fires in the company of an older playmate may have helped the child to digest the experience. Repetition lessens the impact of most strong impressions. It may well be that imaginary fires are also enjoyed for their association with destruction, and have some aggressive import.

Some forms of make-believe clearly stimulate and excite rather than lessen excitement. Every mother knows that such play may end in a whirl of laughter, aggression or tears unless carefully guided. Phantasies may provide their own stimulation in boring surroundings. Individual children differ in the extent to which they resort to it. In a study of older children it was found that those with a rich phantasy life were able to sit still and wait for much longer periods than those with relatively poor imagination, even though the two groups were equally intelligent(329).

There are many examples of play which must be described as wishful or compensatory. There is no doubt that children do sometimes re-enact events not in the way they happened, but as they would have liked them to happen. This is a fact rather than an explanation.

In games such as 'being in the army' or 'being a wind-screen-wiper', by contrast, the child appears to represent to himself concretely a slightly puzzling expression or action. It seems to be part of an effort to make sense of the world. He is trying them out, literally, in action. A great deal of make-believe play, too, is a rehearsal of something the child has experienced. Playing houses, families, shops and schools are the most usual. But any impressive event, such as going to Italy in an aeroplane, may be re-enacted in detail for the next year with frequent appeals to the adults for confirmation about the colour of the aeroplane (now represented by a kitchen stool) or the correct sequence of events.

There is no one function of make-believe play. The child may be exploring his feelings, lessening his fears, increasing his excitement, trying to understand a puzzling event by graphic representation, seeking confirmation of a hazy memory, or altering an event to make it pleasant to himself in phantasy.

Piaget's notion of symbolic play as 'assimilation' of events in symbolic form probably sums up best, at present, the exploring, manipulating, repeating, varying, confirming and classifying of impressions, events and feelings which can be observed in children's make-believe play. If so, make-believe play belongs with all those processes and structures which underly the coding, storing, checking and recoding of information, and which appear to keep the human brain pretty constantly busy. That the rehearsal is overt rather than covert gives imaginative play its distinctive character, coupled with the fact that the repetitions are rarely accurate. Piaget suggests that the variations of play mainly result from an incapacity to order events sequentially or logically. This is probably only partly true. In some of their pretend play, children demand adult corroboration ('My hat is like the lady's, isn't it, Mummy?'). But, on other occasions, the child may violently repudiate any suggestion that his productions are mere reproductions. His jumbled-up nursery rhymes are, to him, new poems; his repetitions of a story are inventions of his own. The child tries to do something and be something different although his success may not be great. Most of the content of make-believe play is pretty stereotyped and repetitive(14). But he tries. To produce changes and differences is quite as necessary to the process of adapting to the world as rechewing the informational cud. We learn more from experiments than from mere observation.

The need to juggle and rearrange applies even more to the beginner's attempt to re-code information. It has been suggested that (for adults) events are constantly re-coded in more economical forms so that they can be 'stored' (i.e. be potentially available for remembering) more easily(269). A delightful counter-example of silly (uneconomic) remembering is that of Miss Bates, a character in Jane Austen's novel *Emma*: she was unable to answer any question without recounting all the events from pigs to petticoats which had accompanied the relevant item. Resorting, realigning and rearranging what has been experienced is essential if information is to be used. The process of resorting is not only likely to be slower and more difficult for the very young, the realignments are also likely to be at a different level. It is no accident that children's word-play and rhymes tend to depend upon clang and sound associations rather than on meaning(302, 313).

CHAPTER SIX

PLAY AND IMITATION

A LOT of play is imitative. Most people would assent to that. It is also illuminating to think of imitation as the converse of play, as Piaget does (see Chapter Two). A good deal of the make-believe play, discussed in the last chapter, involved pretending to be someone else by copying what they did, or imitating, however imperfectly, the functions of objects. Imagination depends on re-combining aspects of events in novel ways; imitation depends (ideally) on reproducing or mirroring events in exactly the same way and in the same sequence as they occur. When this is said, unfortunately, not all is said. Imitation covers a number of different types of behaviour.

At times, children's, and adults', imitations are almost ludicrously involuntary copies of what someone is doing. I have seen a little girl, absorbed in watching her sick mother, put her hand to her side when the mother did so with a heavy sigh on getting up. Only the laughter of some of those present recalled her to herself with a blush of embarrassment.

Köhler(196) gave the example of a chimpanzee stretching up his hand while watching another trying to reach a banana. Yawning and the involuntary kicking movements of people watching football are frequently called 'contagious' behaviour.

Contagious behaviour, like yawning, has been described as 'socially facilitated'. The behaviour of one of a group elicits or intensifies the same behaviour in other group members (359: ch. IV). Chickens fed to satiation in solitude will resume feeding on seeing other chickens eat. But it is necessary to distinguish between the involuntary imitation of movements, and imitation when the behaviour of others is merely the occasion for similar behaviour in group members, and does not involve the same movements at all. Children, seeing others pitching a tent, or constructing a house in a neighbouring garden, will quickly start making a house or tent themselves. Giving one child a piece of paper and crayons brings most others to the spot clamouring for the same activity. But these are not involuntary movements, and each child will draw a slightly different picture, and make his own version of a house with whatever material is to hand.

Learning by observation is another aspect of imitation. It has attracted most of the limited interest experimental psychologists have shown in the subject until quite recently. It means learning something new by watching someone else, without participating actively. An older brother's new trick or game is carefully watched before being tried out. This kind of imitation is neither forced, nor automatic, does not involve emotion communicated by others, nor is it copying something the child can do already, merely called out by someone else's doing it. Learning by imitation (learning by watching another), and learning to imitate (learning how to learn from watching another) have not always been sufficiently distinguished in this kind of research.

Most imitative play, however, belongs to the role-playing and re-enacting of events, common between the ages of two and eight. Children insist on having the same food as the adult, flour and whisk to make cakes like Mummy, spanner and hammer to mend the car like Daddy. But whether the same material, or a given activity, or a certain bodily position is to be important, varies. On occasion, putting on a policeman's hat is all that is required for the impersonation. The scribbles need not be legible. Role-playing does not require the presence of the 'model', the correct imitation of movements, or the communication of excitement. It is symbolic play in which the imitated movement, or someone's belongings, or tone of voice are used as visible or outward props.

Some Theoretical Explanations

Miller and Dollard said in 1941 that there were as many

theories of imitation as there were psychological theories at
all(247). This is still true. Early writers considered the tendency to imitate to be innate. Miller and Dollard set up
experiments in the Hullian tradition showing that rats and
children can learn to imitate the actions of a 'leader' if they
are rewarded for this. Such instrumental learning (see
Chapter Two) generalized to other situations, when different
incentives were given, and with different 'leaders' or
'models'. Before being trained, the rats imitated less even
than would be expected by chance. This was true also of
nursery-school children in the laboratory 'pre-training'
sessions(231, 247). What is surprising is that rats, who do
not usually imitate, and nursery-school children who do,
exhibited all the same characteristics usually found in
instrumental learning (see Chapter Two). It cannot be
assumed that the children were as naïve as the rats about
imitating. They must have known not only how to imitate,
but must already have learned when not to do so. It must be
supposed either that they judged imitation to be inappropriate in the pre-training sessions, or they failed to cotton
on, or had no means of telling what they were to do, i.e. to
take the actions of another as a cue for their own. What the
children learned in the sort of experimental set-up used by
Miller and Dollard and others cannot be very strong support
for the view that imitation is a generalized habit, learned on
the basis of rewards. It is better described by assuming that
the children and the rats learned to attend to the relevant
type of cue in this kind of situation(24, 73, 82, 291). Copying
can be produced by instrumental conditioning, but this
cannot provide the whole explanation for imitative play.
Why, for instance, should 'role-playing' be more prevalent
at one age than another, or why should it occur most in free
play when the child shows least sign of any need, and is least
likely to be rewarded?

Skinner's account(331, 332) of learning by observation is
also in terms of instrumental, or rather 'operant' conditioning (see Chapter Two). Animals and humans are active.
They must do something. Whatever actions the individual

happens to perform at the moment of being trained become the constituents of the novel response he is to learn. At each stage, those actions which most approximate the novel response are rewarded, and the learner goes through a series of approximations until his actions match the desired result. The baby babbles. Anything remotely like a human sound in a given language is greeted by adult delight. As he grows older only closer approximations to what the parent has said will be rewarded, and so on. This account is inadequate for language learning(53, 313), although copying could, no doubt, be produced in this way. Babbling and cooing are better explained in terms of feedback mechanisms (see Chapters Three and Four). Learning a language and its grammar has features which are incompatible with Skinner's view (53, 403).

Traditionally, imitation of the role-playing kind has been discussed under the concept of 'identification' – a term used by Freud to label the process whereby the child tries to impersonate or be like the parent of the same sex in order to resolve his Oedipal conflicts (see Chapter Two). There have been many modifications of this position within the general framework of psychoanalysis(51). One of the most famous of these is Anna Freud's hypothesis that the individual identifies with the aggressor(120). Identification is defensive. It protects the individual from anxiety. Conquered nations adopt the habits and customs of their conquerors, and victims may use the very forms of aggression that have been used against them. But it is difficult, in practice, to disentangle aggression by victims against each other, or against those lower still in the pecking order, from the social prestige associated with mastery and successful aggression which influences imitation (see below). Few non-analytical psychologists have taken the view that identification is innately based, or that 'Oedipal conflict', or other anxieties are preconditions for it. But Freud's assumption that identification with the parent of the same sex is a major factor in the child's taking over, and literally making his own the parent's, and hence society's rules, prohibitions and values, and so in developing inner control or 'conscience', has been widely, if not always explicitly, accepted. The process is, however, more usually explained in terms of one or other of the learning theories, often as instrumental conditioning, with or without invoking mediating mechanisms (see Chapter Two) (162, 206, 325).

Mowrer(254, 256) has described identification in terms of 'classical' conditioning. The mother provides food, comfort and 'primary reinforcements' generally. The pleasurable sensations (internal stimuli) this arouses become associated with the mother's actions and voice, i.e. – stimuli which occur at the same time. These pleasurable sensations generalize to the child's own actions to the degree to which they resemble the mother's and are reproduced by the child for their own sake, i.e. the pleasure they have acquired by association. Imitation, acquired through conditioning, may then be effectively rewarded or punished by others in given situations which the imitator has to learn to discriminate. Mowrer explains vicarious imitation by assuming that the individual imitates someone who is being rewarded, although no reward accrues to the imitator himself, because the imitator experiences some of the same sensory (covert, internal) consequences of the 'model's' behaviour. For instance, what is normally described as 'sympathetic' behaviour, the response of an individual to the pain of another, is explained in the same way as conditioning to other signals paired with pain. If a rat is given an electric shock preceded by shock to another rat, it will come to respond emotionally (gauged by behaviour or physiological changes) to the squeals of another (74). Mowrer's theory depends on the arousal of pleasure or pain in anticipation ('hope' and 'fear'). There is evidence that people who are associated with pleasurable experiences are imitated, while those who dispense punishment only may be avoided altogether. However, the most bullied, weakest member of a gang may imitate the gangleader who bullies him most, and windscreen-wipers (see example in Chapter Five) may serve as perfectly effective models for children on occasion. This requires rather roundabout explanations on this theory. Nevertheless, conditioned associations are important in the processes of attending involved in all forms of imitation.

The Gestalt-school psychologist, Koffka (see Chapter Two) focused on the perceptual aspects of imitating. He distinguished between the immediate execution of an action forced by its perception, and learning how to execute some procedure by watching someone else do it. However, he suggested that the difference is mainly a question of the organism's maturity. Koffka assumed a direct connexion between the physiological structures underlying perception and those underlying the movement so that both would be aroused at the same time. In mature, complex organisms a number of factors intervene which prevent the action following immediately upon the related perception as it does in the young (see Chapter Two). However, while learning by observing is a method of learning which needs itself to be learned, and adults are better at it than children, even adults may show involuntary imitation. Learning a new action by observing another, and involuntarily performing a well-practised action on seeing someone else perform it should be sharply distinguished even if they are both called 'imitating'.

It is doubtful whether any of the above explanations are adequate to explain all forms of imitation. To some extent this is because 'imitation' covers disparate activities. Some of these owe more to conditioned associations, others to situations where the behaviour is contingent upon rewards, while in learning by observation differential reinforcement of the observing responses themselves may be important. Differential reinforcement need not necessarily be thought of as a question of rewards like food or praise. Return information which decreases uncertainty may reinforce observing responses(341). Some conditions are more important than others in different types of imitation. An advance in understanding these is likely to come from experimental investigation of the attentional and feedback processes involved in them.

Developmental Studies of Imitation

A study of 200 children between the ages of two and twenty-one months showed that what is 'imitated' during this period depends on age, and on what the child can do already(146). No child imitated before the age of nine and a half weeks. Mouth movements were copied earlier and more frequently than other stimuli, and imitation of writing did not occur before the fourteenth month. The investigator argued that such imitation is a neurologically-based by-product of rudimentary, involuntary attention.

Valentine's observations on his own three children(367) also led him to describe involuntary imitation as the 'monopolization of attention by some fascinating impression'. Smiling, making sounds, and other actions for which there is an innate tendency, are imitated readily. Indeed, it is possible that in this kind of 'imitation', what the experimenter or what the mother does acts more as a stimulus to the child to do whatever he can do. Its similarity to the adult action may be partly accidental – a result of the adult's selecting a response he knows to have some priority for the child at a given stage of development, and which is easily called out by a given type of situation(119). One of the most prevalent types of imitation in infancy is adults imitating what the child does, rather than the other way about! We do this too when we want to communicate with people whose language we do not know. We try to make the sort of gestures and sounds they make in an attempt to understand them and to make ourselves intelligible.

According to Piaget's theory, 'imitation' is the converse and complementary of 'play' (see Chapter Two). By using imitation in the widest possible sense to refer to any accommodation to external impressions which is not adequately balanced by assimilation, he accounts for different forms of imitating in terms of developmental differences. At the age of just over a month one of his children started crying on hearing another cry, and stopped when he stopped. Piaget considers this a case of 'contagion' – one stage beyond the reflex instigation of an action by a stimulus which the child is unable to discriminate from the stimulus which sets off the reflex. Systematic imitation, on the other hand, is not possible until the fifth or sixth month of life since it requires that the child's various schemas for seeing, hearing, grasping and uttering are integrated. The child must be able to perceive that the result obtained by another is similar to what he does himself. The child makes a sound, the parent imitates him, and the child systematically produces sounds sufficiently like those of the adult to be called 'imitations' usually. Young infants can only imitate actions they can perform already, and do so from the desire to prolong interesting impressions or perceptions. Piaget's child made a sound like 'pfs', the mother imitated him. This made the child laugh and he repeated 'pfs' several times. Until the age of about nine months the child cannot repeat the actions of another which he has not observed on himself, such as putting out his tongue in imitation. A series of discriminations have to be learned by the child before this. When the adult waggles his tongue, the child may make some sort of mouth movement, 'locating' the action. The child may then try out various mouth movements and finally learns to distinguish between tongue and lip. At the age of about one, after the child can experiment with activities he knows already, he is able to imitate all kinds of movements, even when there is a slight delay between his own actions and those of the model.

By the age of eighteen months to two years, the model need no longer be present, and the child's imitations and experimentation need no longer be executed in full.

There is no doubt that children repeat activities 'for fun', or at any rate when there is no possible external coercion or lure to do so. A recent study recording the utterances of a two-year-old lying in his cot prior to going to sleep(373) showed that words and expressions heard during the day, especially if they were new to him, were repeated over and over again with and without variations. At the age of twenty months one of my infants combined physical exercises with these repetitions. While in his cot he would grasp his toes and rock on his back, or try to stand on his head while uttering something he had heard earlier that day, with enormous force of expression, and a ludicrous likeness of tone and cadence, if not of enunciation, to the speaker. At times repetitions of two word phrases he knew, like 'see lorry', 'naughty boy', would take on the quality of a sing-song and be repeated in various keys. At others, the words themselves would be slightly altered, for instance, with different pronunciations of 'lorry' or substitution of words. It is difficult to distinguish between imitation and play in this. Both reproduction of something heard or seen, and variations of it, seem to be typical of imitative play.

Young children do not reproduce the actions of others accurately. Recent investigations of children's speech have found that its inaccuracies and omissions are not random (212). The child's speech is not merely imitation with omissions. Reproducing something he has heard clearly occurs in a child's speech. But the child also says 'I thinked', or 'I thoughted', or 'foots' which he has never heard. This is not imitation, but faulty application of rules about the past tense and the plural of nouns (53). The child must have known (or learned) the implicit rules to be able to make systematic mistakes. Currently, psycholinguists are assuming that children have innate templates of linguistic universals (rules said to underly, universally, any grammar of any human language) by means of which they can progressively assimilate the language they hear. The young child's grammar is not an abbreviated adult form, but is generated from a basic finite grammar which can be infinitely expanded so that the child is not limited by what he hears but can produce any number of sentences of the basic type (72, 72a, 313). Russian psycholinguists tend to assume less in the way of specifically linguistic innate blue-prints, but their research emphasizes the productive aspect of children's speech (403). The extent to which specifically linguistic rules are innate in humans over and above their capacity to order and pigeon-hole events, and to learn rules, is still somewhat controversial.

Learning social roles also involves the learning of rules.

When infant-school children play 'school', the child who takes the role of teacher almost invariably ends up by hitting all the 'pupils'. Infant-school teachers do not hit children as much as this would suggest if the children 'imitated' them. The psychoanalytic explanation would be that the child is working off some extra aggression. This may be so, even if the 'spilling over' of 'pent-up' aggression does not describe it correctly. But whether or not real anger, or aggression which has paid off in the past, are involved, the child who plays 'teacher' is also portraying graphically his concept of teacher as one in authority with the power to punish. Both 'teacher' and 'pupils' are enacting a social rule in this game, culled with some distortion from their experience. The distortion may be due to the fact that the child's concept at this stage is based more on what has particularly impressed him than on consistent essential general characteristics. Enough of the popular stereotype of 'teacher' as someone 'who gives you the cane' survives, too, to account for the portrayal even if there is no conceptual confusion. Schoolchildren's imitative role-playing is not a model of abstraction, but it is not an incoherent medley of confused impressions either. Needless to say, 'teacher' is the preferred role. Even young children quickly learn that it is better to be at the giving than at the receiving end. But the 'pupils' do submit even if not for long. The play of both parties exemplifies a social rule or pattern, and not the imitation of movements, or expression of emotions.

Piaget observed how children's imitations become more accurate as they get older. During the kindergarten and early school years, imitation of adults may only resemble the actual activities very remotely. A child who is capable of forming letters or words will, when imitating a writing adult, abandon such labours altogether and scribble instead. The adult's fluency, apparent ease and importance of demeanour are portrayed rather than actual writing movements. An older child who writes fluently and well can combine these aspects, and may write an actual letter to a friend concurrently, rather than merely 'play at' writing.

Older children are more interested in, as well as more capable of accurate reproductions. Many a younger brother or sister has experienced the frustration of patiently helping an older one with the minute details of the *mise en scène*, for which he or she expects to be rewarded by the game itself, only to find that the particular headgear to be worn, or the rearrangement of the furniture itself has been important rather than acting out some event. The older child abandons play at just the moment of acting when it becomes interesting to the younger one.

Symbolic imitation or representation does not disappear. It becomes a more effective tool in thinking after the age of eight, and abstract models are essential in logical thinking. According to Piaget, when accuracy of imitation is achieved, about the age of eight, the activity no longer ranks as play. Piaget's concept of play essentially involves that of distortion and variation. However, it is probably more correct to say that play, like make-believe and imitative role-playing, disappears or diminishes around about that age because overt actions are increasingly replaced by covert, internal 'thinkings about' whether they are distortions or accurate representations of events.

Some Conditions Favouring Imitation

Bandura has recently contributed and reviewed a number of studies of conditions which favour imitation(18). For instance, adults are more prone to violate a prohibition when they are part of a crowd, or among people of prestige who are engaging in the forbidden act. A man wearing a freshly pressed suit, white shirt and tie, shiny shoes and a hat was imitated more frequently by others (not 'in the know' in the experiment) in disobeying a request to stop and wait at a pedestrian crossing, than when the same man was dressed in soiled, patched trousers, unpressed shirt and worn shoes (209). A number of investigators have found the social standing or prestige of whoever is imitated (the 'model') to be no less important for children. People who are seen to be powerful, or competent at some task, those who are nice to the children and give them sweets and praise, and those who are considered attractive by them, have all been found, under experimental conditions, to make potent models(18).

The individual characteristics of those imitating also make a difference. Children who lack self-esteem, or are over-dependent, or more incompetent, have been found to imitate more than those rated as self-assured or when experimental conditions ensure success rather than failure. And, of course, those children imitate who are rewarded for it(18).

Differences in imitativeness between boys and girls depend to some extent on the sex of the 'model'. By and large, men and boys are more aggressive than women and girls, and also have more prestige in our society, and girls are brought up to be more dependent. This should mean that women and girls imitate more. However, either sex may temporarily dispense the rewards, or be in the ascendant. Predictions about who will be imitated most frequently by whom, and in what respect, vary in different situations. Bandura recorded some interesting experiments testing whether an adult who successfully competes with children for attractive toys, or an adult who dispenses the toys is imitated more. The 'socially powerful' stooge who gave all the attractive toys to the children was imitated, but less when he ignored the other adult than when he gave him something too. Indeed, a 'powerless' ignored stooge was imitated more than a 'powerful' one, especially by the boys if the latter happened to be a woman and the former a man. The sense of what is fair and fitting, the social values as well as the social distinctions already acquired by those nursery-school children, were also factors. What children have experienced at home, and the example set by those with whom they have been most frequently in contact determines to a large extent what and whom they will imitate. Eleven-year-old boys' tendency to enforce rules when others broke them was related to their upbringing six years earlier. There was a close match between the parents' and the boys' attitudes, provided the relationship between them was affectionate and the boys depended emotionally more on the parents than on their age-mates(229, 325, 326).

Apart from the social characteristics of those who imitate and those who are imitated, the behaviour to be imitated is itself a factor in the situation. Aggression and anti-social behaviour rank high on the list. There is plenty of evidence that aggressive behaviour is influenced by learning(31), and by the example of others(20). Aggressive, delinquent boys frequently have fathers who are equally aggressive(19). They will not allow the boys to attack them but encourage them to be aggressive elsewhere. They provide an example, and reward aggression by praise. Among the conforming middle classes, training to inhibit aggression is usually quite severe. If the relationship between adult and child is otherwise affectionate, this is usually successful in inducing anxiety which inhibits aggression. At the same time the very severity of the training may provide the child with a model to follow on 'allowable' occasions(326). In our society, too, a totally unaggressive boy is likely to be punished for his weakness by ridicule (he is a 'sissy'), as well as by being put upon by others.

In play, especially if aggression is expressed against toys, and in phantasy, social sanctions usually do not follow at all. At any rate, aggressive acts are among the easiest to get children to imitate. For instance, in a study comparing the extent to which children imitated the incidental behaviour of a 'model' when she had previously played and talked with them, and then when she had ignored them, there were significant differences in favour of the group with whom the model had previously played in all measures of imitation except of some quasi-aggressive acts. Even the group who had been ignored by her imitated her knocking a doll off its perch(18a).

The person to be imitated need not actually be present. A film or cartoon is equally effective. What happens to the film actor, or the cartoon model makes a difference. The aggressor who is punished is less likely to be imitated than one who gets what he wants. In another study, kindergarten children were shown attractive toys with which they were not allowed to play. One group then saw a film of a child playing with these toys and being fondled by his mother, while another group was shown a film in which the child was rebuked for playing with the toys. When left by themselves with the attractive toys afterwards, the first group disobeyed the injunction not to play with them much more frequently than the second group. The children who had not seen either film were intermediate between the two(20). The effect is on actual behaviour rather than on what children learn or remember. Children who saw a film of an aggressive boy who was punished, subsequently played less aggressively than those who had seen him rewarded, but they remembered the aggressive actions of the villain quite as well. Aggressive behaviour of all kinds, including the actual actions seen, increased after viewing the aggression of others when an occasion for this was given by mildly frustrating the children. 'Social facilitation', or reinforcing or removing social restrictions on behaviour, seems to be the main factor in this.

Since weakness, dependence, inefficiency and low prestige are some of the characteristics of those who imitate most, it is to be expected that, on the whole, children will imitate more than adults, and that those they imitate will be adults, older children, or those above them in a given pecking order. Children's likes or dislikes for certain kinds of food(95), as well as their moral judgements, can be shaped by adult example or expression of opinion, or by merely hearing a relevant story(20). For this to work there must be a social structure in which the imitator finds his level *vis à vis* the model. It presupposes a good deal of social learning.

In most of the investigations, some kind of play session before and after the intervening 'happenings' served as a baseline for the measurement of imitative behaviour. It is likely that in free play, out of the ken of observing, or possibly observing, adults, imitative role-playing follows similar patterns. But in view of the finding that the social rank of monkeys may be different when they are playing than when competing for food (see Chapter Three), who is imitated by whom when children's play is out of adult earshot is probably not the model most followed at a polite tea-party.

Learning by Observing

When it comes to learning something the child could not do before, watching someone else perform the action or solve the puzzle has several advantages over merely having additional tries oneself. The movements of the model emphasize and so draw the child's attention to those parts of a puzzle device which have to be manipulated in order to solve it. If the problem involves a choice, say of one of two boxes, the outcome of the model's choice, whether he receives a reward or draws a blank, conveys additional information to the imitator, and saves him time and labour. In these situations the social standing of the imitated one, or the rewards meted out to him directly or by implication, are probably important mainly in directing the imitator's attention to his actions. Whether the child profits from the one he imitates depends on the extent to which he can translate a visual connexion into appropriate movements. From developmental studies it is clear that this is not achieved all at once. Young children below the age of five or six do not seem to learn much that is really new to them from watching alone, but need also to touch, handle, and try it out themselves (394). This is different from imitating actions which one can perform already, which even nine- to thirteen-months-old babies seem to do perfectly well.

One of the most interesting facts about early experiments with such proverbially imitative creatures as apes is that many investigators failed completely to get them to imitate or to learn from watching others in the laboratory. More recently it was shown that experience of a wide range of materials and tools, and contact with people, are preconditions for imitating. A chimpanzee, Vicky, raised like a child at the house of the experimenters, not only solved a series of puzzles and problems by watching the experimenter, but also showed the full range of imitative play of a one-to-two-year-old child from dusting furniture to applying lipstick. The experimenter's cage-raised chimpanzees which had been reared in a restricted environment and had had only limited contact with humans failed to learn by observing the human models(153). Presumably the 'rich' environment of a human home acquainted Vicky with a variety of objects and materials, with the use of tools, and with the innumerable small daily problems that such an environment presents. If humans are to act as models, a good deal of contact with people must be presupposed, whether this is explained as the building up of an expectation that what will work for the human will also work for the imitating monkey, or in terms of directing and sustaining the animal's attention on the actions of the human experimenter.

Incidental Cues and the Content of Imitative Play

Vicky was not trained to imitate dusting or putting on lip-stick. Such learning must have been largely 'incidental'. Similarly, in the experiment in which children were supposed to choose one of two boxes in imitation of an adult, they also produced the adult's manner of marching into the room, and other bits of odd behaviour(18a). Imitative play, in so far as anything is learned by it at all, is more like this than it is like learning a specific task. When an individual has strong incentives to solve a given problem, or learn to discriminate between objects, the number of things irrelevant to the task in hand which he will notice or remember is reduced(96). Animals learn to respond correctly to more cues when their responses to a compound of these are reinforced at spaced intervals rather than consistently(346). The extent to which the task has been learned beyond what is strictly necessary for adequate performance(392) or has become automatic; the complexity, range, vividness, intensity and relevance of the cues against background 'noise' have effects on how much is noticed (see Chapters Four and Five). This is probably also the case with self-imposed tasks such as build-ing a fort or doing a puzzle.

The term 'imitative play' is applied most often to those situations where the emotional tempo is low, and the chosen task sufficiently undefined to allow for the possibility of using chance and unlikely cues. When a scientist or artist says he is 'playing around' with a problem which will not fit into accustomed pigeonholes, this means that he is attending to what he usually ignores as 'irrelevant', and to chance conjunctions. That is to say, he is deliberately courting the state of more evenly or differently distributed attention more characteristic of children (see Chapters Four and Five). The adult breaks the 'rules' in doing this. Children have not yet learned them. Whatever is attention-catching here and now, or in the immediate past, whether by virtue of its being new, or odd, or striking or incongruous or connected with what is emotionally or socially impressive or part of a known or recurring pattern is likely to be reproduced in imitative play.

Imitative play apes the adult world to a large extent because the child must be active in some way and has few or no ideas or sustained aims of his own as yet. The battles and wars of one generation are the games of the next. Toy soldiers are dressed and named according to the most impressive or latest adult tale. Songs lampooning a conquered foe become nursery rhymes. 'Humpty Dumpty' relates to an incident in the English Civil War. Tricks, superstitions and April Fools Day pranks played by children today have traditions which may go back 200 years or more when they belonged to the adult world(272). Currently famous people and impressive events equally give rise to rhymes and toys.

There is a curious contradiction in children's immense delight with toys that imitate the 'real thing'. Doll's houses with a 'real' lamp that lights, and a switch to turn it on, model cars, Hoovers, even washing machines 'like mother's' apparently sell well in the toy shops. Why not use an actual light switch, clean with mother's Hoover, and help with the washing? A partial answer, no doubt, is that these are precisely things usually forbidden to little ones as dangerous, and therefore only accessible in the form of toys. But the very fact of its being a small replica is also important – whether because it is less frightening, more easily handled, or can be taken in visually more completely than the real, proportionately rather large, object, or whether the sense of being in charge, like an admired adult, is the attraction, is difficult to say. It is possible that all these conditions enter into it in one way or another.

The adult's nostalgia for a paradisical childhood must not blind him to the fact that being a child has, socially, distinctly more disadvantages than advantages. The wish to be grown up and to do something impressive and adult, or failing this, to get as near it as you can here and now, is easily explained in terms of social learning. It fits a good deal of imitative play. When my husband and I speak French to conceal something from the children, they immediately break into gibberish pretending to have a secret we are not to share. If they knew a language we did not, they would employ that. My little girl is beginning to experiment with words which could become a secret code between her and her younger brother. 'Secret' languages, evolved by inventing words or prefacing them with various letters or syllables, are well known to most schoolchildren. But verbal play is almost certainly not merely determined by social incentives, although it is probably reinforced by these.

The Functions of Imitative Play

The view taken here is that imitation refers to at least five different types of behaviour: 1. the involuntary reproduction of a well-practised movement seen on another; 2. the involuntary arousal of feelings appropriate only to the current experience of another, or the contagion or communication of excitement by group members to each other; 3. social facilitation where the behaviour of a group member releases, inhibits or is the occasion for comparable behaviour in others; 4. observational learning, a technique of learning something new by watching someone else do it; and 5. role-playing and the re-enacting of events where the repetition concerns patterns of actions witnessed or heard about. It is doubtful if all these will fit under one tight explanatory umbrella. The classical paradigms of learning: 'classical' conditioning, instrumental or operant learning, and rule learning, certainly apply differently in the five categories, although attentional processes are involved in them all.

Imitative play means mainly role-playing and re-enacting events. It would seem to belong to repeating anything 'memorable', i.e. significant, startling or impressive or exemplifying a rule, which can be observed in most overt play-activities of children. Here the view is taken that it is the overt form of the sort of rehearsal which goes on covertly in adults as part of the mechanism of memory (see Chapter Five). What is repeated and rehearsed in imitative play are the actions of others, and events witnessed and heard of rather than experienced. The child can imitate only to the extent to which he has already learned or become capable of translating visual cues into action.

However, he is not usually learning by watching at the moment of play. Indeed the actions involved may be well practised. But they do have to be selected from the individual's repertoire or even re-combined. For the higher apes and man, ability to match, to utilize regularities and patterns, is probably involved in imitating complex activities, whereas it is quite possible to yawn on seeing someone else do so without possessing a sense of social niceties or an elaborate mental apparatus to cope with complicated information. In imitative play, events are repeated in terms of what has impressed the child, or of the template or stereotype he has already of this kind of situation. The social character of the play is, in a sense, incidental. The child impersonates a dog or an aeroplane with the same zest with which he pretends that he is Daddy or the milkman, except that people and social events are normally the most impressive parts of his experience.

It is quite possible that imitative play has fringe benefits for later social behaviour, and is of more immediate use to the individual in storing and digesting impressions, or in lessening anxiety, or to his group in distilling its rules and sanctions. At any rate, the biological use to a social animal of doing what everyone else in his society does must be considerable. This need not depend upon one kind of mechanism only. Imitative play, in the sense of role-playing and the re-enacting of events, however, seems to be an overt form of rehearsal and 'going over' what has been experienced, which needs investigating in terms of memory mechanisms.

CHAPTER SEVEN

SOCIAL PLAY

The Development of Social Play

WHEN observed in little groups, pre-school children, like very young monkeys, mostly play alone at first. They play with toys, explore, or fiddle with stray objects, or they may watch the play of others without participating. As they get older, they play the same games as other children present, but in parallel, without cooperating with the others; a little later still they may play the same games, using the same objects in the vicinity of others, but still without producing a joint effort(275, 276). Indeed Piaget contends that really cooperative play develops only after the age of seven or eight (283). It is the generally accepted view that solitary play followed by parallel play, associative play and finally by cooperative play, is the sequence in which social play develops with age.

In a sense, however, social play begins much sooner. The social life of a child starts when he is born. He could not survive without being cared for, and this involves innumerable contacts with other humans from the start. Naturally, social play is not initiated by the newborn. But mothers, fathers, grannies, nurses, friends, and even totally strange females, will coo and talk to the baby, touch, kiss, fondle and prod him, wave rattles and teddies at him, or sing him nursery rhymes whenever they get a chance. At first, they are rewarded with little more than the baby's occasional attention, but by the age of six weeks he can smile back, and shows unmistakable signs of appreciating the presence of others. Once he can reach and touch them, a good deal of the baby's play with others consists of exploring in whatever way he can; pulling, pushing or hitting, as he does with

objects. When he is between five and seven months old he
will laugh in games of peep-bo and pat-a-cake, and after a
few more weeks he can even take an active part in these(59,
134). After the age of one, a good deal of his play is imitative.
The toddler enjoys doing whatever those whom he knows
best are doing.

Soon after babies can discriminate strange from familiar
faces, between the ages of five and seven months, they smile
at other babies and strange children even though they no
longer smile at strange adults. Other children are a great
attraction as babies get older. Of course, when hurt, hungry
or thwarted, toddlers will gravitate to their mothers or to
the adults who look after them. But, although this varies
considerably, there are children as young as two-and-a-half
who will be miserable among a heap of attractive toys if
there are no others to play with. This does not necessarily
mean that if children of that age are placed together some
really cooperative game develops. The children may behave
rather like characters in a Greek tragedy. Each acts his
piece without much reference to the others. At the same time,
they do tend to play with the same toys as the others, so that
they can hardly be oblivious of them. When playing with
encouraging adults, or older children whom they know well,
they do participate in current play. Shyness and fear in a
relatively strange situation may have contributed to making
the youngest children merely look on, do nothing at all, or
play solitarily when observed in free play in a nursery school,
as reported in studies of this kind(275). Playing in parallel,
rather than with each other, was most prevalent between the
ages of two and three in this, as in Gesell's longitudinal in-
vestigation(134). Associative play, when the children were
apparently engaged in a game involving the others, but each
one was intent only on his own bit of it, came at a slightly
later stage. Really cooperative play in which the children
joined to make something, or play houses and shops together,
was rare before the age of three.

In a study of children between the ages of six months and
two years, pairs of children, matched in age, were observed

in a playpen after one or the other or each of them had been given a toy, or when a toy was placed between them(242). In these situations children between the ages of six and eight months paid no more attention to each other than to the toys. Between the ages of nine and thirteen months the pen-partner became more important. The babies might roll a ball to each other, or fight for a toy. For children between the ages of nineteen and twenty-five months social contact with the play-partner predominated. What one child did was influenced by the activity of the other.

There is little doubt that children become more capable of cooperating as they get older. The difficulty of the task which depends upon cooperation, as well as ability to communicate with each other, are involved in this. In an investigation in which the apparatus was so arranged that a child could only receive a sweet if his partner pulled a string for it, older children succeeded easily. They simply told the other what to do. Neither the two-and-a-half-year-old, nor monkey, pairs were successful(385). Ability to talk, although it obviously helps, is not essential, so long as some method of communicating with others has been learned and the task is within compass. Even adolescent monkeys have been shown to be able to cooperate on a task by drawing each other's attention to what they wanted by gestures and whines(80). Whether older children cooperated on a task in the laboratory depended chiefly on whether the cooperation paid off, i.e. on the spacing and timing of the reinforcements or rewards. Operant conditioning can be used to increase and maintain cooperation between children(12).

A number of factors contribute to making cooperative play more difficult for younger children. More tasks in themselves are more difficult for them, their methods of communicating with others are more limited, and their means of telling when these are relevant or successful are relatively poor before the age of three.

The size of the group in which children play (258: ch. XV) increases with age (as it does with monkey children). At the age of three, the play-group usually consists of three children at most, and the group does not stay together for long. By the age of five, a play-group may consist of four or five children, and it generally lasts much longer. It has been suggested that before the age of two to three, children are incapable of attending to more than one person at a time. When three little ones are put together, only two of them play together at any given moment(57). This would be another difficulty for them when the group is larger. Add to this that accurate repetition of a sequence of events is difficult for the under threes, and that their attention rarely holds out for long, and it becomes fairly easy to see that games which demand coherent and coordinated sequences of actions, especially if they involve more than two children, should be beyond them.

The familiarity of the context in which the play takes place is important too. Rhesus and other monkey infants cautiously explore and engage in play with others only from the safe vantage point of the mother or familiar substitute before venturing on expeditions of their own (see Chapter Three). The extent to which the environment or the other children are familiar and not frightening, and whether the mother is present or not, are equally important when one is counting the spontaneous social contacts of human infants. Certainly brothers and sisters often pay attention to each other, and play cooperatively with each other, at much earlier ages than those generally reported in experimental studies. Brothers aged eighteen and forty-one months respectively were frequently observed to tumble over one another in contact play like baby bears. My two-year-old cooperated with his four-year-old brother in trying to build as high a tower as possible after they had seen one which delighted them both. The two-year-old who had started the tower waited for the other to put on a brick before placing his own, picked up the other's brick if it happened to be badly placed, and allowed this to be done to his own bricks also.

The frequency and amount of social play at different ages varies with habits and social background. Piaget mainly drew the subjects of his investigations from the Maison des

Petits. The Montessori methods used there tend to encourage solitary occupations more than is customary for American children whom Gesell studied. This would account for the fact that the Swiss children were reported to play in parallel or in association rather than cooperatively at later ages than the American children.

Absence of cooperative social play does not necessarily mean a lack of 'sympathetic' reactions. My eldest boy mainly played solitary games until he was nearly four years old. But already at the age of twenty-three months, his first reaction to hearing his newborn brother cry was to bring him his very 'best' teddy. Conversely, cooperative play does not necessarily presuppose sympathetic reactions to partners in the game. Susan Isaacs, commenting on her observations of children between two and five years in her nursery school in the 1920s, suggests that 'the play of a number of children is little more than the congeries of individual phantasies. When these phantasies happen to overlap, they give rise to common activity, and may, for the time being, weld the players together into a group'(182, p. 215). Several children want to play trains, but each one really wants to be the driver and needs others as passengers simply to make his own role more complete. Again this is probably more typical of children in a nursery school than of brothers and sisters with interesting experiences which coincide.

Of course, if the term 'social' play is to be applied only to play in which toys and activities are shared, or assigned and accepted according to rules, it is clear that young children have a good deal to learn before their play with others can be so called. The demand for playmates does not necessarily mean less quarrelling. Competing for toys or anything else good that is going, asserting oneself over others for good or ill, are consequences rather than causes of social play. Before the age of two outbursts of anger are directed mainly against adults. Between the ages of three and four quarrelling with other children takes precedence(139a). This is the time when playmates tend to become important to children in our society.

Sharing and Competing in Play

Sharing toys and taking turns, two essentials in reducing quarrels, are learned by experience. Susan Isaacs has given a verbatim report of two four-year-olds quarrelling about a tricycle(182). The slightly younger of the two girls ran to tell Mrs Isaacs that the other had had it all the time and would not give it up. The suggestion that they should share only led to further crying and struggles for possession. When Mrs Isaacs said she would go away since they would not accept her suggestion, the younger one agreed to share, but the two girls still struggled for some time until it became obvious that neither would have the benefit of the tricycle. They then started taking turns, and apparently shared more easily ever after this experience. It is probable that the adult's disapproval, conveyed in her threat to leave them to their quarrel, had some effect in addition to the children's proving to themselves physically that their quarrelling did not pay off. Sharing may also come more easily to a child whose desire to play with others is strong. 'Then I won't play any more' is often used effectively by children to induce others to let them have a toy. Like most other socially desirable habits, sharing is learned via a variety of incentives and social pressures. This does not exclude an 'appeal' to or evocation of a child's feeling for, or with another when it is possible to wean the child's attention away from his object for long enough.

Competing with others in order to excel is, of course, encouraged in Western society. The results of an experiment designed to assess the extent to which children of different ages are influenced by others engaged on the same task showed that two-year-olds took little notice of each other when engaged in inserting pegs into peg-boards. The three-year-olds were disturbed by the presence of others. They did less well than when working alone, although there was occasional rivalry. By the age of five, the children worked harder in pairs than alone, with indications that they were trying to rival each other(214). A study of competition in

two- to seven-year-old Viennese children showed a steady
rise in competitive actions and remarks between the two
ages from their almost complete absence at the age of
two(143). Another study(250) found a slightly later start.
Five- or six-year-olds express rivalry with perhaps the least
inhibition. If one of them says that he was given a car for
his birthday, most others will chime in and say that they
have five, or a hundred, cars. By Junior age, the 'need to
achieve' has, generally speaking, been fairly well learned in
our society.

Group and Gang Play

The play-groups of six-to seven-year-olds still shift about a
good deal, and are organized rather loosely. This has often
been described as a 'transitional' age, leading to the 'gang-
age', between the ages of about eight and twelve. Eight- to
twelve-year-olds are said to hate playing on their own.
Rivalry and competition with others, whether individuals
or groups, are important incentives at this age(175). Loyalty
to the gang, and cooperation within it may override individual rivalries. Toys become less important than tools and
realistic implements. Jumping, running, wrestling and all
forms of sport are favourites. Organized games with simple
rules(135), Cowboys and Indians, ball-games, roller-skating
(48), and annoying other people, are later replaced by more
complex games, sports(211) and gang rivalries.

Most of this has been reported of boys rather than girls.
In Western society boys and girls tend to segregate at this
point. Individual secret boy–girl friendships are quite
common, but a boy will rarely acknowledge such to his
mates, and may even 'cut' his girl-friend when he is with
them. In general, an older boy will play with other boys in a
group which stays together with far fewer fluctuations than
before. Individual friendships too fluctuate less as children
get older(355).

Gangs tend to develop fairly rigid pecking orders mainly
based on physical prowess. According to the Kansas study

in the 1920s, older boys liked organized games with rules, and competitive ones like football, boxing and wrestling, more than the girls did. Active, vigorous games were preferred more by boys than by girls even between the ages of five and eight, but the difference was more noticeable after the age of eight. After the age of ten, simpler games tend to be dropped in favour of more complexly organized ones. Hiding and finding, tag and singing games are typically absent from the play of boys over ten.

The segregation of older boys and girls in play may be due to adult pressure: to the idea that girls ought not to be physically as rough as boys, nor be allowed to be away from home and supervision to the same extent. Possibly, too, boys' games may become too rough for the girls, as in the higher apes, so that girls tend to drop out. An interesting current study of play-groups in schools in Israel found that, although there was a drop in the number of mixed boy–girl play-groups between the ages of nine and eleven, mixed groups did still occur, especially in the secular schools. In the religious schools there was more segregation. The number of children playing in mixed groups in the religious schools was only one-third of those playing in mixed groups in the secular schools(98). This suggests that the degree of spontaneous segregation of the sexes in play during this period must, at least to some extent, be a question of social convention and adult approval. Israeli girls, incidentally, are just as liable for compulsory military training as the boys, and, outside the most orthodox circles, inequality of the sexes seems to be stressed less.

The extent to which children congregate in gangs and continue to do so in adolescence is largely determined by the social, cultural and economic nature of the neighbourhood in which they live. Thrasher's famous 1,313 gangs were all in the slum districts of Chicago(360). Thrasher's gangs developed out of play-groups in crowded neighbourhoods. Two or three children who had known each other all their lives would form the nucleus which attracted others. The desire to escape supervision by the family welded some together as against adults. Clashes with other gangs augmented solidarity. In adverse conditions, poverty and unemployment and all that goes with these, the gangs were liable to become delinquent and to continue into early adulthood, although the composition of a gang would shift about. The structure and permanence of these adolescent gangs depended on circumstances, including hostility from the neighbourhood or from other gangs. Hostility against a group generally strengthens its cohesiveness(29).

The leisure-occupations of Thrasher's 'Dirty Dozen' of sixteen- to twenty-year-olds: brawling, fighting, shooting craps, sex, drinking, basketball and football, are perhaps rather different from games of marbles or tag. However, these gangs came together informally without any specified common purpose, unlike, for instance, clubs for tennis or dining, and they were direct continuations of earlier play-groups. The fact that the members of the gangs were sexually mature, while the children in the play-groups were not, must obviously have influenced their activities. This is not to say that younger boys do not play sexual games or fight. Susan Isaacs reported interest in sex, and all bodily functions, in her normal, intelligent and avowedly free nursery-school children(182). If the memories of adults are to be relied upon, since there are no adequate studies, games like touching, hitting, or pinching the opponent's genitals while protecting their own, mutual masturbation and inspection, competitions as to who can urinate in the largest arc as well as 'smutty' talk, and jokes and rhymes about what is usually 'taboo', are quite common among normal, sexually immature boys during unsupervised play in our society, although such games are carefully hidden from adults. In societies which allow sex-play among children, this occurs throughout childhood, while kinship taboos are observed(236). Psychologists have long been delighted by the irony that the only period in life that Freud designated as sexually latent is so only in virtue of social pressures. It goes without saying that the sex-play of the sexually immature cannot be quite the same as the sexual activity of mature individuals. Whether the constituents of the mating pattern which occur pre-pubertally in humans as in most mammals should, or should not, be called 'sexual' when they occur out of context or out of the normal sequence is arguable (27: ch. XXII), but this is not an important issue.

Recently sociologists have laid less stress on economic than on sociological factors in accounting for the existence and activities of gangs. Adolescents have an ill-defined status in Western society, and sexually no defined rolé at all; their striving for adult status, and for an identity in a highly complex, mechanized world is supposed to be responsible for much of the tough behaviour and wild escapades(42). However, the subject is outside the scope of this book.

The Influence of other Children and of Adults upon Play-groups and Gangs

Older children's and adolescents' play-groups and gangs frequently use nicknames, secret languages, badges and special meeting places: street-corners, derelict houses, or playgrounds, depending on the character of the neighbourhood and the kind of gang. Gangs often ape the initiation rites, passwords and other trappings of adult secret societies. In the case of pre-adolescent and adolescent gangs these do not in fact 'protect' them in any way, and are, in this sense, much more like imitative play. They are probably important to each member as signs of belonging – whether or not they also serve individual phantasies. The need to belong, to be a member of some group other than the family, is usually strong in adolescence. To imitate, to do as others of your own age do, and to be influenced by them is an important step towards this. To be different, whether in dress, speech, or anything else is to incur ridicule and even ostracism.

The relative influence of adults and other children changes with age(155). It is not possible to give an absolute age at which the influence of peers becomes more important than that of adults. What is expected of a boy by way of independence varies in different societies, social classes, and sub-groups. Individual children differ in the extent to which they are dependent upon adults, and this is one factor in how they will be influenced (183). One experimental study of nine-year-old boys, for instance, showed them to be more influenced by the judgement of an adult than by one boy only slightly older than themselves, when trying to decide whether a pinpoint of light in a darkened room had moved or not(183). Another investigation required seven- to ten-year-old children to judge which of three lines were equal to another one. After they had heard the unanimous verdict of eight of their age-mates (confederates of the experimenters), they accepted the majority verdict, even when it was wrong(28). A teacher's judgement was accepted less often in this study. Ten- to thirteen-year-olds were less easily influenced by either in this situation. The size of the group giving a suggestion, its standing *vis à vis* the individual, the extent to which doubt about a problem is objectively possible, the degree of unanimity of those trying to influence, and the discrepancy between their judgement and the individual's own, the individual's anxiety, age (the younger, the more easily influenced), and having been previously rewarded for giving incorrect answers, have all been found to affect the extent to which people are influenced by others (29: ch. I). In general, it is probably the case that adolescents are more influenced by members of their group than by adults(20). The need to belong, to be 'one of them', learned to different degrees of urgency in different environments, antedates this, and is quite possibly more important than the particular activity pursued by the play-group or gang who come together informally in childhood and early adolescence.

Competitive Play and Games

Organized games with rules have the advantage of minimizing friction within a group by assigning definite roles and rules of behaviour to the players. They give the group a common aim or goal to which each one can contribute and so feel himself a bona fide member, even if only for the time being. Each individual may also have his own phantasy of playing for England, excelling above all others, being applauded by the girls, saving the group from defeat, or the world from destruction, or exercising a preferred skill. We know little of this with any precision. It seems fairly safe to assume, at any rate, that a society would not encourage pursuits whether 'serious' or not, of which it disapproved.

The theory that games simulate the serious pursuits of a society in order to practise skills necessary to it(304) is another version of Groos' theory of play as practice (see Chapter One). On the face of it, this seems plausible enough. A martial society must keep its men fit, and must also encourage the young to learn the measure of self-denial and cooperation with his fellows necessary for concerted action. Mock battles are fought with all the appurtenances of military operations by our armed forces, but it may be doubted whether military commanders would rank these as play.

Huizinga's famous theory of play(172) is, in some respects, the converse of the previous theory. Play, according to Huizinga, is older than culture forms. Indeed civilization derives from play. On the basis of his analysis of the meaning of the word 'play' in different civilizations, Huizinga came to the conclusion that in most of these 'play' has some connexion with strife and contest, and also with (illicit) love-play. Play is basically fighting or hostility checked by friendship. This encourages social virtues like chivalry, loyalty and courage and the urge to be first in skill and knowledge. Philosophy has its roots in the sacred riddle game, poetry in social games like teasing and mocking songs between the sexes; myths and poetry are play with language. Huizinga also considers play to be identical with magic, as, for instance, in the ritual combats which announce divine decisions, or in the sacred miming of divine intervention in human affairs: making rain when there is a drought, or rituals to induce fertility in the soil. In spite of Huizinga's unpromising statement that play is not reducible to other terms and that no biological explanation can deal with it, it should be possible to translate some of his suggestions into testable form. For instance, his assertion that social play is hostility checked by friendship is interesting in the light of observations of some of the social play of mammals (see Chapter Three). But the suggestion that competition is the main basis of games, although, no doubt, partly true, is hardly enlightening, since competition is itself learned within a social context, possibly even through play and games. An analysis of organized games and sports would be beyond our present subject, but some current studies on the relation between games and social learning will be discussed in the next chapter.

CHAPTER EIGHT

THE INFLUENCE OF INDIVIDUAL AND SOCIAL DIFFERENCES UPON PLAY

HUMAN behaviour can be investigated by assessing the reactions of individuals to systematically changed characteristics of the external world. For instance, the type of task, or the kind, number and timing of some current physical stimuli can be varied and manipulated experimentally. It is also possible to compare groups of people differing in age, sex, intelligence, social or economic standing, or cultural background with respect to a given item of behaviour. The manner in which these 'individual difference' variables have been found to relate to play will be discussed in this chapter.

1. *The Play of Intelligent and of Retarded Children*

Individual children at any age vary in the efficiency and speed with which they can tackle complex tasks, especially those involving language or the use of symbols. The degree to which children rate higher on solving complex problems and puzzles of all kinds, the larger the range of their information, and the wider their vocabulary in comparison with their age-mates, the higher is their score on an 'intelligence' test made up of these items. By convention, those who succeed on all tests which about two-thirds of their age-mates can pass, are given a score of 100 ('intelligence quotient' or I.Q.). This, plus or minus about fifteen points is 'normal', i.e. the majority of children fall into this group, and there are proportionately fewer children, the further away from the norm you get.

The extent to which achieving high or low scores on intelligence tests depend upon the child's inherited constitution, and how much is due to his opportunities in the past to learn about the world in which he lives, is still controversial. We do know that both are important. Brain-damage, especially early in life, decreases ability to score highly. Members of the same family tend to rate similar scores on intelligence tests, and, by and large, the closer the genetic link, the more closely do the ratings coincide. At the same time, numerous studies show that opportunities to learn about the world, contact with educated and informed adults, the presence of books in the home, the variety of sources of information available to the child, the social, economic, cultural and educational standing of the parents, and all that goes with this, are related to a child's rank on intelligence tests compared with his age-mates (67: ch. X, 111).

For practical purposes, the extremes, the very bright or very dull, have been singled out for special study, and there are some, although by no means adequate, observations about their play.

The best-known study of gifted children is Terman's exhaustive long-term investigation in the 1920s in California of children with I.Q.s between 140 and 200(353). This highly selected group, now in their late forties, is still being followed up. The investigation of their intellectual achievements, health, physique, early history, family background and personality also included a survey of their play interests, and the kinds of games they played, or knew about. This survey was mainly in the form of questionnaires and checklists which were compared with similar material from a group of unselected children of the same age whose I.Q. scores ranged from the dull to the bright, the majority being of average intelligence.

A number of differences were found between gifted children's play and that of their contemporaries. The gifted children's play interests included, as might be expected, far more intellectual as opposed to physical activities, and correspondingly less interest in boisterous games, and slightly greater preference for quiet pursuits. Their play was more like that of older children and they preferred playmates slightly older than themselves. They showed a less marked preference than their less gifted contemporaries for one or the other sex in choosing a playmate, and less preference for competitive games. A good deal of the gifted children's time was spent in playing with other children, but they played alone slightly more than the control group. Imaginary playmates, and living in imaginary countries was common among these gifted children between the ages of two and five. Their physique, physical and mental health, general stability and social adjustment was significantly above the average. Similar results were reported in other studies of the play of bright children(211). One study(44) showed that intelligent children played about fifty minutes a day more than retarded children, spending nearly an hour more in 'mental recreation': reading, looking at atlases, encyclopedias and the like, from choice.

In some cases very bright children who have no age-mates equalling them intellectually may have social difficulties in play. There is a report of a boy with an I.Q. of 187, i.e. near the ceiling of any test, who was unpopular with his age-mates because he insisted on making the games too complicated, but was unacceptable to older children because they considered him too little to join in their play. In Terman's sample, however, the gifted children were as popular as the control group with their age-mates. In general, the play of intelligent children has been characterized as more varied, versatile(210), resourceful and mature. Intelligent children were more rather than less active in play and extra-curricular activities than their more average contemporaries.

By contrast, retarded children show less originality in their play activities, prefer games without complicated rules, and games more usually played by younger children. For instance, retarded ten- or eleven-year-olds still liked games of tag, hide and seek, 'drop the handkerchief' and 'the farmer's in his dell', which intelligent girls of that age had dropped in favour of reading, hiking, dancing or playing an instrument. Retarded children tended to prefer social activities slightly more than intelligent children(211). Mentally defective children of eleven chose construction materials less often than normal seven-year-olds of the same mental age, and chose toys and games which led to definitely prescribed activities more often than the younger normal children(169).

By and large, when children choose spontaneously, they go for activities within their compass. This is not to say that all children choose in play whatever is easiest as has sometimes been suggested. On the contrary, even to get sweets, children may prefer a more distant or difficult to an easier route(71).

Intellectual ability is clearly important in the choice of toys and games. But opportunity, and what is socially accepted also play a part. For instance, both intelligent and retarded boys stated that they disliked playing with dolls and playing the piano.

Retarded children within a normal group are likely to be of inferior status within it. They are less likely to be chosen for play, as friends, or as companions on the way home. A large number of different studies show a definite association between a child's ability and the extent to which he will be chosen by his peers to participate in play and leisure activities(90). This is true of young chimpanzees too (see Chapter Three), and is consistent with the assumption that playmates are at least partly valued for the stimulation and interest they provide.

2. *Differences Between the Play of Boys and Girls*

In most societies differences in play between boys and girls are not merely expected, but actively encouraged. In our own culture, only very young boys may be allowed to play with their sisters' dolls occasionally without ridicule or remonstrance. And even they are rarely given dolls of their own, although teddies and stuffed animals may be allowed. A seven-year-old boy who enjoys tucking teddies up in cots is likely to be ridiculed if he does it too often. Similarly, girls do enjoy playing with toy cars and train sets, but are rarely given these as presents. Older girls particularly are discouraged from playing boisterous games and may be labelled 'tom-boys' if they do not conform to the quieter, gentler, less aggressive activities expected of them. Boys who eschew rough games, or prefer reading or playing the piano are in danger of being labelled 'sissy'.

It is fairly well established that the upbringing and discipline of boys and girls in Western society is very different, but also that individual children are exposed to the relevant attitudes and training methods in different degrees (27: ch. VII). North American three-year-olds already showed sex differences in the aggressiveness with which they played with miniature dolls. Four-year-old boys engaged more in romping and activities involving the large muscles, girls tended to play houses or paint. Not all measures used, for instance, preference for pictures of toys and play that the experimenting adults considered 'masculine' and 'feminine' respectively, were equally reliable, or correlated highly with observation of the children in play. A recent ethological study of English three-year olds also found that boys did far more playing-fighting than girls. Laughter and jumping up and down acted as signs that the fights were friendly(399).

An earlier study of older children found that the majority of children's games are played by both boys and girls(211). The greatest difference was found in the manner of play. Boys, by and large, are more boisterous and energetic than girls. Although there are differences between sexually immature boys and girls in weight, height, and rates and 'spurts' of physical development, the precise relation of these to differences in play is not at all clear. A recent study of the adult role of hermaphrodites (people constitutionally endowed in varying degrees with a bisexual apparatus, as judged by sex chromatin pattern, morphologically determined gonadal sex, hormonal sex which relates to secondary sex characteristics, and external or internal reproductive structures) showed that the sex which was assigned to them at birth, and the role in which they were consequently reared, determined to a large extent the sex-role which they successfully carried out, and even the masculinity or femininity of their appearance (27: ch. VI). The greater leniency towards the aggressive and boisterous behaviour of boys than to that of girls, prevalent in most societies, presumably has an effect on their manner of play. But variations between boys and girls in amount of activity, even before puberty, are probably shaped or intensified rather than created by social training.

Competitive games too were more popular among boys than girls in studies in the 1920s, especially games involving trials of muscular skill, dexterity and strength, like football, wrestling, boxing, snowball fights or track events. Girls were less likely to participate in organized games, or in playing games which involved conforming to accepted rules. Visiting, reading, writing, teasing and other games involving language, were more popular with girls than with boys between the ages of eight and fifteen(211). Girls are, generally speaking, linguistically more skilful from an early age than boys in our society, and when they are aggressive tend to use their tongues rather than their fists.

It is possible that the boys' greater freedom to range beyond the home, in contradistinction to the closer surveillance of the girls, fosters the ganging together of the former, and makes girls rely less on their peers. A study of a community in the south-west Pacific showed a very different treatment of boys and girls respectively from the time they were weaned, onwards (27: ch. VIII). The boys were turned out into the village and played in age-groups under the general surveillance of village elders. The girls stayed at home by the side of an older woman. In Europe and America too, girls are allowed less freedom of movement, are more closely supervised, and kept nearer home more frequently than boys are, although this is gradually changing. A recent investigation(308) of games played by American boys and girls respectively showed that while girls still play games traditionally considered 'feminine', typically 'masculine' games like baseball and basketball no longer show a difference between the sexes. Girls (between the ages of six and thirteen) play them too. Earlier studies showed, if anything, more variety in the play of boys compared with the girls.

The study in the 1960s found a much greater variety of activities engaged in by the girls. Differences in the play of boys and girls have changed to some extent within the last forty years.

3. The Influence of Early Social and Intellectual Stimulation upon Play

The question to what extent and how permanently experiences occurring in infancy affect later behaviour has been investigated in many contexts and over a variety of species (see Chapter Three). The fact that results are influenced(357) by the intensity, frequency, and types of experiences, the ages at which they occur, and the ages at which measurements of behaviour are made, differences in genetic strains, and species differences, makes generalizations difficult. On human children most, if not the most reliable, evidence comes from studies comparing ordinary children with those deprived of their parents by death, desertion, or illness, and brought up in institutions.

Almost all the early studies found institution infants to have drastic handicaps in intelligence, social skills, and language development when compared with children brought up in their own homes(43). Infants in institutions were reported to be apathetic, uninterested in their surroundings, and to play much less than ordinary children. When play did occur it was immature, stereotyped, and lacking in inventiveness. The original, rather global view, was that this was due to loss of mothering and mother-love. The early studies were criticized on methodological grounds (267). However, these emotionally biased views had an excellent effect in that some of the conditions which 'maternal deprivation' actually covered(75, 389) began to receive public attention and amelioration. Among these were lack of toys, lack of opportunity for being stimulated either socially or intellectually, brief, intermittent contacts with a number of different, busy care-takers, and little opportunity for the children to attach themselves permanently to any one of them. The older type of institution had relatively few, and frequently changing, staff whose many domestic duties left them with little or no time to talk to, or play with, individual children. Hygienic precautions forbade them to hold and fondle young babies, and lack of funds often made it impossible to provide much in the way of equipment. The children's experiences before being taken into care, which might include cruelty, neglect, undernourishment, overstrict or inconsistent discipline, a generally impoverished environment, or any combination of these, provide other sources of differences between them and normally reared children. It is probable too, that proportionately more children from families with genetic weaknesses will be found among those coming into care.

The major questions have been about what mainly determines the adverse effects, and whether they need be permanent. For instance, is the comparative absence of spontaneous play, the stereotyped rocking, the lack of inventiveness, reported of some deprived children due to lack of stimulation, or to grief, or because it has been impossible for them to acquire strong affectional and social motives so that they have few incentives to explore, play and learn? Can they be brought to a normal level of achievement by subsequent training, even after prolonged early deprivation?

In recent studies, lack of opportunity for stimulation has been stressed. The white walls, quiet, hygienic rooms, absence of toys and of adults playing with them, and the minimum handling typical of most early institutions caring for young babies, have been likened to conditions of sensory deprivation. These might easily account for listlessness, apathy and retardation in physically admirably cared-for babies. One recent study, comparing infants in an institution with children of the same age living with their own families(292) found many differences in the amount of stimulation the two groups received. An institution baby could see his cot, his own hands, a toy, another baby and could vary this scene a little by moving about in his cot. Babies in their own homes were lifted up more often, were cuddled more frequently, and were talked to more. The adults in the institution tried to make as little noise as possible, and the infants did not cry or babble much. As toddlers, the institution children rarely left their nursery, and went without the car-rides or outings which formed a normal part of the lives of children living in their own homes.

The greatest differences between children brought up in the institution compared with those living in their own homes were in language development and social skills, and the least in motor development. This is usually found in studies of this kind(111). The institution babies mouthed less, showed little preference for one toy over another, explored less and played less. They started playing with their hands at the normal time, but this was not followed by elaborating these activities as is usual with normal infants. Children who were subsequently placed in foster homes showed great improvements. Improvements in skills of all kinds were also found in another study when children, at the toddler stage, moved into a relatively more stimulating day-nursery after their first year of life had been spent in the exceedingly restricted environment of the baby-room of a somewhat primitive institution which had retarded them(89). Supplementary experiences, even for relatively brief periods, seem to lead to improvements of the test scores of deprived infants(314).

Differences in amount of stimulation in the environment as between institution and home children can be found even when the institution is modern and enlightened. Three-month-old babies living in their own families were talked to five times as often, were fed four times as often during observational periods, were played with seven times as much, were out of their cots twice as often, were held more often; they also had many different toys while the institutional three-months-olds had one tied to each cot(298). Apparently, these institutional babies did play spontaneously with their hands almost as much as the home children played with toys, and did manipulate objects that were given to them. Their 'social responsiveness' to the experimenter was indeed significantly greater than that of the home children. It is not possible on this evidence to say whether this was because they had not yet learned to discriminate familiar from strange faces, while the home children had, or whether they reacted more positively because of their previously greater social deprivation. All that is shown is a difference in social response.

Generally speaking, comparative studies show that children from the more stimulating institutional homes score more highly on tests of all kinds than children from deprived homes (263: ch. VI). The extent to which the adults caring for them teach, play and pay attention to individuals, as well as the variety of toys and play materials available to them, are involved in this. Exploring and playing increases in stimulating environments.

It is unlikely that sensory stimulation, in the form of toys to see and handle, objects to explore, and noises to hear, is the only important constituent of maternal care. Being cared for by a large number of different people rather than by one person alone has been studied as a possible factor(299). Eight of sixteen six-months-olds in an institution were given two months 'mothering' by the experimenter during which time she alone performed all the care-taking; feeding, bathing, nappy-changing and playing with them, while the remaining babies continued under their normal régime in which routine care-taking was done by several nurses at different times. The 'experimental' babies were much more socially responsive than their controls after the two months, although they had started out level on tests before the experiment began. However, in communally living 'Kibbutzim' in Israel everyone's babies are cared for in a common nursery by several nurses without ill effects on tests in adolescence (294). There may be a number of reasons for this discrepancy. The social standing and attitudes of the adults in charge, and, consequently, the minutiae of their behaviour towards the children, are bound to be better if communal nursing is the accepted social norm and is expected to reap the best results than if the society regards communal care as a '*pis-aller*', whatever the adults may do, and the children as objects of pity and the receivers of charity. The Kibbutzim mothers, although they see their children for relatively brief periods only, and do none of the care-taking, do see them regularly. Kibbutzim staff do not change as frequently, and so on.

Some early investigators stressed the lack of cuddling and bodily contact characteristic of institutional care as a major detrimental factor. This was subsequently severely criticized for lack of evidence, but, since Harlow's finding on baby monkeys' need to cling to something soft (see Chapter Three), may have to be reconsidered. The familiar, oft-repeated and invariably recurring, particular constellations of sounds, sights, smells, touches and tastes which make up a given mother may stimulate, or help to organize the developing infant's perceptions; or they may reduce fear and excitement and so keep his as yet poorly organized system on a more even keel. As mentioned (in Chapter Three) young chimpanzees when they are frightened cling to other chimpanzees, or to familiar humans, and this clinging inhibits, or at any rate lessens, signs of stress and fear(239).

Physical contact which reduces stress is probably a factor in the attachment between human infant and mother also. However, contact play between a human child and his mother almost certainly occurs when the baby is not frightened. Also, it stimulates, rather than soothes the baby. The type of contact is quite different in the two cases. A frightened human infant will respond to being totally and tightly surrounded by his mother's arms, and will snuggle up to her as much as possible. In play, human infants escape from such embraces, but try to nuzzle and rub themselves against the mother, jump up and down on her, clamber all over her, and so on. In monkeys this kind of play has been described as exploration. Human infants do explore their mothers also, but the movements in jumping up and down, clambering all over, and rubbing themselves against her are different in the assurance and confidence the child shows, while exploratory movements tend to be more uncertain and tentative. It looks much more like 'taking possession', asserting mastery, or confirming either of these, as well as enjoyment of the mild physical shocks occasioned by it. Mild physical shocks, like other mildly increased stimulation, seem to be 'rewarding'. A report which indicates that smiling at babies, talking to them, and other forms of stimulation may be more important than feeding and care-taking for the babies' attachment to their nurse has come from a study in the U.S.S.R.(193). This is similar to the findings of a study on puppies (see Chapter Three). Mild forms of stimulation certainly seem to be important in the development of social 'bonds'.

The relative importance of familiarity, body-contact, sucking, feeding, having discomforts alleviated which reduce excitement, and of contacts which stimulate: chirruping noises, catching the baby's eye, touching, talking and playing with him, as well as the frequency and timing of these, in the development of the baby's attachment to his mother, is not yet clear. A good deal is now known about the cues actually available to the infant in different types of interaction with an adult, and how they impinge upon the infant's repertoire of learned and unlearned responses. But we need far more detailed research before we can assess their relative effects. Playing with the infant may contribute to his attachment to his mother by providing a social situation, or to his alertness and tendency to explore through stimulation. At any rate, it seems to contribute to his playing more.

Conversely, social incentives are important in young children's learning(342) and probably for play. It has frequently been assumed that they derive solely from the infant's attachment to his mother or substitute. On learning theory, this is easily accounted for on the principle that responses learned to one set of stimuli will generalize to others in proportion as they resemble or are associated with the original set. It has also been held that children who have not become attached to their mother or care-taking adult during infancy will be incapable of forming lasting attachments to their peers later(43). Broken homes are more frequent in the background of those who are emotionally disturbed and emotionally 'shallow' than of their more fortunate peers. But so are a number of other adverse conditions. Some severely deprived children show an exaggerated, restless, short-lived friendliness to every adult stranger they meet, paralleled by equally indiscriminate, short-lived interest in objects. In the playroom, they pick up every toy in turn only to drop it the next moment for something else, without ever settling down to consecutive, constructive individual, or cooperative social play. These are extreme cases, and may represent only the reactions of children who are constitutionally labile, or have specific, not necessarily obvious, kinds of brain damage, or where adverse conditions are in fact still present, and the children are unhappy, or bewildered.

According to Harlow, being together with other infants is at least as important as being with their mothers for the social reactions of monkeys to each other (see Chapter Three). As far as human children are concerned, there is one report of deprived children staying together in an environment where they had constant changes of care-takers. The children formed strong and lasting attachments to each other(122).

Whether it is, in principle, possible to 'reverse' or totally efface the effects of a childhood experience is controversial. The answer must ultimately depend upon findings about the detailed physical and physiological arrangements upon which long-term memory depends. If, as seems likely, chemical changes in the brain are involved for long-term effects (130, 205) these may be overlaid, become inaccessible, 'fade' or disintegrate, and may not, in any case, be brought about by brief experiences. It is not possible to discuss these questions in detail here. However there are differences in the effects experiences have on immature and mature brains respectively. In practice, the question turns upon the measurable effects upon behaviour which an experience may have, and whether this remains measurable – for how long, and under what conditions. From the available evidence about adverse effects upon measurable behaviour of children deprived of social and intellectual stimulation, there is every indication that subsequent care before puberty to compensate for this, can succeed to a surprising extent. This is important, even if it were merely to reflect the crudity of our present behavioural measurements.

4. Some Influences of Parental Attitudes upon Play

In spite of the multiplicity and complexity of the factors involved in relating methods of child-rearing to children's subsequent behaviour, there have been a number of significant findings which are relevant to children's play. Generally speaking, studies of this kind employ detailed rating scales of parental attitudes and practices in a given population, based on individual interviews with the parents. These are correlated with ratings of the children's behaviour in various situations, based on observations, tests and reports. Differences in family attitudes and practices are reflected in the amount of activity, originality and social content of children's play(15, 16, 325). Homes which have been labelled 'permissive', because the parents consulted each other about decisions, explained the reasons for rules to their children, and tried to avoid being arbitrary while providing adequate control, produced children who were socially outgoing (in an aggressive as well as a friendly way), inquisitive, original and constructive in their play and general behaviour. Autocratic homes which emphasized clear-cut restrictions without much consultation between the partners, and expected relatively unquestioning obedience from the children, tended to have children who were quiet, unaggressive, conforming, and restricted in curiosity, originality and fancifulness. Over-indulgence, over-protection and a tendency to 'baby' the children was accompanied by their fearing physical hazards and lacking in physical skills.

The type of play situation in which the behaviour is measured is probably important. For instance, one study showed that nursery-school children who were frequently punished at home by their mothers were less aggressive to others in free play than children who had experienced only relatively mild punishments(324). A study relating aggression in doll-play to the amount of punishment and frustration nursery-school children experienced at home, on the other hand, found that those who were spanked, scolded or isolated more and had fewer of their requests granted at home were considerably more aggressive in doll-play than children whose homes rated low on the amount of punishment and frustration they encountered(167). Aggression to dolls is not the same as hitting another child. How anxious the parents are, and their warmth of manner towards their children made a difference to whatever type of upbringing they used.

The presence or absence of the parent upon whom the child 'models' himself (see Chapter Six) affects his play. Boys whose fathers were absent from the home played less aggressively than boys whose fathers were present. Their play was more like the play of girls. Girls' play, on the other hand, was not affected by the absence of the father(323). Perhaps it is unnecessary to stress the obvious effects parental attitudes and practices do normally have on their children. It is, however, interesting to find that even pre-school children whose mothers encourage their attempts to achieve success are more likely spontaneously to choose for their play activities such as painting, making clay-models or reading, in which 'achievement' may be said to matter(79).

The current presence or absence of adults also has an effect upon play, mainly in the direction of allowing increased aggression in the relatively harmless context of doll-play (215, 328), when the adult allows this. Observation of mothers playing with their three- to six-year-olds showed that direct interference, control and criticism of the child's play was related to non-cooperation or inhibition of play on the part of the child, and this tended to generalize to his attitude in subsequent play with a 'neutral' adult(40).

5. Child-rearing Norms and Games

Recently an attempt has been made to link child-rearing

practices in various cultures with the games most common in each(305). Reports of games in a number of 'primitive' tribes and the results of studies rating the severity or indulgence with which the tribes treat their young over such matters as training in toilet habits, obedience, responsibility and the like, were compared. Games, for this purpose, were divided into three main categories, each with a number of subdivisions. Games of physical skill formed one of the major divisions. Marathon races, hoop and pole games belong to this. Games of strategy which involved skill in making rational choices among alternatives, such as chess or poker, formed a second category. The third comprised games of chance: dice games, gambling, and the like. A survey of the distribution of games in a number of societies showed some link between physical games and environmental factors, such as climate, temperature and diet(304). However, the authors also suggest that most games are imitations of a society's major activities. For instance, games of strategy simulate war and combat. They occur mainly in societies with complex political and social structures. Games of chance simulate religious practices such as divining, and a belief in occult or supernatural intervention in human affairs.

Several statistically significant relationships were found between the type of game most usually played, and ratings on child-rearing practices. Games of physical skill were found in societies which stressed achievement and success as the children's most important goals. Games of strategy were played in societies which ranked high in training their children to be clean, obedient and independent, using severe punishments as a deterrent, and affection as reward. Games of chance occurred in societies which rewarded responsible and adult behaviour in the young: poor societies which needed the children to work early. The authors suggest that the links between the type of early training and games are to be explained partly on the basis that playing games is a direct training ground for the skills expected later.

Roberts' and Sutton-Smith's(347) major suggestion,

however, is that individuals play games as an outlet for the personal inner conflicts which their particular type of childhood training has precipitated. They call it the 'conflict-enculturation' hypothesis. This explains the association between severity of obedience training and games of strategy by assuming that the complexity of the society in which such games are mainly played necessarily makes demands upon obedience. The frustration and anger aroused in children by this training are displaced upon games and satisfied in the unreal combat of games of strategy, while the child still remains obedient in reality. The association between games of chance and early training in responsibility for the children is held to be due to the conflict aroused in children of poor societies who must perform economically necessary routine chores that leave little scope for initiative. Games of chance are the individual's response to his passive role, and provide an outlet for the irresponsibility which is inadmissible in his daily life. Games of physical skill were found to be associated with parental emphasis on achievement and success. Some support for the theory was derived from findings that boys and men in our society receive less severe training in obedience and responsibility than girls, while greater stress is laid upon their achieving success. Boys and men do play games of physical skill more than girls; women and girls apparently prefer games of strategy and chance(347).

Unfortunately, it is a little difficult to interpret these interesting findings confidently because of methodological weaknesses of which the authors are well aware. For instance, absence of a game in a given society may have been due to omissions by the compiler of the lists, and the criteria by which games are assigned to various categories are not always unambiguous. But even the most unequivocal association between variations in childhood training and certain types of games could give rise to no more than speculation about the direction of the influence. Certain types of games might as easily be the cause of children being trained in certain ways as to result from it, or both may be associated solely in virtue of being a consequence of a given society's norms of behaviour. The findings do not necessitate an assumption of relief from inner conflict as the basis of involvement in a game, although they would be compatible with it.

The Opies' delightful compilation of children's lore(272) gives an idea of the extent to which similar games are played by children of widely different backgrounds, geographical locations and generations. Tongue-twisters like Peter Piper are at least 200 years old. Humorous insults, from the ancient Greek story of a youth calling a herding woman a 'mother of asses' and being greeted with 'Good morning, my son' to the modern English 'Same to you with a ton of atom bombs on top of you', may show something of the sameness of the human condition. But the form of a game and the immediate reason for which it is played are not necessarily directly connected.

6. Social, Economic and Cultural Differences in Play

There are considerable differences in what is the fashionable doctrine on how to bring up children in different social classes(84) and different generations. American parents of the mid-twentieth century have been some of the most patient and cooperative subjects for studies of the relation between different child training practices and child behaviour. Their handling of weaning, toilet training, the degree of sexual modesty they expect of young children, whether they use physical punishments and material rewards or verbal praise and reproof, give affection or withhold it for good and bad conduct, differs according to whether they belong to the 'middle' or 'lower' classes(325). A number of factors contribute to these differences. For one thing, middle-class parents have usually had a longer period of education, and more access to books on the latest theory of how to bring up Johnny. But there are more important effects. Middle-class parents talk more to their children, have more information to impart on a greater variety of topics, are more able to provide appropriate toys and

materials on which the children can experiment, can give
the children more opportunity for travel, and are in other
ways more able to provide intellectually stimulating environments which affect play (see above). Different methods of
handling social training have effects on the children's style
of expressing aggression, the degree to which they depend on
other children, opportunities to be together with other
children without adult supervision, and other ingredients of
social play.

More interesting, perhaps, are differences in the play of
children which emerged from an extensive study of six
societies(381) belonging to totally different social and cultural groups. A Gusii community in Kenya, the Nyansongo,
living a relatively traditional life 5,000 to 7,000 feet above sea
level in thatched roof huts, was one of the societies investigated
in this anthropological field study. Another was that of the
Rajputs of Khalapur, an Indian village some ninety miles
north of Delhi. The third study was conducted in the village
of Taira on the north-east coast of Okinawa, the largest of
the Ryukus islands which are one of a chain on the western
rim of the Pacific Ocean. They have cultural ties with Japan,
Korea and China, countries accessible by small boats.
Annexed by Japan at the end of the nineteenth century, they
came under American influence after the Second World
War. The fourth study was of an Indian-speaking community
in southern Mexico and the fifth of two settlements in the
Philippines. Finally, there was a study of the northern part
of Orchard Town – a typical New England town in the
United States – with its two-storey houses, garages, central
heating, electric light, telephone, television, bathrooms and
W.C.s, showers and rooms for everything and practically
everybody.

Free Time and Toys in Four of the Different Communities

The difference which strikes one immediately in the reports
on the play of children in the New England community and
in the other societies is the time and toys available to the

former. The Nyansongo, who depend mainly upon agriculture and some animal husbandry, supplemented by employment of the men outside the community, have a reasonable standard of living in that they are better fed and clothed than most peasants in Africa. Nevertheless, there is economic anxiety, and the women particularly work extremely hard. The children must help. Training in obedience and responsibilities frequently starts as soon as a younger brother or sister is born, and in any case when the children are about three years old. They are expected to run errands, carry dishes of food from one house to another within the homestead (between the houses of the father's co-wives or those of his elder brothers), and they even help their mothers in hoeing the field for short periods. By the age of six or seven they do a considerable amount of hoeing. Boys then are trained to herd cattle by their fathers or elder brothers, if the family owns cattle. The little boys tag along under the supervision of the oldest uncircumcised (pre-adolescent) boy. The herding groups consist of boys from several homesteads, and whoever is the oldest dominates the rest and assigns tasks to them. In homesteads that own cattle, the oldest boy, even if he is only six years old, is responsible to his father for the welfare of the cattle. Girls and children under six are expected to remain within the homestead under the supervision of the oldest uncircumcised girl, usually within calling distance of the mother who works in the nearby fields. Girls carry out household tasks, help with hoeing, weeding and harvesting, are taught to chuck corn, grind eleusine and cook porridge. They help to wash clothes at the stream, fetch water and they mind the younger children, carrying the very little ones on their backs. Child nurses between the ages of five and nine are severely punished by their mothers if they neglect their charges.

Few Nyansongo children go to school. A child's free time is not merely limited by the tasks he or she is expected to perform, but it has to take second place to duty whenever an older child or an adult requires it. Whether as a result of this, or for some other reason, girls who are kept in or around the homestead and whose society is mainly confined to their siblings and other related children in the homestead, may be quite inactive during a pause – sometimes prolonged – between tasks. Their play consists mainly of cuddling each other or kissing and tickling the infants in their charge, or whispering and giggling with each other. They rarely fight. Children who go herding range farther afield, are out of adult earshot, and the tasks involved in herding cattle do not take all their time. In the intervals they climb trees, shoot at birds with home-made slings, watch the traffic and tussle with one another. When they have led the cattle down to the stream to drink, they may splash in the water, and sometimes swim. The only toys are the boys' home-made slings with which they shoot at birds, or occasionally at each other with berries. Only twice did the observers, who lived with the Nyansongo from 1955 to 1957, see children play an imaginative game. Once a six-year-old fashioned a plough to which he yoked his younger brother, and once a ten-year-old herding boy built a house of reeds. Toys are equally rare. Once a mother gave her infant a gourd rattle to shake to distract him from his pain when he had burned himself badly. The mothers of older children told the observers that they used to give them leaves or tins to play with when they were little. But the observers who took part in many of the community's activities never witnessed this.

The contrast with American children is obvious. They have any number of indoor and outdoor toys. Stuffed animals, miniature trucks and cars, dolls, teddies, doll's prams and trucks to pull, toy-soldiers, guns, musical instruments, tri-cycles, wagons, scooters at the pre-school level, and bi-cycles later. In addition, a number of families have sand-pits, wading pools and swings in their gardens. Fathers help their children to fly model aeroplanes, and play games with them in their spare time. The parents take the children to the zoo, to museums, circuses and other entertainments. Pre-school children are never expected to do regular chores at home, although they are encouraged to pick up their own toys and may occasionally fetch things around the house for their mothers. Their time is spent playing, they busy themselves with their toys, scribble, draw, do puzzles and other ready-made games, or they may have neighbouring children in to play with them. They are allowed considerable freedom in watching television.

Compulsory schooling starts at the age of six, and this is considered to be the child's work. Everything is done to make school enjoyable for them. It is regarded as the duty of adults, parents and teachers alike, to promote the happiness of the children. The free time of schoolchildren is regulated by the school time-table. 'Recesses' or break-times are spent in the playground, running about, chasing each other, or playing a number of games organized among themselves. Boys may gang up with a physically powerful, often intellectually somewhat backward, leader, and playfully charge others who do not belong to the same group. Actual playground fights are promptly stopped by the teacher and are punished. Girls are more likely to play games like jumping over ropes. After school, the children's time is more or less their own, spent in play with other children. They rarely have regular chores, although girls of twelve may be left in charge of younger brothers or sisters, or may baby-sit for neighbours. The congregation of large play-groups in the house or back-garden is discouraged by the mothers.

As they get older, children are progressively less under the supervision of adults. Too much interference by adults is not considered to be good for boys who are encouraged to 'stand up' for themselves, but parents will interfere if there is too much rough-housing or risk of someone getting hurt. Older children may spend their play-time away from home in the surrounding woods and fields, collecting birds' eggs, fishing, swimming, and so forth. For the older ones there are an increasing number of organized activities such as scouts, church choirs, baseball teams, and the like. There are also dancing classes where children from the age of ten onwards are supposed to learn to behave like young ladies and gentlemen towards each other. In Orchard Town play is encouraged, and toys and time are available in plenty. Adult direction in both is by no means lacking. Nyansongo children have free time simply when there are no chores for them to do. They have no toys and no encouragement from adults to play. Adult direction of play is confined to discouraging aggression and physical hurt.

The other communities fall somewhere in between these two extremes. The landowning, farming Rajputs of India claim descent from warrior-rulers, and their concept of themselves is as landlords rather than as workers, even though they may have to perform most of the tasks themselves. The wealthiest families employ lower-caste servants to work their fields, and each Rajput family is served by water-carriers, sweepers, carpenters, barbers, potters, washermen and leather-workers, whose work belongs to lower castes. They have a rich cultural heritage in art, music and literature. Bhudana, a famous centre of Islamic learning, is only four miles away from the village. The women, especially those of high social standing, observe purdah. They are secluded in their homesteads with mothers- and sisters-in-law and do not work in the fields, but are occupied in preparing food, ginning cotton, spinning and mending clothes. By custom, children are not required to work if there is an adult who can perform the task. Consequently, the extent to which children work depends on the wealth of the family. Those who can afford hired labour send their children, or, at any rate, their boys, to school. Education of children was little valued until recently, but now literacy is becoming important in business transactions. Rajput boys form the majority of castes represented in the school. But attendance is irregular, and children are seldom forced to go if they want to play truant.

Pre-school children are free to play most of the time, and have no chores assigned to them. Sometimes, if no older child is available, a four- or five-year-old may be sent shopping or with a message to the men's gathering place, since the women are confined to their courtyard. But generally little is expected of children below the age of seven. They are supposed to learn by imitation and observation rather than by direct teaching. Sometimes an uncle or grandfather who is too old to work in the fields may mind a three-year-old boy, taking him along to watch work in the fields. Mostly, the younger children tag along with the five- to seven-year-olds who play in the streets or in the fields just outside the village with children from other households. The women prefer their children to play in groups rather than alone. The children chase and tease each other, climb on vacant carts or play see-saw on some wagon wheel that happens to be lying around.

Rajput pre-school children seem to have as much free time as their American equivalents and rather more freedom, but there is a difference as to toys. Figurines tend to be for ornament and display, rather than for use as toys for children. Some children have rag dolls or cloth balls made by the newest bride to come to the homestead, and a few have hoops or toy-carts made by the village carpenter or by themselves. Girls from the wealthier homes may have sets of toy eating utensils, or toy grain-grinders or scales. Some infants are given plastic rattles and painted wooden animals.

Children above the age of seven from poor households have an increasing number of chores: field-work and looking after cattle for the boys, and housework and child-minding for the girls. The herding boys play hockey with their herding sticks and a ball. Schoolboys, who have no chores at home, run off to play after school. Tree-tag, pitching shells into a hole, jacks (tossing and catching shells), and a variety of hopscotch are popular. Older boys play competitive games, but do not take winning or losing very seriously. There is less free time for the older children, and they usually have some chores to perform regularly. Boys tend cattle, help with field work or run errands for the men after school. Girls, fewer of whom are sent to school in any case, wash dishes, sweep, bring food to the men's gathering place or to the fields, and mind the baby. However, the Rajput regard themselves as the descendants of rulers and warriors, and work is not regarded as something inherently desirable. It is done when necessary. The Rajputs see no need to instil 'good work habits' into their children, unlike Western communities who often foster and justify play for its educational value as training in manual, intellectual or social skills.

A different picture still emerges from the study of Taira in Okinawa, on the western Pacific. The adults, on being asked, said that young children, even those of school age, could not be expected to work much. Young children will beg to be allowed to perform chores such as accompanying the older children to collect giant snails after a heavy rainfall. Hunting grasshoppers or frogs is considered play by the adults. In fact, however, these are fed to the chickens, and when chicken-feed is scarce the children are scolded for neglecting to gather food for them. Girls as young as six-years-old are expected to care for younger children or babies, and carry them about on their backs for long periods. But this baby-minding is so habitual that it was not even mentioned by the adults when they described to the observers the chores they expected their children to perform.

However, Okinawan children do seem to have a good deal of free time. Schooling has been compulsory for some time. It is mainly on the Japanese system, and was introduced by them in 1891. There is time to play during breaks and after school. The younger children between the ages of two and six go to an American-style kindergarten. In spite of the Japanese and American influence, the social organization belongs to the old Okinawan order with a good many holidays based on agricultural and local religious events. These are spent at uninhibited social gatherings with food, drink, traditional music, elaborate dances, displays of skill, in playing with words, in mimicry and in acting. Japanese-style athletic games and wrestling matches take place, and sports events may last for several weeks.

Few parents in Taira could afford to buy toys for their children, neither do they make them. Nevertheless, the children play with toys. They use any available object: discarded household utensils, empty cans, boxes, stones, leaves, and so forth. They make themselves helmets of cabbage leaves, pistols of bamboo sticks, trucks and boats out of empty boxes, and use stones and peas as marbles for play. Boys and girls play traditional Okinawan games of skill, or marbles, and pretend games. Girls learn traditional Okinawan dances by watching their elders, or coached by an older sister, a friend, or by their mothers. Boys practise skills in sports, copying the men's wrestling, high jump and relay running games.

Phantasy and Imitative Play in Different Societies

Perhaps the most surprising result of these cross-cultural studies is that phantasy and imitative play is practically absent in some societies, and immensely rich and varied in others. Economic factors, although clearly important in the number and variety of bought toys children are given, and in the amount of free time they have at all, are almost certainly not entirely responsible for whether they play imitative and pretend games. The children of Taira do not come from wealthy homes, and are given few or no toys, yet they fashion for themselves what they lack, and, from the report, their play sounds perhaps the most varied and imaginative of all. Possibly, what is most important for the play of children is the community's traditional culture, and the extent to which this is a genuine part of the adults' lives. The only instances of imaginative or imitative play reported in the whole two years of observational study among the Nyansongo were the one occasion on which a six-year-old made some sort of plough to which he yoked his brother, and the other when a ten-year-old built a house of reeds. Both the parents' and the children's lives are narrow, and they have few contacts outside the extended family circle. There is little formal social life, and apart from circumcision celebrations, and the beer-drinking parties and occasional soccer games of the men, adults have few recreations. There are some traditional musical instruments and dances, but they do not seem to be often used. Even the ornaments of the Nyansongo are few. This contrasts particularly vividly with the variety of adult recreations among the people of Okinawa (see above), and the prevalence of imitative and imaginative play among their children, especially between the ages of four and ten, before a girl is deemed old enough to do the housework herself. They play 'houses' on the beach, in the yards, or in uninhabited houses, 'shops' for buying and selling, prepare elaborate 'meals', and so forth. The girls take their young charges with them when they are playing, and although babies are not expected to take part in the games, the younger children sometimes act as pretend children in lieu of dolls which the girls of Taira do not possess. They imitate their mothers, visiting each other ceremoniously, mimic their voices, and so on. Boys are more likely to play robbers, but occasionally pretend to be salesmen. The variety of toys they make for themselves out of the most unlikely material has already been mentioned.

Rajput children play imitatively, but, apparently, without a great deal of imaginative adumbration. Pre-school girls play at cooking, making mud-breads at the village pond. Pre-school boys make elaborate imitation fields, and irrigate them. Conversation is the main form of adult recreation, and children are told stories by the adult women in the evenings. A centre of Islamic learning is near, but whether this farming community with its warrior-landlord ideal of itself is really steeped in its cultural heritage, or how it is transmitted to the children is not clear and far from self-evident. We need to know far more before any generalization about the prevalence and variety of imaginative play among children of different societies can be made with confidence. What these studies suggest is that its content and variety depends on adult pursuits both in work and recreation to a much greater extent than studies of the imaginative play of European and American children alone would lead one to believe. The ability to juggle around with perceptions and ideas may be built into the works, as it were, but its spontaneous exercise seems to depend very much on what, and how much, the environment provides.

Children who dance in a ring and chant 'Ring a ring o' roses,/ A pocketful of posies,/ A-tishoo, a-tishoo/ We all fall down' have no idea that it may refer to the symptoms and effects of cholera, the Black Death of the Middle Ages. They have heard it, can follow its rhythm and simple actions in a game which brings them together with others. Falling down and getting up, chanting, and the other repetitive constituents make it interesting. Even the Black Death was a 'happening', at all events.

Toys

The number and kinds of toys which are around at any given moment make a difference both to the manner and the kind of children's play. A study of schoolchildren's behaviour with different amounts of equipment in the playground(185) showed that with fewer toys around children made a greater number of social contacts with each other. Undesirable behaviour also increased, and there was more play with sand and dirt. Large amounts of play-equipment discouraged social contacts, but had a stimulating effect on individual exploration, constructions, and the like. This fits in well with the assumption that the value of playmates lies at least partly in their ability to stimulate or interest.

Different kinds of toys also differ in the extent to which they encourage or discourage social contacts between children or between adults and children. Communal games like housey-housey or snakes and ladders are obvious examples of material which is likely to encourage contact with others. It has been found that pre-school children talk more in doll-play and while colouring with crayons than when they are painting, cutting with scissors, or looking at books(3). Miniature sets of dolls and equipment which allow the child to build up a 'world' of people, houses, cars, traffic, animals, fields and roads in a sand-tray, have long been found best for the kind of imaginative story play used in projective tests and some forms of play-therapy(216, 226). Swings, climbing frames, tricycles and equipment which exercises the large muscles are often used by children in their phantasy play, but lend themselves less to adult participation. The effects of confronting children with equipment already tidily organized according to someone else's idea rather than allowing them to arrange it in their own way has already been mentioned. Children play more destructively in the first case(287).

It is often assumed, probably quite correctly, that teddies, soft toys, or woolly blankets are used as comforters by human infants and some older children. We do not, as far as I know, have any experimental evidence to show that cuddling soft toys reduces anxiety in human children, is resorted to more in frightening situations, or acts as a substitute for the mother. The resemblance of a human mother to some of the rags which children insist on taking to bed with them would not seem to be overwhelming. Nevertheless, one would expect young children, in the absence of their mothers, to cling to a familiar soft object in preference to handling a new one. But we do not know whether a familiar spiky or hard one would be preferred to a novel soft one in this situation. Whether the perceptual characteristic of an object (i.e., its look, feel, smell, warmth or softness to the touch), or the activity itself (clinging, sucking, etc.), or on the other hand past associations with reassurance are most important in reducing stress, is not clear for human children. Young children's preference for dolls is apparently based more on their feel and flexibility than on their facial features(99). Chimpanzees brought up on surrogates, i.e. cloth contraptions from which they had obtained milk through a nozzle, clung to familiar objects such as rag mops or a stuffed toy, but not to people(239), when they were frightened.

Repetition, familiarity, regularity of occurrences, stimulation which is gradual and mild rather than abrupt and sudden, are all known to reduce excitement (see Chapter Four). Repetitive activities on the part of the child may have the same effect. Repetitive rocking, thumb-sucking, or particular activities like clinging, probably reduce anxiety. Crawling into hiding places, or building small houses with which to surround themselves may have the same effect although such play is not necessarily a sign of anxiety. Of course, there are other methods of overcoming a child's fear and shyness. Generally speaking, distracting his attention, provided it is gently done, is the most successful with normal young children.

Familiarity with an object, possibly some pleasant or reassuring association, or the fact that it has been marked by the owner as 'his', as in the literal depositing of its scent-mark upon an object by the badger (see Chapter Three), is one class of characteristic of play objects among mammals. But toys, including soft teddies, are almost certainly not solely used for their comforting or reassuring character-istics. Both boys and girls may use a teddy in the traditional role of the doll, as a baby or child in pretend games. It used to be assumed that looking after dolls was based on little girls' 'maternal instinct'. There is little evidence for this. It is possible that a combination of characteristics such as pro-portionately small size, different body proportions from the adult figure, and so forth, are innately 'appealing' to humans. It has been suggested that infants' physical characteristics – size and childish proportions, whether in animal or human infants – produce innately different reactions on the part of adults than do animals with adult physical characteristics (223). On the whole, however, it seems unlikely that humans have such detailed innate blue-prints of characteristics to which they respond, or even if they did, that this would be more evident in pre-adolescent than in adolescent children. The dolls' characteristics do not prevent them from being pushed to the bottom of the toy-box, trailed by the hair – or dismembered, if that happens to be the current interest. Child-minding, and being actually in charge of babies or younger children, does not seem to be related to play with dolls as pretend babies. Nyansongo girls, who have a great many child-minding duties, apparently do not play with dolls. But the girls of Taira are also child-minders, and have to carry their charges with them when they run off to play. This does not prevent them from using younger children as 'pretend children' in their play, although they are not given bought dolls. The conclusions of the American psychologist,

Hall, from his investigation in 1896, are probably correct. He wrote that 'the parental instinct is far less prominent in doll-play than is commonly supposed' (99, p. 189), and that doll-play 'reveals the child's mind'. In other words, doll-play is imaginative play in which the child acts what he thinks and feels, with 'props'.

Hall's conclusions were based on a study using questionnaires for parents and teachers as well as reminiscences by adults between the ages of fourteen and twenty-four. Dolls came in all shapes, sizes and materials, some more preferred than others. Plaster-of-paris dolls rated rather low. A variety of other objects were treated as dolls: bottles, pillows, kittens, pieces of cloth, clay, mud, toothpicks, potatoes (with matchstick legs) and other vegetables, nails, spoons, marbles, orange peel, a water-bottle, one corner of a blanket while the other was the mother, carrots, and a knife, fork and spoon were 'servants'. Few of these Western children never played with dolls, and there was plenty of evidence that boys liked dolls, and played games in which objects rated as people. Dolls were most common between the ages of four and twelve. Before the age of three children rarely gave them names, but simply referred to them as 'dolly'. Young children cared more about the softness and flexibility of the doll, than about its facial features, and perhaps surprisingly, few dolls were in fact used as 'babies'. Most of them were pretend adults. More recent studies found that dolls were used also as older children, or children of the same age as the players (216). Treatment of the doll, and feeling towards it, were in many ways unlike the way the child would treat, and feel about, a real baby according to Hall. Nevertheless, dolls were certainly invested with feelings, generally those most prominent in the child. Dolls feared thunder and lightning, or ghosts, were naughty, got punished, and so forth. Hall considered that children are not fully aware of the fact that it is they who 'animate' the doll, but half, or fully believe that these objects have feelings. (For the problems involved in this view, see Chapter Five.) Further investigations will have to start from the fact that dolls are not used for one kind of play only. They may be 'props' in imaginative play, provide realistic trappings to imitative role-playing, or function as lay figures on to which the child projects his feelings, and may also act as a comforting familiar when the child is afraid.

Most recent studies of doll-play have assumed that dolls are used projectively (as vehicles for the child's feelings about himself and others), and have concentrated on the conditions under which feelings are expressed(216) rather than upon the characteristics of dolls. Doll-play has been used mainly as a method to study personality rather than as a subject in its own right requiring investigation, except in so far as its reliability, validity and usefulness for that particular purpose has been in question. As a research method, in this sense, doll-play has been used mainly since the 1930s (216). Under these conditions there are some preferences for one doll over another. The mother doll is used more frequently than the father doll by girls. Boys use them equally. There are some reports that six-year-olds show greater preference than four-year-olds for dolls of the same sex as themselves, and that children who are brought up in permissive homes use the adult dolls more in their phantasy play. Although the play equipment used in the investigations differs considerably from study to study, the majority use small dolls from one to six inches tall, realistically dressed as father, mother, children, etc., and flexible so that they could be made to stand, sit or lie down.

Like the games children play, toys, figurines, effigies and dolls apparently belonged to the adult world before they were used as playthings for children. Hall quoted a number of studies to that effect. In Europe, for instance, dolls are of comparatively recent origin and derive from wooden statuettes of empresses. Dolls in Japan were of religious or quasi-religious significance. Images of the emperor, empresses and court, in wood or enamelled clay, were bought for each daughter. The daughter would take these with her when she got married and give them to her children. On a special feast day of the dolls, the girls made offerings of sake and dried rice to the effigies, and then spent the day with the toys imitating the whole round of Japanese feudal life. The boys had a day of feast for flags with effigies of heroes, commanders, and so on, a set of which would be bought for each boy born into the family. On the feast day there would be a display of these. Dolls for play were apparently imported to Japan by the Dutch. In China, theatrical performances with puppets preceded their use as playthings for girls.

The link between the religious use of effigies as gods and doll-play is not a direct one, according to Hall. Some societies dread making tangible representations (for religious reasons), but the little girls may nevertheless dress up puppies, and play with them as Western children would with dolls. Unfortunately, it is not possible here to say more about the fascinating propensity of humans to make 'images' and concrete effigies for themselves. The most reasonable explanation at present seems to be that it occurs in proportion as people are able to think in abstract terms. One would expect it to be absent unless there is some ability to imagine and mentally represent situations and objects, and to occur little at bare subsistence level, when all available time is taken up with minute-to-minute practical considerations. It should also occur little where abstract thinking has become a smooth running part of the system. Image-making in this sense, is well illustrated by Menon's story 'The Prevalence of Witches' in which the local chief, in order to follow the missionary's tale of his home and family, places a stone on the ground for each person mentioned. Actually, model-making is not so infrequent among sophisticated scientists either: building electronic machines to imitate human problem-solving in order to understand this function better, for instance.

Toys are not, of course, merely used in pretend and make-believe play. Objects that can be explored, that 'do' things, or are aids to skills, whether of movement or perception, or materials which can be used to create different effects, are equally important to the child. The characteristics of objects likely to attract children will vary with growing skills and greater familiarity (see Chapter Four). There are a number of books giving practical advice on what toys, materials, and games to choose at different ages(3, 192).

One exceedingly successful toy I have seen for a two-and-a-half-year-old boy was an eight-foot-long, cuddly, soft snake made of nylon fur, with villainous red squinting eyes, and a long red tongue poised to sting. It was used to attack and frighten others during the day, and taken to bed as a comforter at night: a nice combination of thrilling and soothing characteristics.

CHAPTER NINE

PLAY THERAPY

Forms of Play Therapy

'NOBODY ever does anything just for fun', said a psycho-
therapist lugubriously to the parent of a backward little
boy whose habit of laughingly slamming the door in her
face had been under discussion. The parent dined out on the
story for years. But she took the point that to understand an
action it is not sufficient to suppose that it was enjoyed.
Further questions – for instance, why this game rather than
another, can be asked.

Play was first used incidentally by Freud (see Chapter
Two) in the treatment of a normal, healthy, and intelligent
little boy whose sudden, rather violent fear of horses worried
his father, a friend and former patient of Freud's(124).
'Little Hans', as he became widely known in psychoanalytical writings, was not treated directly by Freud, but via his
father who recorded as much as possible of the child's spontaneous behaviour, including his talk, dreams, and also his
play, and submitted these records to Freud for interpretation
and guidance. Freud saw the case in terms of his theory of
emotional development which predicts certain difficulties
at given ages or stages of development (see Chapter Two).
An overt fear of horses, even when triggered off by a real
event such as seeing a horse fall down under a load in the
street, would be taken to express also covert, but to the child
more important, anxiety about himself and his feelings
towards his father, mother and the new baby. His spontaneous play at being a horse, letting toy-horses fall down,
and so forth, was taken as symptomatic not so much of the
fear inspired by the real event, but of those fears and adjustments with which the boy was trying to cope at the time,

and which were assumed to find their overt expression in a fear that, for him, symbolized these by association.

A follower of Freud's, Hermine Hug-Hellmuth used play in treating disturbed children for the purpose of observing and understanding them. Her actual treatment consisted in trying to influence their behaviour directly, as a parent or teacher might.

Melanie Klein started psychoanalysis of children in 1919 (194). She considered direct education to be useless in readjusting emotionally disturbed children. In their case, as in the case of adults, the disturbances would disappear only if the child had been made aware of the emotional conflict which generated them. Spontaneous play was used by her as a direct substitute for the verbal free association used by Freud in the treatment of adults. She assumed that what the child does in free play symbolizes the wishes, fears, pleasures, and conflicts and preoccupation of which he is not aware. The therapist stands in a special relation to the child, acting as a sort of lay figure to whom the child assigns a number of roles that his real relations to other people, or his feelings about them, have made a focus of difficulties for him. The therapist has the job of making the child aware of this by interpreting his play to him.

Melanie Klein first used miniature toys – mainly representations of family figures – for projective play. At various times she protested vigorously against the misconception that interpreting meant assigning a specific symbolic meaning to particular games. A game played by a child at a given moment, like verbal free association, can be interpreted only within the context of a child's general play, and what, at the time, preceded and followed it. The theoretical framework of psychoanalytical theory would serve as a sort of guiding line, suggesting, but not prescribing, the kind of conflicts for which an analyst might look (Comment, 226). The analyst's job is to understand what the child feels, and to convey this to him. For instance, a child may play with bricks in a way which indicates that individual bricks stand for people, perhaps members of the child's family. If so, the analyst says so to the child, who may assent, deny this, or may simply go on playing. The analyst infers from the manner of the assent, or the denial, and from the child's subsequent play, whether her guess has been correct. An over-anxious acceptance of a suggested interpretation might disconfirm it as much as a calm denial. Violent or agitated denial might lead a therapist to suspect that the trail was at least 'warm', while being plainly ignored would probably induce the salutary caution which is its normal consequence in social intercourse. In any case, the individual child's usual style of reacting would have to be taken into account. Melanie Klein's view of development diverged from the original Freudian picture. For instance, she credited children with a kind of 'conscience' and guilt feelings as early as towards the end of the first year of life, rather than after the age of three or so, and also assumed an ability to symbolize objects at this age. It is fair to say that very intelligent children may show symbolic ability at surprisingly early ages.

Freud's daughter, Anna, abided more filially by Freud's view of emotional development, but modified his technique of treatment a good deal to adapt it to children. Unlike Melanie Klein, she considered child therapy as radically different from the adult variety(121). For instance, whatever difficulties at home produced the emotional disturbance originally might still be present. They have to be ascertained, and if possible, manipulated and improved. The child's parents are usually still alive so that it is neither possible nor desirable for the analyst to be a passive lay figure on to whom the child can project his image of the parent. 'Analysis', that is, uncovering and redirecting 'fixated libido' (by making the child aware of his conflicts), is only one part of therapy. In the case of children, the therapist's job is also educational, and for this he must actively enlist the child's confidence and affection. Play, according to Anna Freud, is not necessarily symbolic of anything. If a boy builds a lamp-post, this may simply be because he has happened to see one that impressed him. Children do play phantasy games, but whether a particular game is symbolic, or what the motives behind it may be, has to be built up from evidence about the child's situation at home, his current experiences, trivial as well as important, and a knowledge of his wishes, hopes and fears which adults can only gain with familiarity and with the child's confidence. Play as such is of secondary importance.

These approaches to the treatment of disturbed children marked the beginning of the techniques known as 'play therapy' (called 'child psychotherapy' by those who use play incidentally only). An enormous number of different kinds of therapy have grown up, some with only tenuous links to the original concepts or techniques. They vary in the degree to which the therapist considers his role to be active or passive; the extent to which the parents are brought into the treatment, and the child's environment is altered; the frequency of the treatment; how play is conceived to function in the treatment; and whether and to what extent verbal explanations of it are given to the child. Some, in the tradition of Anna Freud, stress the child's relationship to the therapist as the most important therapeutic agent, relieving the child of anxiety, allowing him to come to terms with his conflicts and re-educating him within a benign social relationship between adult and child. Those in the tradition of Melanie Klein depend more upon interpretations to the child of his symbolic play. Some therapists use play merely in order to communicate with the patient, as a talking point, and for the social situation it can create. Others restrict the child to a few toys, encouraging him to re-enact certain scenes known or suspected to have been traumatic to him, so as to reduce the child's fears about them quickly. This is said to be useful in dealing with phobias(208).

There has been some change in the type of conflict or area of anxiety for which psychoanalytically oriented therapists look out. Freud and his followers in the early days tended to concentrate upon what may, very roughly, be called conflicts of conscience. Anxiety over doing what is forbidden may be learned so well and so intensely that it extends to associated but normally permitted activities, feelings and wishes. (In psychoanalytic jargon: a too severe 'Superego' or unconscious conscience repressing the unconscious, instinctive, libidinal impulses of the 'Id'.) More recently, the child's ability to respond to and cope with his environment have received greater attention (in jargon: the 'strength' of the 'Ego' which relates the child's impulses to 'reality'). An instance is the problem of learning to defer the satisfaction of desires(103a).

The majority of play therapists have been eclectic. Rather than follow any one theoretical line very rigidly, they use whatever ideas, techniques or suggestions seem most appropriate in particular cases. An early example of this is Lowenfeld's 'world picture' technique(226). The material consists of miniature replicas of people, animals, fences, houses, trees, bridges, and so forth. Water and sand-trays with three different kinds of sand are available, and the child is told to play with these as he likes. The resultant confections or miniature 'worlds' may consist of mountains and valleys, a scenery with people or animals; or they may be realistic replicas of little towns with neat little rows of houses, or quite phantastic with wild animals rushing all over the place, or contain no people or animals at all. The child is asked to explain the 'world' he has built up to the therapist as to an ignorant Martian, and to say what will happen next. Content, style and amount of movement in what is 'happening' were supposed to reveal the degree of the child's disturbance, and to get some inkling what it was about.

Doll-play is not the only kind of play activity which has been used for therapeutic purposes. Dramatic play, such as acting out particular social situations together with others, has been considered to have a 'releasing' effect by expressing emotions, or to be conducive to social learning. For instance, children might learn to respond to others in dramatic or pretend play where in an ordinary setting they would have been too shy, or, by playing the part of an adult they may learn at first hand the difficulties an adult might have in coping with a fractious child. In art-therapy, drawings and paintings are interpreted by the therapist as in doll-play, or used as expressions of feeling which are considered to be therapeutic in their own right. Music, too, has been held to have therapeutic effects.

Free play, without any direction or interpretation from adults has been held to cure emotional disturbances by the followers of 'non-directive' or 'client-centred' therapy. This conceives the therapist's role to be entirely passive, limited to creating an atmosphere of friendliness and acceptance within which the patient can come to terms with his difficulties. Applied to the treatment of children(11) this means that most emphasis is put upon the child's play. He is given almost complete freedom to choose his own activities in a playroom in the presence of an approving, permissive therapist who allows the patient to take the initiative. It is assumed that he will 'act out' his conflicts and socially unacceptable impulses in play. Play is held to be 'cathartic'. It is assumed that a 'discharge' of emotions through play in a secure atmosphere will reduce the child's anxiety after which he will be able to adjust to normal social demands more easily(350).

By now the play techniques with disturbed children are as varied and prolific as the theoretical assumptions of the therapists. These are not, now, by any means solely or even mainly derived from psychoanalysis. Gestalt and Field theories (see Chapter Two) conceive personality development to consist of growing differentiations within the individual. Play is the child's method of exploring and coming to terms with the world, and of learning physical coordination, the use of symbols and phantasy. The adult, by sharing the child's play and make-believe reassures him of the validity and meaningfulness of what he does. Non-directive therapy, which considers play as itself therapeutic, has already been mentioned. Play has been used educationally, to modify the child's behaviour or to help him with his current problems of adjustment(152), such as the birth of a brother, failure at school, not being able to get on with other children, and so forth. In the more analytical tradition play is regarded as a reflection of 'libidinal' development (279), as substitute behaviour for what cannot be achieved in reality, or as pretend mastery over the anxieties which provoked the play that gives the child the opportunity to meet similar disturbances later with greater assurance(103, 142).

Therapeutic processes (although not play specifically), as well as many psychoanalytic concepts were translated into learning-theory terms as instrumental learning by Neal Miller(94). Mowrer(255) re-described many of the hypotheses in terms of conditioning of autonomic processes (e.g. changes in breathing, heartrate, sweating, stomach contractions, etc., consequent upon excitement) as well as instrumental learning via rewards. Some of the autonomic changes, involuntary accompaniments of anxiety and excitement, persist long after a person's outward behaviour has ceased to give any indication of it. They can be aroused not merely by the original object of fear, but also by associated cues. For humans, words and symbols can arouse anxiety or excitement very effectively.

A natural reaction to this 'embarras de richesse' of techniques and theories about what is happening in the course of them would be to indict them indiscriminately. However, the success or failure of therapeutic techniques, the accuracy or otherwise of facts discovered in the course of them, and the adequacy and usefulness of a given theoretical description are quite separate questions.

The fact that people may feel better, or indeed be better, after a given course of action is totally irrelevant to whether the theory which suggested it is its most accurate description. It could probably be demonstrated that the majority of a primitive tribe could be cured of most of their ailments by a witch-doctor's magic, and that using a combine harvester of the most modern pattern always hindered their harvesting. The first example would not show that the witch-doctor's explanation of what he was doing was correct, nor would failure of the harvest show the combine harvester to be of the wrong make. Even if a therapy turned up trumps every time, the theory which inspired it might be outmoded or inadequate. By the same token, therapeutic failures do not invalidate the theory from which the technique derived.

They merely show the techniques themselves to be faulty, badly applied, useless, or irrelevant. Freud's theory is now inadequate, not because not enough cures can be achieved, but because the picture of behaviour being driven by one or by a number of instincts, which can be dammed up, spark over, erupt in unsuitable places, and so forth, is misleading, inaccurate and inadequate to describe what is now known about the workings of the homeostatic systems that regulate the organism's functions (see Chapter Two). This, of course, applies to treatments derived from other theories as well. Unless a therapy is designed in the form of an experimental test with adequate controls to ensure that results, whether positive or negative, could not have been due to extraneous factors (difficult enough to do in laboratory procedures, let alone in the context of a bona fide treatment), it cannot be held either to support or to disconfirm the theory which suggested the procedure.

Similarly, facts are not automatically rendered invalid because they fit in with an out-moded or unfashionable theory, or were suggested by methods which lacked scientific rigour. But they do have to be corroborated by independent evidence. For instance, Freud's suggestion that people can be affected by experiences of which they are unconscious was, at one time, considered self-contradictory (although the idea of degrees of consciousness goes back at least to Leibniz's seventeenth-century philosophical system). Nowadays, the notion of different degrees of awareness, 'arousal', and alertness is commonplace. It has long been possible to measure different degrees of 'arousal' in terms of physiological changes, e.g. in breathing and heart-beat rate. Electric potential recordings of changes in the sweat glands or skin resistance have been used very extensively for this, although individuals vary as to which physiological indicator is the most potent(204). Techniques of recording electrocortical changes (changes in distinctive rhythms from the brain) have shown that these vary with the person's 'alertness' to stimuli, during relaxation, and in concentrating on intellectual work. Different levels of awareness and depth of

oblivion have been demonstrated when people are asleep
as well as during waking(220, 274). People may show differences in their outward behaviour in response to stimuli
when they are quite unaware of this and are unable to describe or remember them afterwards(144). Such 'unconscious' physiological reactions as the dilation of small blood-
vessels can be conditioned to external cues, including words
(295). Noticing stimuli varies with background 'noise', with
the degree of uncertainty about the stimuli(348), and their
probability in given contexts (see Chapter Four). These advances make nonsense of the early quibbles as to whether
'unconscious sensations' was good English, good German,
or good sense or not. At the same time, they show the
metaphor 'the unconscious' to be both superfluous and
misleading. Play is undoubtedly influenced by many experiences of which the child may have been only dimly or not
at all aware. But whether we should tell him about these,
even when we know what they are, is quite a different
question.

Another psychoanalytical prediction which has been
assumed to be true of play is that feelings, such as anger,
which are aroused but denied expression, may be 'displaced' upon unsuitable objects, or expressed symbolically,
or after delay. This has been shown to hold in certain circumstances. But such findings as that students, who were
annoyed and then given an opportunity to write aggressive
stories, were less aggressive afterwards than those who had
no opportunity to express anger, or the commonplace that
a man, reprimanded by his superior, may go home to shout
at his wife, can be explained on other than 'overspill'
theories. Neal Miller accounted for anger as a response to
frustration, and its displacement in terms of learning theory
as a function of generalization(247, 248, 248a). (The argument rests on the demonstration that the gradient of generalization is steeper for avoidance than for approach when
there is a conflict between these). Reinforcement of the
opportunity to attack has been another explanation. Squirrel
monkeys, taught to pull a chain for some toy which could be

attacked, did so far more when they had just received a painful shock than at other times(13). It is possible to argue that pulling the chain (the only possible action in this laboratory set-up) may have become associated with cessation of the shock, or that excitement facilitated activity of all kinds, and this was the 'nearest' thing to do.

Berkowitz(31) has pointed out that not being allowed to express anger is a form of frustration which may arouse additional aggression – that for humans, what instigated or was associated with aggression might be present symbolically all the time; and that expressing anger might be associated with anxiety which would inhibit its repetition. Any adequate theoretical description must cover at least all these possibilities. It is likely to re-describe the facts. But this does not alter the findings at the level at which they were investigated. Not all play consists of substitutions, but aggression may be expressed to substitute objects in play, and substitute actions may express it. At any rate, such behaviour may look 'playful'.

The practical application of theories, and of the facts and connexions they suggest, is yet another matter. Play has been used in the diagnosis of disturbed children. Is it, in fact, possible to judge the social and emotional adjustment of a child by the way he plays?

The Play of Maladjusted Children

There would be no problem about diagnosis if all types of maladjustment found expression in distinctive and unequivocal play-forms. This is certainly not so. There are severely disturbed children whose behaviour is so odd that it leaves even the layman in no doubt about it, whether this is during 'play' or 'work'. Some of these children are almost completely inactive. In a playroom full of toys they find nothing to interest them, and either huddle in a corner, or produce stereotyped, bizarre, repetitive finger or body-movements. Frequently, they are so out of touch with their surroundings and with other people that the distinction between 'play' and other activities simply does not apply. This condition has been described as self-absorbed or 'autistic'. It is not yet known whether this covers only one or a number of syndromes, or what their causation is. However, the most typical cases do show recognizable peculiarities of play. Apathy, rocking and head-banging are common, but are also found in some quite different or much less severe conditions. More typical is the highly repetitive, often 'ritualistic' nature of their play, and the obsessive concern with certain objects – often light-switches and mechanized contraptions of various kinds. This has sometimes been compared with the stereotyped, repetitive behaviour found in captive animals living in very restricted conditions. But autistic children do not seem to have grossly abnormal environments. The children are unresponsive in social situations, probably mainly because it is difficult to 'get through' to them, i.e. to gain and hold their attention. There is also evidence that autistic children tend to avoid complex stimuli, possibly because they are over-aroused already(177). If they speak at all, they show odd speech habits. The condition is relatively rare, and probably caused rather differently from the more usual types of difficulties which are referred to Child Guidance Clinics or outpatient departments. This is true also of some of the 'hyperactive' children who fail to play because they are continually rushing to and fro, unable to settle to any consecutive activity.

Apart from these extremes, the term 'maladjustment' covers a variety of behaviour which deviates from what is usually expected of a boy or girl at a given age. Educational difficulties despite a normal or high I.Q., difficulties in relation to adults either at home or elsewhere, or to other children; being over-aggressive, solitary or timid to an unusual degree; lying and stealing excessively; refusing to go to school; unreasonable fears of animals or objects; speech difficulties; bed-wetting or soiling; refusal to eat; and a number of other problems have been given such labels as 'emotional disturbances', 'social maladjustment', 'habit disorders', and so forth.

In severity, such conditions may vary from a simple mis-apprehension on the part of the adult in charge as to what he should expect or do, to being intolerable to child and adult alike. Some show a single difficulty, such as fear of dogs or bed-wetting. In others, practically everything the child does or says, or fails to do or say, is a source of anxiety, chagrin or irritation to all concerned.

It is not surprising that there is no one play-form which distinguishes them all from 'normal' children. Nor is the play of such children always obviously typical of the be-haviour for which they are referred. The favourite game of an extremely aggressive nine-year-old persistent thief I knew, who swore like a trooper and truanted from school, was to creep into an empty toy-cupboard with the largest, softest teddy he could find. A timid little stutterer with a sheltered, middle-class background and a choleric father, painted unmentionable words on the window-panes. But it does not go by contraries either.

According to Murphy(261), it is not the content of play which differs from that of ordinary children, but its structure, style and cohesion. Perfectly ordinary children play the most hair-raising games of drowning and mutilating toys that, by their own accounts, stand for their mothers, fathers, brothers, sisters or anyone who has incurred their temporary displeasure. The intensity rather than the frequency of such play seems to differentiate disturbed from better-adjusted chil-dren(253). Indeed, in this particular study, the normal four-year-olds expressed more open and direct hostility to their siblings than the disturbed group, but the intensity ratings for such expressions were significantly greater for the latter.

A great many difficulties, whether in their relation to adults, to other children, over controlling their aggression, or over irrational fears or anything else, have a depressing effect, and make children listless and miserable. This will reduce a child's general activity, and the vigour and inven-tiveness of his play. Conditions of general timidity or anxiety have similar effects. A frustrating experience, even if only temporary, has been shown to make children play less con-

structively, and at a more immature level(21). Many
disturbed children, in spite of sometimes high intelligence,
will persistently play as only much younger children would.
For instance, an intelligent but highly excitable and anxious
six-year-old I knew, perfectly capable of painting the kind
of houses, people and trees usual at about that age, rarely
produced anything but a smear of colours like a two-year-old.
Anxiety makes for lowered efficiency on complex tasks(187).

Signs such as these in play may give clues about a child's
general behaviour. For instance, a six-year-old girl referred
to me for a head-shaking tic, so severe that it was painful to
watch, showed an extreme fear of dirt, sand and water during
the initial play-hour. There were a great many hand-washings
and demands to have her clothes changed although they were
perfectly clean. Her mother said that she had forgotten to
mention this behaviour because she was so used to it at home.
The girl's gradual (unobtrusively encouraged) acceptance
of sand and water as permissible playthings at first extended
to enjoying dirtying her own and her mother's clothes at
home, before settling down to a more reasonable attitude
to dirt and cleanliness. (Her head-shaking tic disappeared
soon after. This may have been fortuitous, or there may have
been the connexion between tics, obsessional behaviour and
cleanliness training envisaged in the hypothesis which first
suggested the treatment. Alternatively, getting rid of a strong
fear may have had a generally relaxing effect.) The girl's behaviour in play during the period of change in her attitudes
to dirt was paralleled or followed by similar behaviour at
home as reported by her mother. The differences in play
were relatively obvious in this case.

Play with standardized toys, during which specific bits of
behaviour can be scored and compared, has been used in
the form of objective personality tests and as an experimental
situation in which variations in the set-up could be measured.
It has already been mentioned that the reliability of these
doll-play methods was high when assessing specific behaviour like aggression (see Chapter Five), that it correlated
well with ratings of the children's (aggressive) behaviour

elsewhere, and remained consistent across different measures used, and at different times. But this was when testing the normal range of children. For extremes, the very timid and the very aggressive, the correspondence of behaviour in play-tests and otherwise, held only with qualifications. Maladjusted children's responses are more variable and unreliable even on cognitive tests than those of samples of the general population of children, let alone on personality tests(128). More than one test is usually used, therefore, in any one case. The main advantage of play is that it can be used to assess the reactions of an individual child to a variety of concrete situations which are less easy to reproduce otherwise, in a medium that is familiar and liked in childhood.

Perhaps the most extensive use of play has been made in the treatment of disturbed children. Derived from a wide variety of theoretical considerations (see above), some techniques aim at making the children aware of conflicts and anxieties within themselves; others use play as a form of social learning, or to 'work off' difficulties, as a means of establishing friendly contact, or to present them with the kind of situation suspected to be difficult for them so as to reorientate or re-educate them. The object of them all is to make the child 'better'. Whether this is achieved is controversial as yet.

The Use of Play in Therapy

The question whether play is effective in treating different kinds of 'maladjustment' in children has hardly been tackled objectively so far at all, although there have been more investigations on adults since Eysenck showed that previous studies had failed to find psychotherapy more effective in relieving psychological disorders than no treatment at all save an initial interview(106). Presenting successful cases is, of course, not enough. It must be shown that these form a substantial proportion of all similar cases treated, and that the therapy was better than doing nothing, or doing something different. Since then research into psychotherapy has become more sophisticated in teasing out some of the many factors which contribute to the very complex situation which a series of interviews between a 'therapist' and a 'patient' presents(93, 241). Among these are the personal characteristics of the therapist and the patient, and all the minutiae of gesture, tone of voice and type of communication possible within this social situation. The length of treatment, number of sessions, the effect of 'non-directive' statements, i.e. passive reiterations of what the patient has said, versus active directions by the therapist, have been the subject of study. Operant conditioning with different schedules of reinforcement, such as the therapist's making approving noises to some, rather than to others of the patient's statements at specified intervals, has also been applied in therapy.

In assessing the effects of any complex situation, a simple counting of heads is unlikely to produce sensible assessments or reliable predictions. Control groups who do not receive the treatment in question are a necessary check on its results. But control groups only confer credibility on the data if those who are treated, and those who are not, are matched on as many points as possible. Similarity in age, sex, intelligence, education and social standing of the parents are minimal requirements. For children, the school they attend, the kind, number and severity of symptoms, how long they have shown disturbances, whether the parents approve of the treatment, and temporary changes in the child's environment must also be taken into account. It is difficult to match all these when comparing treatment and waiting groups. Even when those who receive therapy and those who do not are selected primarily for the purpose of comparison, it would require a very large number of patients indeed from which to pick out the matched pairs. There is also the question as to what is to count as improvement or 'success' and how to assess it. 'Losing' a symptom is an obvious candidate, but difficult to assess objectively if the 'symptom' is being over-aggressive without particular temper outbursts, being difficult to manage in general, unduly anxious and timid without fear of a specific object.

One experimental study of children cut through the difficulties of matching control and experimental groups by simulating clinical conditions rather than using an actual patient population. Sixteen children who ranked lowest on various personality tests and behaviour ratings given to two age-grades in a school were divided into two matched groups, only one of which received play-therapy. Tests given to both groups after one year and again eighteen months later showed some significant differences between the social adjustment scores on tests in favour of the treated group(327). This, of course, tells us little about what, in particular, brought about what changes there were.

Children's play, like other behaviour, may be altered by quite slight signs of approval or disapproval shown by the adult in charge. But the type of change which is predicted from well-established data on adults is not always corroborated when the subjects are children. For instance, it was assumed, perfectly reasonably on the basis of other findings, that smiling at a child, repeating what he said, or describing what he was doing, would reinforce whatever the child was doing at the time. In fact, four- to five-year-olds did play significantly more with the miniature adult dolls after play with them had been reinforced in this way, but their play with the child doll was not affected by the reinforcements(17). Whatever the reason for this (it could be a practical problem of procedure rather than a theoretical question), predictions for children from apparently similar situations for adults may not always be fulfilled even when the set-up is experimental rather than clinical. It is hardly surprising that the generally much less precise studies on the effectiveness of 'play-therapy' – when this may mean any of the kinds mentioned – should leave the question open still.

Until recently, therapies which used play in one form or another were virtually the only form of behaviour treatment for young children. Most frequently they were considered forms of learning. There are now a growing number of therapies using the strategies of various kinds of learning theories directly: classical and instrumental conditioning, gradual acclimatization, aversion therapy and others(107). Cures of bed-wetting, especially in older and not maladjusted children have been achieved with a conditioning procedure. For other disturbances in children, it is thought that operant conditioning, i.e. shaping their actual ongoing behaviour by reinforcing what is acceptable may be more successful(108). A number of cures have been reported.

Some forms of play-therapy in which play is conceived as a means of reorientating and re-educating a child, do, in fact, amount to much the same thing in practice: the shaping of spontaneous behaviour by the therapist's regulating the reinforcements contingent upon it. Playing with a child, whether this is a make-believe game or dominoes, involves the continuous process of an adult's reactions to what the child is doing. Attending to and playing with children act effectively as reinforcers(342). In behaviour therapy, however, the reinforcements would be pre-arranged by what is known about reinforcement contingencies, rather than being left to the judgement of the moment.

There are differences between 'play' and direct training techniques. One would suppose that all the advantages lie with the latter. Curiously enough, in practice, play has been used extensively in the teaching of young children. Its history in education is as long as any that has ever been written. The reasons for this probably vary with what play is supposed to involve. Between calling a particularly tedious chore of learning 'a game', and leaving children completely to their own devices in the belief that they are bound to learn something about something, there are innumerable ways of getting children to learn by providing materials, suggestions, and directions for their play, enlisting their preferred activities, and reinforcing what they are doing by participating in it or attending to them. In play, ostensibly at least, the children can opt out, and can change their activities with changes of attention. They are less unequal to the adult socially. Adult direction is bound to be unobtrusive – and indirect. With young and with anxious children this may be necessary.

Concretely representing events, situations or objects (as in play with toys or in make-believe) conveys more information in the sense in which experimenting conveys more information than mere observation. Make-believe play in the presence of a reassuring therapist can be used to get a child accustomed to something he fears, etc. These and other aspects of play are not mysterious, but they need to be tested separately and systematically for their effectiveness. To some extent this is happening now with techniques derived from experimental set-ups. It is probable that, with the present resurgence of interest in problems of attention and communication, future developments in therapy will focus on these.

CHAPTER TEN

WHY PLAY?

THE most usual question to ask if people's behaviour is puzzling is why they act in such a way. This suggests an answer in terms of something that impelled or 'drove' them. It is the business of psychologists to be puzzled by every action, but if the questions are formulated so that they require answers in terms of special motives, they soon become unsatisfactory. For instance: 'Why do animals eat? They are driven by hunger. Why do they drink? They are motivated by thirst. Why do they play? They have needs to be active and to explore.' When they are not vacuous, such answers misleadingly imply a passive system being pushed into action, unless further questions are asked about the detailed conditions under which the behaviour occurs and the mechanisms or structures necessary for it. When all these are known, questions about motivation become redundant. For instance, thirst is often called a 'motivational system', but a great deal is now known about the maintenance of water-balance in organisms, the physiological, neural and central nervous systems involved, and some of the effects of water deprivation on behaviour. To call the whole organization a 'motivational' system is to add nothing. Even to call these arrangements a 'system' is mainly a device for classification to make the subject manageable. Not all the structures involved in keeping the organism's water-balance steady are uniquely involved in that alone, and the states of other 'systems' are concerned in it; for instance: temperature-control, salt and carbohydrate intake, and excretion. The mouth is part of the digestive system, but also part of the speech mechanism, and so forth.

'Motivation' or 'drive' is also used to refer to the fact that, within limits, the longer an animal is deprived of food, the harder it will work at some task which procures it, and that behaviour which is followed by food after deprivation tends to be repeated. So long as the term 'motive' is used merely to label such facts, it is unexceptionable. However, to infer a separate 'motive state' whenever faster performance or new learning follows a given stimulus pattern more or less consistently in certain conditions is either misleading, or does nothing more than label the stimulus pattern as 'reinforcing'. It reiterates the facts but does not explain them. The possibility of moving after inactivity, seeing pictures, hearing sounds, manipulating puzzles, and other ingredients of play have been shown to be reinforcing. In so far as this makes play into a 'motive' it is a label for what is not known about it rather than for what is known.

The word 'motive' has been used in such different ways that I shall simply state how I use the terms 'cause', 'motive' and 'reasons for an action'. The 'causes' of a given behaviour are all the conditions, structures and functions in the absence of which the behaviour fails to occur (or is modified) and which are sufficient for its occurrence. 'Motives' are those causes which result from activity within a living organism, which could potentially come under its voluntary control. A man's reasons for his behaviour are those motives of which he is aware, which he controls or uses, and which form part of his plans or strategies for action. (The models which probably best approximate the latter at present are analogies with self-regulating, self-instructing electronic devices which can select from incoming information and from a number of programmes.)

No infallibility is claimed for these definitions, but they serve to delineate 'play' a little. 'Play' is not used of actions known to be uncontrollable, nor of actions known to be the result of a plan although plans may be used in play. 'Play' is most usually applied to behaviour which, to the observer, appears to be neither the reasonable result of a plan, nor out of the person's control. This does not make it a candidate for a special motive, however. On the contrary, the conditions which reinforce play are far from uniform. A new toy, a familiar toy, an event which is not frightening and events which have frightened a child, boredom as well as stimulation may lead to more play. In any case, on the definition of 'motives' used here, they are not necessarily the kind of conditions for which it is sensible to look first.

It has been argued all along that play is not a uniform activity. It may be violent and all over the place, or quiet and concentrated. It may involve exploring, aggression, parts of sexual behaviour, be social or solitary. There is, however, one characteristic which distinguishes each kind of play from the behaviour from which it takes its name. The fact that, in each case, there is a paradoxical difference between play and the corresponding serious behaviour. In some cases play looks like an incomplete version of some other recognizable pattern of behaviour. Aggressive play stops short not only of killing, but also of routing the opponent, intimidating him to the point of giving up, and so forth. More importantly, it occurs in the wrong context. Aggression is unfriendly. Aggressive play occurs only between friends, or in a friendly social context. Imitation is often used to mean learning by observing. But in imitative play the person imitated is usually not even present. Any part of sexual behaviour may be called sex-play, but not coitus itself if adults are involved. Typically, exploring is of unfamiliar surroundings. Objects which are new to a monkey are sniffed, chewed, licked and manipulated. Handling, trying out, and manipulating (apparently) well-known objects, and hunting around in familiar surroundings, is usually called playing. Play looks biologically useless because it is misclassified as belonging to behaviour patterns with recognizable biological functions when the similarity of the behaviour is confined to particular actions. Attack is useful in protecting the animal, or procuring and securing to him his mate, food or brood. Hitting, biting, threatening, wrestling or pursuit in play have none of these functions, and may appear only in a modified form. What biological functions play-fighting has can only be established conclusively by experimental analysis of the behaviour in different species.

From the kind of evidence there is at present (see Chapters Three and Seven), it seems likely that the details of 'play-fighting' are different in different species, and serve diverse functions within given social contexts; possibly ranging from those which acquaint the members of a social group and cement friendships, to dominance fights barely confined to play by social sanctions or other checks. Dominance fights are not play. Play-fighting, as such, mainly has different biological uses than has aggression.

Why should one look for biological functions for play at all? Perhaps it is a mere by-product, useful neither to the animal nor the species? Even within the framework of evolutionary theory this is not impossible. It is, however, unlikely. Behaviour which is common to a very large number of different species, and varies within these according to age, social habits, type of feeding, and so forth, like certain types of play, is most likely subject to the environmental pressures that ensure survival or extinction. At any rate, it cannot safely be assumed that it is not, and need therefore not be studied. This does not mean that if one can think of a biological function for play at all, it must necessarily be the correct one. Play-fighting has often been considered useful to the young for learning and perfecting fighting and hunting skills. But it is now known that for a number of mammalian species play-fighting would be quite unnecessary if learning or perfecting aggressive or hunting movements were its function.

Not all play that looks biologically useless is necessarily misclassified. Exploratory play with familiar objects may look paradoxical simply because the observer does not know that aspects of the object are still unfamiliar or 'undigested' for the explorers. For instance, the young are relatively slow to adapt, and to classify information returned from their exploration of objects, and they may need to handle objects when an adult merely has to look to know what it is and does. An observer may easily underestimate the time they need for this. At the same time, continued play with an object cannot always be assumed to be a form of exploring or even of assimilating information. Clutching at, sucking, clinging to or repeated touching of familiar objects also serves to reduce excitement. This is of quite a different biological use in stabilizing the organism. Biological functions cannot be assumed without an experimental analysis of the minutiae of the behaviour in question and the conditions under which these occur.

One category for which to establish this is general activity. A great deal is known about the conditions which influence general activity, but the criteria for when it should rank as play are not obvious. It is possible to call any non-specific activity play. If so, boisterous play is part of the picture of behaviour seen in conditions of 'arousal'. Whatever alerts and excites an organism (short of producing fear) without at the same time giving its actions a specific direction must then also be assumed to be a condition for boisterous play. The physiological mechanisms and structures involved have been studied a good deal. Loosely speaking, these concern the autonomic nervous system and subcortical controlling centres, particularly when there is a lack or disturbance of integration with the highest cortical centres. In terms of overt behaviour, excited animals or humans do whatever is most typical of the species and of the individual in question. Horses canter, human infants flap their arms and legs and squeal, five-year-olds jump and skip. Gross bodily movements are frequently involved, especially in the young.

There are several reasons why boisterous play should occur more in the young than in older animals. For instance, movements are less integrated and controlled in young mammals, and changes in the pattern of stimulation are likely to set off diffuse reactions more often than in the adult. The possibility that boisterous play reduces excitement is not the only function that could be ascribed to it. It might be a means of preparing for action, limbering up for what might be required should the changes turn out to herald danger, food, mates or playmates. Mild 'toning up' is especially beneficial for children's motor development. There is little doubt that the basic skills required for moving in space develop in the absence of special training. Nevertheless, in the absence of stimulation and exercise even adult animals get out of condition. Although surprisingly little stimulation suffices for development in the young, gross lack of it does retard.

The 'need' to move, jump, shout and 'let off steam' generally recognized in the young is not, however, merely a reaction to exciting stimulation although the latter may be an occasion for it. The fact that children find it less easy than adults to sit still for long periods, not to bang their heels against the chair, not to jump up, or move their arms, or touch objects, to execute fine movements with their fingers and modulate their voices, is not a question of having more energy to spill, but of comparative lack of integration and control of the movement systems. The precise and fine movements required, for instance, for writing between narrow lines, sitting upright, or whispering, cannot be sustained for long by the very young without considerable strain. It seems sensible to assume that those movements would tend to be felt as pleasurable which are, generally speaking, biologically useful or beneficial to the animal. There is not really any very precise evidence about this aspect of 'pleasure in functioning' one way or another. But there is no doubt that movement and exercise, when they do not impose a strain, are conducive to health and fitness.

The largest category of mammal children's play is social play. No specific activity characterizes this. The young do whatever they are capable of doing – with or alongside others. Play-fighting and wrestling, or at any rate physical contacts, seem to be the most commonly reported, but higher ape and human children's play is by no means confined to that. Intelligence as well as the opportunity to encounter a wide variety of activities determines this variety of play.

Perhaps one of the most surprising findings of anthropological investigations is the difference in the variety and intensity of play activities in different communities. The evidence suggests that this is mainly a function of the diversity and richness of the cultural lives of the adults in the different societies. Clearly, climate, diet, and other conditions affecting health and activity will have to be equated before this can be a firm conclusion. Neither adults nor children in a chronically underfed community will have energy for anything more than the bare necessities for living, and the link between the poverty of adult leisure pursuits and the lack of variety in children's play may simply be a question of poor health. Play activities are unlikely to be of the first priority for survival even if they are biologically useful. But, given reasonable health, good diet, sufficient sleep and no worries, those children play most and with the greatest variety who have had the most varied experiences and have contact with adults whose interests are varied.

Different social habits also largely determine the extent to which children play with one another. Even quite nearly related animal species, like the moose and elk, differ in the extent to which the very young play with others. For these animals this is partly a question of the time at which the dam and her young are re-integrated with the herd, and partly one of migratory and feeding habits. Monkey and ape mothers' attitudes to other children or adults wanting to touch, or to entice their young to play, also differ according to the species and the social structures they have evolved. Baboon mothers interfere with their children's play much more than langurs and howlers do, for instance. Baboons live a more exposed life in the plains than langurs and howlers. Human communities and individuals vary very greatly in the extent to which they allow or encourage their young to congregate with others, especially without adult supervision and control, and this differs according to the age and sex of the child.

But there are also age changes in social play which seem to cut across species differences and differences in social habits. Typically, play with others among mammals seems to occur most in the childhood period before puberty, much less in early infancy and babyhood, and to decline after puberty. The first type of play usually reported can be classed with exploration. It often consists in gentle touching, pawing or biting at objects in the immediate environment. Of course, there are bound to be differences between species in this according to their capacities at birth. However, infants as different as foals, baby rhesus monkeys and human babies are actively restrained from indiscriminate exploring by their mothers when they first become capable of it. Fear or caution apparently comes a little later, and during this time babies are more hesitant in their actual approach to new objects, more fearful in strange environments, and take longer to habituate to them than older children, adolescents and adults. Harlow (see Chapter Three) has suggested that the social play of monkeys results mainly from the increasing exploration of the young when they are no longer restrained by their mothers, but are even actively rejected, and are at the same time much less afraid of pursuing what attracts their attention, for instance, the innumerable changes of stimulation due to the moving and squealing of another child. Fear of the strange checking exploration may be one ingredient which prevents human infants from playing socially to the extent that older children do. It is likely that the complexity of the tasks which are involved, and what is demanded in terms of sustained attention are probably concerned also in the extent to which cooperative play is possible. Human infants are rarely left alone together to do whatever they like. When they are, they explore the other by poking his eyes, pulling his hair and other methods of gathering information which will set the weaker one howling. This soon brings adult supervision and restraint. Playing with others is likely to be influenced by such events from the outset to some extent. Whether, or how soon, the attraction of other children as the focus of interesting changes and novelties is supplemented by social motives learned through being cared for by adults or in the course of exploring, or the relative weight which must be given to these, is not yet clear. There can be little doubt that human social behaviour is complexly determined. To ask whether social motives are learned through play (e.g. on the playing fields of Eton), or whether play is learned via social motives (e.g. via symbols or signs of relief from discomfort or pleasure associated with other human beings), confuses the issue. The alternatives are not mutually exclusive.

Unlike most social situations, social play has neither a formal structure, nor can it be defined by one or a given number of common activities. If children meet together mainly for a specific purpose: for games of football, or to play chess – they are no longer said to be 'playing'. Social play is at once the most and the least social of occasions; the most social in so far as what is done is wholly secondary to being together; and the least social in so far as the get-together is informal, optional and generally temporary. A group which is more or less permanent and has evolved its own structure and aims may be a gang, but it is no longer a play-group. The social play of mammals generally declines fairly sharply at puberty. This can hardly be because the animal has become less 'socially motivated'. It has been suggested that social play declines in adolescence in some species because the fighting and wrestling become too rough and painful to most of the participants. However, this will hardly do for humans. Boys do not necessarily hit each other relatively harder in adolescence, nor do their play-groups inevitably break up. But the structures and activities of the play-groups tend to become more explicit and defined. Young men are no longer said to play. To say of an adult that he 'plays' is to speak contemptuously. Unorganized activities not only occur less in adulthood, but are actively discouraged in the community by ridicule. A prime minister may play golf, but he must not just 'play'.

Probably questions about the decline of social play in mammals round about puberty should be asked generally in connexion with the integration of behaviour into adult patterns. Greater cortical control, and, at the behavioural level, the channelling and streamlining of activities into more general plans or strategies with different priorities, occur round about that time. College students in America apparently spent as much time in leisure pursuits as schoolchildren, but their activities were fewer in number and less diffuse in character.

The play of humans as of other mammal children includes parts of behaviour patterns which form biologically coherent sequences in adulthood. Some of this type of play has been shown to have consequences for adult social behaviour in some species. The biological use of such activities is different and less obvious in childhood than it is in the adult sequence.

To register changes in the environment, their timing, spacing and regularity, is essential if organisms are to keep intact and maintain themselves. Mammals, and particularly the higher apes and humans, have very efficient, elaborate devices for perceiving, classifying, coordinating, testing, remembering and using this information. Some forms of play must be classified with these activities. Play that takes the form of searching, and manipulating objects to produce changes in the pattern of stimulation, has been considered a form of exploring, or gathering information. It seems quite probable that the only difference between 'exploring' and a good deal of what is called 'exploratory play' is often simply a question of the ignorance of the observer in not realizing that the object does still present relatively novel or puzzling aspects, or that the activity belongs to the processes of testing out and confirming information which has been newly coded. There is, of course, a distinction between searching for something in particular under the aegis of activities that have priority for the animal at the time, and searching around when there is no other ongoing activity of any urgency. Only the latter could be called play. There is a good deal of evidence that for primates, at any rate, scanning the environment for changes and trying out and testing effects produced by the animal or human goes on pretty constantly during waking, provided the environment is relatively familiar. It is easily checked by totally new, intense or abrupt stimulation and takes a different form when it becomes part of a coordinated sequence or pattern. There are fewer such patterns, or they are less coordinated in childhood than in adulthood. This may be one reason why general searching and manipulation is more in evidence in the young. Other factors which produce differences with age must be looked for in connexion with reactions to danger signals, the slower habituation to stimuli found in the young of many mammals, the facts that more objects and events are likely to be new to the young, and that they have fewer means of coding, classifying and assimilating information, if only because there is less to which it can be assimilated.

Exploratory and movement play seems to require a number of subdivisions. The lack of movement control which leads to 'squirming' in the young – the fact that they are rarely still – is often labelled play. This needs to be distinguished from sudden spurts of activity. These also happen more often with young animals, since they are more easily excited, and are aroused by all sorts of 'incidental' and 'irrelevant' novel stimuli. Practice play, on the other hand, from the earliest circular reactions to variations and elaborations of newly acquired skills, needs to be investigated mainly in terms of the arrangements for feedback or return information at different phases of development. This would also apply to one of the phases of sensory-motor play viewed in terms of the external stimulations. If exploring play occurs in response to changes which are only relatively unfamiliar, abrupt or intense, and 'manipulative' play labels the producing of changes which yield further information, 'practice' play will depend to some extent upon the further changes which can be brought about in and by the activity itself. Some aspects of repetitive play with and without variations will be more relevant to the assimilation and storing of the experiences concerned. The lengthy contact with objects, the manipulations and repetitions which appear as play, are probably to some extent a result of various aspects of children's much poorer 'immediate memory' spans. However, manipulating objects often reduces them to pulp. This may help babies to masticate rather than to learn.

In classifying the play of human children, the four categories used as provisional pigeonholes for the play of animals no longer suffice. Make-believe and symbolic play, both the imitative and the imaginative variety, needs a category whatever explanation of the development of symbolic behaviour is adopted. Some of the play of the higher apes, and any other play which involves learned behaviour with regard to symbols of objects not present at the time, needs to be included. Thinking is at one, or several, removes from perceptions. Its biological use is an extension of present adaptations (e.g. to anticipate changes). If Piaget is right, symbolic play functions like practice play except that symbols rather than objects are manipulated. Certainly repetition and repetition with variations characterize both. The seemingly endless repeating of words or phrases newly heard, and asking apparently unnecessary questions are of the same order as exploring, testing and practice. Repetitive questioning 'for its own sake' often merely means that the child has repeatedly formulated his questions inadequately, so that all the answers he gets are unsatisfactory. According to Freud endless questioning is always a query about sex which the child dare not formulate. Some of them probably are. But formulating any question correctly is by no means easy even when there is no anxiety about taboos. Piaget considered endless, pointless questions to be practice with symbolic forms. This fits a good deal of intellectual play, from simple chanting of patterns of words recently heard to juggling with elaborate abstract puzzles.

Make-believe is symbolic play, but it uses concrete objects symbolically, and translates impressions into concrete actions. It is a rehearsal and re-alignment or re-classifying of events which goes on overtly either because the activity is still difficult, or because translating into actions precedes other more economical forms of coding. This need not mean that make-believe does not involve the child's feelings. On the contrary, the way an event 'feels', the excitement, pleasure, pain or fear it arouses is probably the first means of classifying it. Similarly, the use of toys and effigies may be seen as a means of organizing impressions and feelings using some concrete object or action which concentrates or labels them for the time being.

The picture of play which emerges is of activities which

occur before a given behaviour is fully organized, or when there is some lack of organization. This may be due to an absence of environmental and internal pressures which would suppress them or integrate them into a coherent sequence, or occur in childhood before such sequences become fully controlled and while attention is relatively unselective. This would not necessarily make them useless by-products of an inevitably active organism. They probably perform 'off-duty' functions that are necessary and beneficial but are relatively easily suppressed. Play activities would not be unique in this. Body-cleansing, for instance, preening and scratching are responses to skin irritations, but they do not occur during fighting or mating unless a temporary check is met. It is unlikely that all play activities have a unitary function, but their usefulness is probably connected with the fact that they tend to occur at relatively early stages in the organization of major behavioural trends. For instance, creeping into enclosed spaces (boxes, Wendy-houses, etc.), and carrying about a favourite toy may, like clinging, reduce excitement. This would be useful to the young to keep them on a relatively even keel at a time when their 'steady-state' mechanisms are as yet insufficiently developed. Make-believe play may perform this function too – but may also be needed to organize impressions by providing concrete props at a time when manipulating abstract symbols is only just being learned.

However, questions about the biological use of activities, like questions about individual motivation are better answered by a series of other, more detailed, indirect questions about the minutiae of the behaviour, and the conditions under which it occurs. These conditions are evidently not uniform for all types of play, nor are they exactly the same as the conditions for the activities from which different kinds of play take their names. Once this is accepted it is seen that a great deal is already known about playing, or can be put in the form of questions that can be answered by experimental tests.

Play is paradoxical behaviour. Exploring what is familiar,

practising what has already been mastered, friendly aggression, sex without coition, excitement about nothing, social behaviour not defined by a specific common activity or by social structure, pretence not intended to deceive: this is play. The paradox may simply be due to a mistake. What is supposedly familiar may not be so for the explorer. Excitement may seem to be about 'nothing' to the observer, simply because he does not know that the conditions for it are present. The paradox may be due to misclassification. Behaviour may be labelled 'aggressive' when it is, in fact, friendly, solely because it embodies actions also used in (the biologically more important sequence of) hunting or fighting. A deliberately clumsy or exaggerated movement(401) looks paradoxical on the assumption that the animal or child wants to get from point to point, but not if it is recognized as a device for attracting another's attention. The pretence of make-believe is not a cloak for something else, or behaviour intended to mislead, but thinking (re-coding and rehearsal) in action with real objects as props.

The apparent paradoxes of various kinds of play arise mainly in conditions which leave behaviour relatively unorganized, or before it is fully organized, integrated or streamlined. The conditions which favour relatively unselective and unorganized behaviour can occur at any time of development or maturity. But they are characteristic of the childhood of mammals. Adults sometimes just 'play', but children just 'play' far more.

BIBLIOGRAPHICAL REFERENCES

Abbreviations used for Psychological and other Journals (World list of Scientific Periodicals, Butterworth, 1964).

Acta Psychol. *Acta Psychologica*
Am.Anthrop. *American Anthropologist*
Am.J.Ment.Defic. *American Journal of Mental Deficiency*
Am.J.Orthopsychiat. *American Journal of Orthopsychiatry*
Am.J.Psychiat. *American Journal of Psychiatry*
Am.J.Psychol. *American Journal of Psychology*
Am.Nat. *American Naturalist*
Am.Psychol. *American Psychologist*
Am.Sociol.Rev. *American Sociological Review*
Anim.Behav. *Animal Behaviour*
Ann.N.Y.Acad.Soc. *Annals of the New York Academy of Sciences*
Ann.Rev.Psychol. *Annual Review of Psychology*
Biol.Rev. *Biological Review*
Br.J.Med.Psychol. *British Journal of Medical Psychology*
Br.J.Psychol. *British Journal of Psychology*
Br.Med.Bull. *British Medical Bulletin*
Br.Vet.J. *British Veterinary Journal*
Child Dev. *Child Development*
Comp.Psychol.Monogr. *Comparative Psychology Monographs*
Genet.Psychol.Monogr. *Genetic Psychology Monographs*
Hum.Factors *Human Factors*
J.Abnormal Soc.Psychol. *Journal of Abnormal and Social Psychology*
J.Appl.Psychol. *Journal of Applied Psychology*
J.Child Psychol.Psychiat. *Journal of Child Psychology and Psychiatry*
J.Comp.Physiol.Psychol. *Journal of Comparative and Physiological Psychology*
J.Comp.Psychol. *Journal of Comparative Psychology*
J.Consult.Psychol. *Journal of Consulting Psychology*
J.Educ.Psychol. *Journal of Educational Psychology*
J.Exp.Analysis Behav. *Journal of the Experimental Analysis of Behaviour*
J.Exp.Child Psychol. *Journal of Experimental Child Psychology*
J.Exp.Psychol. *Journal of Experimental Psychology*

J.Genet.Psychol. *Journal of Genetic Psychology*
J.Mammal. *Journal of Mammalogy*
J.Nerv.Ment.Dis. *Journal of Nervous and Mental Diseases*
J.Personality *Journal of Personality*
J.Soc.Psychol. *Journal of Social Psychology*
Percept.Mot.Skills *Perceptual and Motor Skills*
Pr.Roy.Soc. *Proceedings of the Royal Society*
Psychoan.Stud.Child *Psychoanalytic Study of the Child*
Psychol.Bull. *Psychological Bulletin*
Psychol.Issues *Psychological Issues*
Psychol.Forsch. *Psychologische Forschungen*
Psychol.Monogr. *Psychological Monographs*
Psychol.Rep. *Psychological Reports*
Psychol.Rev. *Psychological Review*
Psychosom.Med. *Psychosomatic Medicine*
Q.J.Exp.Psychol. *Quarterly Journal of Experimental Psychology*
Rev.Suisse de Zool. *Revue Suisse de Zoologie*
Scand.J.Psychol. *Scandinavian Journal of Psychology*
Scient.Am. *Scientific American*
Symp.Soc.Exp.Biol. *Symposia of the Society for Experimental Biology*
Symp.Zool.Soc.Lond. *Symposia of the Zoological Society of London*
Vop.Psikhol. *Voprosy Psikhologii*
Z.Psychol. *Zeitschrift für Psychologie*
Z.Tierpsychol. *Zeitschrift für Tierpsychologie*
Z.vergl.Physiol. *Zeitschrift für vergleichende Physiologie*

1. ABEL, T. M. 'Unsynthetic Modes of Thinking Among Adults: a Discussion of Piaget's Concepts', *Am.J.Psychol.*, 44, 123–32, 1932.

2. ALBE-FESSARD, D., and FESSARD, A. 'Thalamic Integrations and Their Consequences at the Telencephalic Level', in G. Moruzzi, A. Fessard, and H. Jasper (eds.) *Brain Mechanisms: Progress in Brain Research*, Vol. 1, Elsevier, 1963.

3. ALSTYNE, D. VAN *Play Behavior and the Choice of Play Materials of Pre-school Children*, University of Chicago Press, 1932.

4. ANOKHIN, P. K. 'The Multiple Ascending Influences of the Subcortical Centres on the Cerebral Cortex', in M. A. Brazier (ed.) *Brain and Behavior*, Vol. 1, American Institute of Biological Sciences, 1961.

5. ANOKHIN, P. K. 'Features of the Afferent Apparatus of the Conditioned Reflex and their Importance for Psychology', in N. O'Connor (ed.) *Recent Soviet Psychology*, Pergamon Press, 1961.

6. ANOKHIN, P. K. 'Systemogenesis as a General Regulator of

Brain Development', in W. A. Himwich and H. E. Himwich (eds.), *The Developing Brain*, Elsevier, 1964.

7. ARMSTRONG, E. A. *A Study of Bird Song*, Oxford University Press, 1963.

8. ARMSTRONG, E. A. *Bird Display and Behaviour: An Introduction to the Study of Bird Psychology*, Dover, 1965.

9. ATTNEAVE, F. *Applications of Information Theory to Psychology: a Summary of Basic Concepts, Methods and Results*, Holt, Rinehart & Winston, New York, 1959.

10. AUSUBEL, D. P. 'A Critique of Piaget's Theory of the Ontogenesis of Motor Behavior', *J.Genet.Psychol.*, 109, 119–22, 1966.

11. AXLINE, V. *Play Therapy*, Houghton Mifflin, Boston, Mass., 1947.

12. AZRIN, N. H. and LINDSLEY, O. R. 'The Reinforcement of Cooperation between Children', *J.Abnormal Soc. Psychol.*, 52, 100–102, 1956.

13. AZRIN, N. H., *et al.* 'The Opportunity for Aggression as an Operant Reinforcer during Aversive Stimulation', *J.Exp.Analysis Behav.*, 8, 171–80, 1965.

14. BACH, G. R. 'Young Children's Play Fantasies', *Psychol. Monogr.*, 59, 3–31, 1945.

15. BALDWIN, A. L. 'Socialization and the Parent-Child Relationship', *Child Dev.*, 19, 127–36, 1948.

16. BALDWIN, A. L. 'The Effect of Home Environment on Nursery School Behavior', *Child Dev.*, 20, 49–62, 1949.

17. BALDWIN, C. P., and LEVIN, H. 'Reinforcement of Agents of Action in Doll-Play', *J.Abnormal and Soc.Psychol.*, 68, 328–30, 1964.

18. BANDURA, A. 'Social Learning through Imitation', *Nebraska Symposium on Motivation*, University of Nebraska Press, 1962.

18a. BANDURA, A. and HUSTON, A. C. 'Identification as a Process of Incidental Learning, *J. Abnormal Soc. Psychol.*, 63, 311–18, 1961.

19. BANDURA, A., and WALTERS, R. H. *Adolescent Aggression*, Ronald Press, New York, 1959.

20. BANDURA, A., and WALTERS, R. H. *Social Learning and Personality Development*, Holt, Rinehart & Winston, New York, 1963.

21. BARKER, R. G., DEMBO, T., and LEWIN, K. 'Frustration and Regression: An Experiment with Young Children', *University of Iowa Studies in Child Welfare*, 18, 1–314, 1941.

22. BARTOSHUK, A. K. 'Human Neonatal Cardiac Acceleration to Sound: Habituation and Dishabituation', *Percept.Mot.Skills*, 15, 15–27, 1962.

23. BATTERSBY, E. 'Do Young Birds Play?', *Ibis*, 86, 225, 1944.

24. BAYROFF, A. G., and LARD, K. E. 'Experimental Social Behavior of Animals', *J.Comp.Physiol.Psychol.*, 37, 165–71, 1944.

25. BEACH, F. A. 'Current Concepts of Play in Animals', *Am.Nat.*, 79, 523–41, 1945.

26. BEACH, F. A. 'Instinctive Behavior: Reproductive Activities', in S. S. Stevens (ed.) *Handbook of Experimental Psychology*, John Wiley, 1951.

27. BEACH, F. A. (ed.) *Sex and Behavior*, John Wiley, 1965.

28. BERENDA, R. W. *The Influence of the Group on the Judgments of Children*, Kings Crown Press, New York, 1950.

29. BERG, I. A., and BASS, B. M. *Conformity and Deviation*, Harper, 1961.

30. BERKOWITZ, L. 'Some Factors Affecting the Reduction of Overt Hostility', *J.Abnormal Soc. Psychol.*, 60, 14–21, 1960.

31. BERKOWITZ, L. 'Aggressive Cues in Aggressive Behavior and Hostility Catharsis', *Psychol.Rev.*, 71, 104–22, 1964.

32. BERITOFF, J. S. *Neural Mechanisms of Higher Vertebrate Behavior*, Churchill, 1965.

33. BERLYNE, D. E. 'Uncertainty and Conflict: a Point of Contact between Information-Theory and Behavior-Theory Concepts', *Psychol.Rev.*, 64, 329–39, 1957.

34. BERLYNE, D. E. *Conflict, Arousal, and Curiosity*, McGraw-Hill, 1960.

35. BERNSTEIN, I. S. 'Response to Nesting Materials of Wild Born and Captive Born Chimpanzees', *Anim.Behav.*, 10, 1–6, 1962.

36. BERTALANFFY, L. VON 'Modern Concepts on Biological Adaptation', in C. McC. Brooks and P. F. Cranefield (eds.), *The Historical Development of Physiological Thought*, Hafner, New York, 1959.

37. BINGHAM, H. C. 'Parental Play of Chimpanzees', *J.Mammal.*, 8, 77–89, 1927.

38. BINNS, B. 'Individual Differences in Human Neonates' Responses to Stimulation', *Child Dev.*, 36, 249–56, 1965.

39. BIRCH, H. G. 'The Relation of Previous Experience to Insightful Problem-solving', *J.Comp.Psychol.*, 38, 367–83, 1945.

40. BISHOP, M. B. 'Mother-Child Interaction and the Social Behavior of Children', *Psychol.Monogr.*, 65, Whole N: 328, 1951.

41. BLISS, E. L. (ed.) *Roots of Behavior: Genetics, Instinct and Socialization in Animals*, Harper and Row, 1962.

42. BLOCH, H. A., and NIEDERHOFFER, A. *The Gang: A Study in Adolescent Behavior*, Philosophical Library, New York, 1958.

43. BOWLBY, J. *Maternal Care and Mental Health*, World Health Organization: Monograph series, New York; H.M. Stationery Office, 1951.

44. BOYNTON, P. L., and FORD, F. A. 'The Relationship between Play and Intelligence', *J.Appl.Psychol.*, 17, 294–301, 1933.

45. BRAINE, M.D.S. 'The Ontogeny of Certain Logical Operations: Piaget's Formulations Examined by Non-verbal Methods', *Psychol.Monogr.*, 73, Whole N: 475, 1959.

46. BREUER, J., and FREUD, S. *Studies on Hysteria*. The Standard Edition of the Complete Psychological Works of Sigmund Freud, Vol. 2, Hogarth Press, 1955.

47. BRIDGER, W. H. 'Sensory Habituation and Discrimination in the Human Neonate', *Am.J.Psychiat.*, 117, 991–96, 1961.

48. BRITT, S. H., and JANUS, S. Q. 'Toward a Social Psychology of Human Play', *J.Soc.Psychol.*, 13/14, 351–84, 1941.

49. BROADBENT, D. E. *Perception and Communication*, Pergamon Press, 1958.

50. BROADBENT, D. E. 'Vigilance', *Br.Med.Bull.*, 20, 17–20, 1964.

51. BRONFENBRENNER, U. 'Freudian Theories of Identification and Their Derivatives', *Child Dev.*, 31, 15–40, 1960.

52. BROWN, J. 'Some tests of the Decay Theory of Immediate Memory', *Q.J.Exp.Psychol.*, 10, 12–21, 1958.

53. BROWN, R. and FRAZER, C. 'The Acquisition of Syntax', in C. N. Cofer and B. S. Musgrave (eds.), *Verbal Behavior and Learning: Problems and Processes*, McGraw-Hill, 1963.

54. BROWNLEE, A. 'Play in Domestic Cattle in Britain: an Analysis of its Nature', *Br.Vet.J.*, 110, 48–68, 1954.

55. BRUSH, E. S. *et al.* 'Effects of Object Preferences and Aversions on Discrimination Learning in Monkeys with Frontal Lesions', *J.Comp.Physiol.Psychol.*, 54, 319–25, 1961.

56. BÜHLER, C. *From Birth to Maturity: An Outline of the Psychological Development of the Child*, Kegan Paul, 1935.

57. BÜHLER, C. 'The Social Behaviour of Children' cited by N. L. Munn, *The Evolution and Growth of Human Behaviour*, Harrap, 1965.

58. BÜHLER, C., *et al.* 'Die Affektwirksamkeit von Fremdheitseindrücken im ersten Lebensjahr', *Z.Psychol.*, 107, 30–49, 1928.

59. BÜHLER, C. and HETZER, H. 'Das erste Verständnis von Ausdruck im ersten Lebensjahr', *Z.Psychol.*, 107, 50–61, 1928.

60. BURTON, M. *Infancy in Animals*, Hutchinson, 1956.

61. BUSS, A. H. 'Reversal and Non-reversal Shift in Concept

Formation with Partial Reinforcement Eliminated', *J.Exp.Psychol.*, 52, 162–66, 1956.

62. BUTLER, R. A. 'Incentive Conditions Which Influence Visual Exploration', *J.Exp.Psychol.*, 48, 19–23, 1954.

63. BUTLER, R. A. and HARLOW, H. F. 'Persistence of Visual Exploration in Monkeys', *J.Comp.Physiol.Psychol.*, 47, 258–63, 1954.

64. CANTOR, G. N. 'Responses of Infants and Children to Complex and Novel Stimulation', in L. P. Lipsitt and C. C. Spiker (eds.) *Advances in Child Development and Behavior*, Vol. 1, Academic Press, New York, 1963.

65. CANTOR, G. N. and CANTOR, J. H. 'Discriminative Reaction Time Performance in Pre-school Children as Related to Stimulus Familiarization', *J.Exp.Child Psychol.*, 2, 1–9, 1965.

66. CANTOR, G. N. and CANTOR, J. H. 'Discriminative Reaction Time in Children as Related to Amount of Stimulus Familiarization', *J.Exp.Child Psychol.*, 4, 150–57, 1966.

67. CARMICHAEL, L. (ed.) *Manual of Child Psychology*, John Wiley, 1954.

68. CARPENTER, C. R. 'A Field Study of the Behavior and Social Relations of Howling Monkeys', *Comp. Psychol.Monogr.*, 10, 1934.

69. CARPENTER, C. R. 'A Field Study in Siam of the Behavior and Social Relations of the Gibbon (*hylobates lar*)', *Comp.Psychol.Monogr.*, 16, 1940.

70. CARPENTER, C. R. *Naturalistic Behavior of Nonhuman Primates*, Pennsylvania State University, 1964.

71. CHILD, I. L. 'Children's Preferences for Goals Easy or Difficult to Obtain', *Psychol.Monogr.*, 60, Whole N: 280, 1946.

72. CHOMSKY, N. 'Syntactic Structures', The Hague, Mouton, 1957.

72a. CHOMSKY, N. *Aspects of the Theory of Syntax*, M.I.T. Press, 1965.

73. CHURCH, R. M. 'Transmission of Learned Behavior Between Rats', *J.Abnormal Soc. Psychol.*, 54, 163–5, 1957.

74. CHURCH, R. M. 'Emotional Reaction of Rats to the Pain of Others', *J.Comp.Physiol.Psychol.*, 52, 132–4, 1959.

75. CLARKE, A. D., and CLARKE, A. M. 'Some Recent Advances in the Study of Early Deprivation', *J.Child Psychol.Psychiat.*, 1, 26–36, 1960.

76. COFER, C. N., and FOLEY, J. P., JNR 'Mediated Generalization and the Interpretation of Verbal Behavior', *Psychol.Rev.*, 49, 513–40, 1942.

77. COOPER, J. B. 'An Exploratory Study on African Lions', *Comp.Psychol.Monogr.*, 17, 1941/42

78. CRAIG, G. C., and MYERS, J. L. 'A Developmental Study of Sequential Two-choice Decision Making', *Child Dev.*, 34, 483–93, 1963.

79. CRANDALL, V. J., and KATKOFSKY, W., *et al.* Cited in Chapter 9, Mussen, Conger, and Kagan, *Child Development and Personality*, Harper & Row, 1964.

80. CRAWFORD, M. P. 'The Cooperative Solving by Chimpanzees of Problems Requiring Serial Responses to Colour Cues', *J.Soc.Psychol.*, 13, 259–80, 1941.

81. CROSSMAN, E. R. F. W. 'Information Processes in Human Skill', *Br.Med.Bull.*, 20, 32–7, 1964.

82. DARBY, C. L. and RIOPELLE, A. J. 'Observational Learning in the Rhesus Monkey', *J.Comp.Physiol.Psychol.*, 52, 94–8, 1959.

83. DARCHEN, R. 'Sur l'activité exploratrice de Blattella germanica', *Z.Tierpsychol.*, 9, 362–72, 1952.

84. DAVIS, A., and HAVIGHURST, R. J. 'Social Class and Colour Differences in Child Rearing', *Am.Sociol.Rev.*, 11, 698–710, 1946.

85. DAVITZ, J. R. 'The Effects of Previous Training on Post-frustration Behavior', *J.Abnormal Soc.Psychol.*, 47, 309–15, 1952.

86. DELL, P. 'Reticular Homeostasis and Critical Reactivity', in G. Morruzzi, A. Fessard, and H. M. Jasper (eds.), *Brain Mechanisms: Progress in Brain Research*, Vol. 1, Elsevier, 1963.

87. DEMBER, W. N., and EARL, R. W. 'Analysis of Exploratory, Manipulatory and Curiosity Behaviors', *Psychol.Rev.*, 64, 91–6, 1957.

88. DENISOVA, Z. V. 'On the Problem of the Perception of Complex Stimuli in Pre-school Children', *Vop.Psikhol.*, 4, (Abstract), 1961.

89. DENNIS, W., *et al.* 'Infant Development under Environmental Handicap', *Psychol.Monogr.*, 71, Whole N: 436, 1957.

90. DENTLER, R. A., and MACKLER, B. 'Mental Ability and Sociometric Status among Retarded Children', *Psychol.Bull.*, 59, 273–83, 1962.

91. DEVORE, I. (ed.) *Primate Behavior: Field Studies of Monkeys and Apes*, Holt, Rinehart & Winston, New York, 1965.

92. DIETZE, D. 'The Facilitating Effect of Words on Discrimination and Generalization', *J.Exp.Psychol.*, 50, 255–60, 1955.

93. DITTMANN, A. T. 'Psychotherapeutic Processes', *Ann.Rev. Psychol.*, 17, 51–78, 1966.

94. DOLLARD, J. and MILLER, N. E. *Personality and Psychotherapy:*

An Analysis in Terms of Learning, Thinking and Culture, McGraw-Hill, 1950.

95. DUNCKER, K. 'Experimental Modification of Children's Food Preferences through Social Suggestion', *J.Abnormal Soc. Psychol.*, 33, 489–507, 1938.

96. EASTERBROOK, J. A. 'The Effect of Emotion on Cue-utilization and the Organization of Behavior', *Psychol.Rev.*, 66, 183–201, 1959.

97. EIBESFELDT, EIBL 'Über die Jugendentwicklung des Verhaltens eines männlichen Dachses (Meles meles L.) unter besonderer Berücksichtigung des Spieles', *Z.Tierpsychol.*, 7, 327–55, 1950.

98. EIFERMANN, R. R. '*School-children's games*', Research Report 1964, Hebrew University, Jerusalem.

99. ELLIS, A. C. and HALL, G. S. *A Study of Dolls*, Pedagogical Seminary, 4, 129–75, 1896.

100. ELKIND, D. 'The Development of Quantitative Thinking: A Systematic Replication of Piaget's Studies', *J.Genet.Psychol.*, 98, 37–46, 219–27, 1961.

101. ELLINGSON, R. J. 'Studies of the Electrical Activity of the Developing Human Brain', in W. A. Himwich and H. E. Himwich (eds.), *The Developing Brain*, Elsevier, 1964.

102. ENGERS, T., *et al.* 'Olfactory Responses and Adaptation in the Human Neonate', *J.Comp.Physiol.Psychol.*, 56, 73–7, 1963.

103. ERIKSON, E. H. 'Clinical Studies in Childhood Play', in R. G. Barker, J. S. Kounin, and H. F. Wright, *Child Behavior and Development*, McGraw-Hill, 1943.

103a. ERIKSON, E. H. 'Identity and the Life Cycle', *Psychol.Issues*, I, 1–171, 1959.

104. EPSTEIN, W. 'Experimental Investigations of the Genesis of Visual Space Perception, *Psychol.Bull.*, 61, 115–28, 1964.

105. ETKIN, W. (ed.) *Social Behavior and Organization among Vertebrates*, University of Chicago Press, 1964.

106. EYSENCK, H. J. 'The Effects of Psychotherapy', *J.Consult. Psychol.*, 16, 319–24, 1952.

107. EYSENCK, H. J. (ed.) *Experiments in Behaviour Therapy*, Pergamon Press, 1964.

108. EYSENCK, H. J., and RACHMAN, S. J. 'The Application of Learning Theory to Child Psychiatry', in J. G. Howells (ed.), *Modern Perspectives in Child Psychiatry*, Oliver and Boyd, 1965.

109. FANTZ, R. L. 'The Origin of Form Perception', *Scient.Am.*, 204, N:5, 66–72, 1961.

110. FARWELL, L. 'Reaction of Kindergarten Children to Constructive Play Materials', cited by Bühler (see ref. 56).

111. FREEBERG, N. E., and PAYNE, D. T. 'Parental Influence on Cognitive Development in Early Childhood: a Review', *Child Dev.*, 38, 65–87, 1967.

112. FEIGENBAUM, K. D. 'Task Complexity and I.Q. as Variables in Piaget's Problem of Conservation', *Child Dev.*, 34, 423–32, 1963.

113. FERSTER, C. B., and SKINNER, B. F. *Schedules of Reinforcement*, Appleton-Century-Crofts, 1957.

114. FESHBACH, S. 'The Drive-reducing Function of Fantasy Behavior', *J.Abnormal Soc.Psychol.*, 50, 3–11, 1955.

115. FISKE, D. W. and MADDI, S. R. (eds.) *Functions of Varied Experience*, Dorsey Press, Homewood, Illinois, 1961.

116. FLAVELL, J. H. *The Developmental Psychology of Jean Piaget*, Van Nostrand, Princeton, New Jersey, 1963.

117. FOREL, A. *The Social World of Ants*, Putnam's Sons, New York, 1928.

118. FOSS, B. M. (ed.) *Determinants of Infant Behaviour*, Methuen, 1961.

119. FOSS, B. M. 'Imitation', in B. M. Foss (ed.), *Determinants of Infant Behaviour*, Vol. 3. Methuen, 1965.

120. FREUD, A. *The Ego and the Mechanisms of Defence*, Hogarth Press, 1939; International Universities Press, New York, 1946.

121. FREUD, A. *The Psychoanalytical Treatment of Children*, Hogarth Press, 1946; International Universities Press, New York, 1964.

122. FREUD, A. and BURLINGHAM, D. *Infants without families*, Allen & Unwin, 1944.

123. FREUD, S. *Creative Writers and Day-dreaming*, in the Standard Edition of the Complete Works of S. Freud, Hogarth Press, 1959.

124. FREUD, S. *The cases of 'Little Hans' and the 'Rat Man'*, Complete Works, Vol. 10, Hogarth Press, 1955.

125. FREUD, S. *Formulation on the Two Principles of Mental Functioning*, Complete Works, Vol. 12, Hogarth Press, 1958.

126. FREUD, S. *Beyond the Pleasure Principle*, Complete Works, Vol. 18, Hogarth Press, 1955.

126a. FREUD, S. *An Autobiographical Study*, Complete Works, Vol. 20, Hogarth Press, 1959.

127. FRISCH, K. V. 'Tranzsprache und Orientierung der Bienen', Springer-Verlag, Berlin, 1965.

128. FRIEDMANN, S. 'Intelligence Tests as Measures of Personality', *Durham Research Review*, 2, N:10, 3–16, 1959.

129. FULLER, J. L. 'The Genetics of Behaviour', in E. S. E. Hafez (ed.), *The Behaviour of Domestic Animals*, Ballière, Tindall & Cassell, 1962.

130. GAITO, J. 'A Biochemical Approach to Learning and Memory', *Psychol.Rev.*, 68, 288–92, 1961.

131. GARNER, W. R. *Uncertainty and Structure as Psychological Concepts*, John Wiley, 1962.

132. GEORGE, F. H. *The Brain as a Computer*, Pergamon Press, 1961.

133. GESELL, A., *et al. The First Five Years of Life*, Methuen, 1955.

134. GESELL, A., and THOMPSON, H. *Infant Behaviour: Its Genesis and Growth*, McGraw-Hill, 1934.

135. GESELL, A., and ILG, F. *The Child from Five to Ten*, Hamish Hamilton, 1946.

136. GESELL, A., ILG, F. L., and BULLIS, G. E. *Vision: Its Development in the Infant and Child*, Hamish Hamilton, 1949.

137. GLANZER, M. 'Curiosity, Exploratory Drive and Stimulus Satiation', *Psychol.Bull.*, 55, 302–15, 1958.

138. GOLLIN, E. S. 'Developmental Studies of Visual Recognition of Incomplete Objects', *Percept.Mot.Skills*, 11, 289–98, 1960.

139. GOODENOUGH, F. L. *The Measurement of Intelligence by Drawing*, World Book Co., Yonkers-on-Hudson, 1926.

139a. GOODENOUGH, F. L. *Anger in Young Children*, University of Minnesota Press, 1931.

140. GRANIT R. 'Receptors and Sensory Perception', Yale University Press, 1955.

141. GOODMAN, A. E. and DENNY, J. 'The Autogeny of Choice, Behavior in Probability and Sequential Programs', *J.Genet. Psychol.*, 102, 5–18, 1963.

142. GREENACRE, P. 'Play in Relation to Creative Imagination', *Psychoanal.Stud.Child*, 14, 61–80, 1959.

143. GREENBERG, P. J. 'Competition in Children: an Experimental Study', *Am.J.Psychol.*, 44, 221–49, 1932.

144. GREENSPOON, J. 'The Reinforcing Effect of Two Spoken Sounds on the Frequency of Two Responses', *Am.J.Psychol.*, 68, 409–16, 1955.

145. GROVE, A. J., NEWELL, G. E., and CARTHY, J. D. *Animal Biology*, University Tutorial Press, 1961.

146. GUERNSEY, M. 'Eine genetische Studie über Nachahmung', *Z.Psychol.*, 107, 105–78, 1928.

147. HAFEZ, E. S. E. (ed.) *The Behaviour of Domestic Animals*, Ballière, Tindall & Cox, 1962.

148. HALVERSON, H. M. 'An Experimental Study of Prehension

in Infants by Means of Systematic Cinema Record', *Genet.Psychol. Monogr.*, 10, 107–286, 1931.

149. HARLOW, H. F., *et al*. 'Learning Motivated by a Manipulation Drive', *J.Exp.Psychol.*, 40, 228–34, 1950.

150. HARLOW, H. F., *et al*. 'Manipulatory Motivation in the Infant Rhesus Monkey', *J.Comp.Physiol.Psychol.*, 49, 444–8, 1956.

151. HARLOW, H. F. 'The Nature of Love', *Am.Psychol.*, 13, 673–85, 1958.

152. HARTLEY, R. E., *et al*. *Understanding Children's Play*, Routledge & Kegan Paul; Columbia University Press, 1952.

153. HAYES, K. J., and HAYES, C. 'Imitation in a Home-raised Chimpanzee', *J.Comp.Physiol.Psychol.*, 45, 450–59, 1952.

154. HEATH, R. G. 'Pleasure Responses of Human Subjects to Direct Stimulation of the Brain: Physiologic and Psychodynamic Considerations', in R. G. Heath, *The Role of Pleasure in Behaviour*, Harper & Row, 1964.

155. HEATHERS, G. 'Emotional Dependence and Independence in Nursery School Play', *J. Genet.Psychol.*, 87, 37–57, 1955.

156. HEDIGER, H. *Wild Animals in Captivity*, Butterworth, 1950.

157. HEDIGER, H. *Studies of the Psychology and Behaviour of Captive Animals in Zoos and Circuses*, Butterworth, 1955.

158. HELD, R. 'Exposure-history as a Factor Maintaining Stability of Perception and Coordination', *J.Nerv.Ment.Dis.*, 132, 26–32, 1961.

159. HELD, R., and HEIN, H. 'Movement-produced Stimulation in the Development of Visually Guided Behavior', *J.Comp.Physiol. Psychol.*, 56, 872–76, 1963.

160. HERRING, A., and KOCH, H. L. 'A Study of Some Factors Influencing the Interest Span of Pre-school Children', *J.Genet. Psychol.*, 38, 249–79, 1930.

161. HILGARD, E. L., and MARQUIS, D. G. *Conditioning and Learning*, revised by G. A. Kimble, Methuen, 1961.

162. HILL, W. F. 'Learning Theory and the Acquisition of Values', *Psychol.Rev.*, 67, 317–31, 1960.

163. HINDE, R. A. 'Factors Governing the Changes in Strength of a Partially Inborn Response, as Shown by the Mobbing Behaviour of the Chaffinch (Fringilla coelebs)', 1 and 2, *Proc.Roy.Soc.*, 142, 306–31 and 331–58, 1954.

164. HINDE, R. A. 'The Nestbuilding Behaviour of Domesticated Canaries', *Proc.Zool.Soc.*, 131, 1–48, 1958.

165. HINDE, R. A. 'Energy Models of Motivation', *Symp.Soc. Exp.Biol.*, 14, 199–213, 1960.

166. HINDE, R. A. 'Behaviour', in A. J. Marshall (ed.), *Biology and Comparative Physiology of Birds*, Vol. 2, Academic Press, New York, 1961.

167. HOLLENBERG, E. and SPERRY, M. 'Some Antecedents of Aggression and Effects of Frustration on Doll-play', *Personality*, 1, 32–43, 1951.

168. HORN, G. 'Physiological and Psychological Aspects of Selective Perception', in D. S. Lehrman, R. A. Hinde, and E. Shaw (eds.), *Advances in the Study of Behavior*, Vol. 1, Academic Press, New York, 1965.

169. HORNE, B. M., *et al.* 'A Comparative Study of Spontaneous Play Activities of Normal and Mentally Defective Children', *J.Genet.Psychol.*, 61, 33–46, 1942.

170. HOUSE, B. J., and ZEAMAN, D. 'Reward and Non-reward in the Discrimination Learning of Imbeciles', *J.Comp.Physiol.Psychol.*, 51, 614–18, 1958.

171. HOWARD, I. P., *et al.* 'Visuomotor Adaptation to Discordant Exafferent Stimulation', *J.Exp.Psychol.*, 70, 189–91, 1965.

172. HUIZINGA, J. *Homo Ludens: A Study of the Play Element in Culture*, Routledge and Kegan Paul, 1949.

173. HULL, C. L. *Principles of Behavior*, Appleton-Century-Crofts, New York, 1943.

174. HULL, C. L. *A Behavior System*, Yale University Press, 1952.

175. HURLOCK, E. B. 'The Use of Group Rivalry as an Incentive', *J.Abnormal Soc.Psychol.*, 22, 278–90, 1927.

176. HUTT, C. 'Exploration and Play in Children', *Symp.Zool. Soc.London*, 18, 61–81, 1966.

177. HUTT, C. and HUTT, S. J. 'Effects of Environmental Complexity on Stereotyped Behaviours of Children', *Anim.Behav.*, 13, 1–4, 1965.

178. INHELDER, B. 'Some Aspects of Piaget's Genetic Approach to Cognition', in W. Kessen and C. Kuhlman (eds.), *Thought in the Young Child*, Society for Research in Child Development, 1962.

179. INHELDER, B., and PIAGET, J. *The Growth of Logical Thinking from Childhood to Adolescence*, Routledge & Kegan Paul, 1958.

180. INHELDER, E. 'Zur Psychologie einiger Verhaltungsweisen – besonders des Spiels – von Zootieren', *Z.Tierpsychol.*, 12, 88–144, 1955.

181. INHELDER, E. 'Uber das Spielen mit Gegenständen bei Huftieren', *Rev.Suisse de Zool.*, 62, 240–50, 1955.

182. ISAACS, S. *Social Development in Young Children: A Study of Beginnings*, Routledge, 1946.

183. JAKUBCZAK, L. F., and WALTERS, R. H. 'Suggestibility as Dependency Behavior', *J.Abnormal Soc.Psychol.*, 59, 102–7, 1959.

184. JEFFRESS, L. A. (ed.) *The Hixon Symposium: Cerebral Mechanisms in Behavior*, John Wiley, 1951.

185. JOHNSON, M. W. 'The Effect on Behavior of Variation in the Amount of Play Equipment', *Child Dev.*, 6, 56–68, 1935.

186. JONES, E. *Sigmund Freud: Life and Work*, Vol. 1, Hogarth Press, 1956.

187. JONES, H. G. 'Learning and Abnormal Behaviour', in H. J. Eysenck (ed.), *Handbook of Abnormal Psychology*, Pitman, 1960.

188. KENDLER, H. H. 'Reversal and Nonreversal Shifts in Nursery School Children', *J.Comp.Physiol.Psychol.*, 53, 83–8, 1960.

189. KENDLER, H. H., and KENDLER, T. S. 'Inferential Behavior in Pre-school Children', *J.Exp.Psychol.*, 51, 311–14, 1956.

189a. KENDLER, J. H., and KENDLER, T. S. 'Vertical and Horizontal Processes in Problem Solving', *Psychol. Rev.*, 69, 1–16, 1962.

190. KENDLER, H. H. and D'AMATO, M. F. 'A Comparison of Reversal Shifts and Nonreversal Shifts in Human Concept Formation Behaviour', *J.Exp.Psychol.*, 49, 165–74, 1955.

191. KENDLER, T. S. 'Concept Formation', *Ann.Rev.Psychol.*, 12, 447–72, 1961.

192. KEPLER, HAZEL *The Child and his Play: A planning Guide for Parents and Teachers*, Funk and Wagnalls, New York; Mayflower, 1952.

193. KISTYAKOVSKAYA, M. Y. 'Stimuli that elicit positive emotions in infants', *Vop.Psikhologii*, (Abstract), 1965.

194. KLEIN, M. 'The Psychoanalytic Play-technique', *Am.J. Orthopsychiat.*, 25, 223–37, 1955.

195. KLÜVER, H. 'The "Temporal Lobe Syndrome" Produced by Bilateral Ablations', in G. E. W. Wolstenholme and C. M. O'Connor (eds.), *CIBA Foundation Symposium on the Neurological Basis of Behaviour*, Churchill, 1958.

196. KÖHLER, W. *The Mentality of Apes*, Kegan Paul, 1925.

197. KOFFKA, K. *The Growth of the Mind*, Kegan Paul, 1946.

198. KONISHI, M. 'Effects of Deafening on Song Development in American Robins and Blackheaded Grosbeaks', *Z.Tierpsychol.*, 22, 584–99, 1965.

198a. KONISHI, M. 'The Role of Auditory Feedback in the Control of Vocalization in the White-crowned Sparrow', *Z.Tierpsychol.*, 22, 770–83, 1965.

199. KLOSOVSKII, B. N., 'The Development of the Brain and its Disturbance by Harmful Factors', Pergamon Press, 1963.

200. KRECH, D. 'Effects of Experience on Brain Chemistry and Anatomy', *Acta Psychol.*, 23, 169–70, 1964.

201. KUENNE, M. R. 'Experimental Investigation of the Relation of Language to Transposition Behavior in Young Children', *J.Exp.Psychol.*, 36, 471–90, 1946.

202. KUO, Z. Y. 'The Genesis of the Cat's Responses to the Rat', *J.Comp.Psychol.*, 11, 1–35, 1930/31.

203. KYLE, H. M. *The Biology of Fishes*, Sidgwick and Jackson, 1926.

204. LACEY, J. I., *et al.* 'Autonomic Response Specificity', *Psychosom. Med.*, 15, 8–21, 1953.

205. LANDAUER, T. K. 'The Hypotheses Concerning the Biochemical Basis of Memory', *Psychol. Rev.*, 71, 167–79, 1966.

206. LAZOWICK, L. 'On the Nature of Identification', *J.Abnormal Soc.Psychol.*, 51, 175–83, 1955.

207. LEATON, R. N. 'Exploratory Behavior in Rats with Hippocampal Lesions', *J.Comp.Physiol.Psychol.*, 59, 325–30, 1965.

208. LEBO, D. 'The Development of Play as a Form of Therapy: From Rousseau to Rogers', *Am.J.Psychiat.*, 112, 418–22, 1955/6.

209. LEFKOWITZ, M. M., *et al.* 'Status Factors in Pedestrian Violation of Traffic Signals', *J.Abnormal Soc.Psychol.*, 51, 704–6, 1955.

210. LEHMAN, H. C. and WITTY, P. A. 'The Play Behavior of Fifty Gifted Children', *J.Educ.Psychol.*, 18, 259–65, 1927.

211. LEHMAN, H. C., and WITTY, P. A. *The Psychology of Play Activities*, Barnes, Cranbury, New Jersey, 1927.

212. LENNEBERG, E. H. *New Directions in the Study of Language*, M.I.T. Press, 1964.

213. LEONT'EV, A. N. 'Learning as a Problem in Psychology', in N. O'Connor (ed.), *Recent Soviet Psychology*, Pergamon Press, 1961.

214. LEUBA, C. 'An Experimental Study of Rivalry in Young Children', *J.Comp.Physiol.Psychol.*, 16, 367–78, 1933.

215. LEVIN, H., *et al.* 'The Influence of the Mother's Presence on Children's Doll-play Aggression', *J.Abnormal Soc.Psychol.*, 55, 304–8, 1957.

216. LEVIN, H., and WARDWELL, E. 'The Research Uses of Doll-play', *Psychol.Bull.*, 59, 27–56, 1962.

217. LEVIN, K. *A Dynamic Theory of Personality*, McGraw-Hill, 1935.

218. LINDAUER, M. 'Ein Beitrag zur Frage der Arbeitsteilung im Bienenstaat', *Z.vergl.Physiol.*, 34, 299–345, 1952.

219. LINDAUER, M. 'Angeborene und erlernte Komponenten in der Sonnenorientierung der Bienen', *Z.vergl.Physiol.*, 42, 43–62, 1959.

220. LINDSLEY, D. B. 'Attention, Consciousness, Sleep and Wakefulness', in Field, Magoun and Hall (eds.), *Handbook of Physiology* Vol. 3, American Physiological Society, 1960.

221. LINDZEY, G. 'Thematic Apperception Test: Interpretative Assumptions and Related Empirical Evidence', *Psychol.Bull.*, 49, 1–25, 1952.

222. LING, B-C. 'A Genetic Study of Sustained Visual Fixation and Associated Behavior in the Human Infant from Birth to Six Months', *J.Genet.Psychol.*, 61, 227–77, 1942.

223. LORENZ, K. 'Die angeborenen Formen möglicher Erfahrung', *Z.Tierpsychol.*, 5, 235–409, 1943.

224. LORENZ, K. *On Aggression*, Methuen, 1966.

225. LOVELL, K. *The Growth of Basic Mathematical and Scientific Concepts in Children*, Philosophical Library, New York, 1961.

226. LOWENFELD, M. 'The World Picture of Children', *Br.J. Med.Psychol.*, 18, 65–101, 1939.

227. LURIA, A. R. *The Mentally Retarded Child*, Pergamon Press, 1963.

228. LYNN, R. *Attention, Arousal and the Orienting Reaction*, Pergamon Press, 1966.

229. MACCOBY, E. E. 'The Taking of Adult Roles in Middle Childhood', *J.Abnormal Soc.Psychol.*, 63, 493–503, 1961.

230. MACCOBY, E. E., and HAGAN, J. W. 'Effects of Distraction upon Central Versus Incidental Recall: Developmental Trends', *J.Exp.Child Psychol.*, 2, 280–89, 1965.

231. MCDAVID, J. W. 'Imitative Behavior in Pre-school Children', *Psychol.Monogr.*, 73, Whole N: 486, 1959.

232. MCFARLAND, D. J. 'Hunger, Thirst and Displacement Pecking in the Barbary Dove', *Anim.Behav.*, 13, 293–300, 1965.

233. MCGRAW, M. B. 'Neuro-motor Maturation of Anti-gravity Functions as Reflected in the Development of a Sitting Posture', *J.Genet.Psychol.*, 59, 155–75, 1941, and *J.Genet.Psychol.*, 58, 83–111, 1941.

234. MACKINTOSH, N. J. 'Selective Attention in Animal Discrimination Learning', *Psychol. Bull.*, 64, 124–50, 1965.

235. MAGOUN, H. W. *The Waking Brain*, Charles C. Thomas, Springfield, Illinois, 1958; Blackwell, 1960.

236. MALINOWSKI, B. *Sex and Repression in Savage Society*, Routledge & Kegan Paul, 1949.

237. MARSHALL, A. J. 'Bower Birds', *Biol.Rev.*, 29, 1–45, 1954.

238. MASON, W. A., *et al.* 'Sex Differences in Affective-social Responses of Rhesus Monkeys', *Behaviour*, 16, 74–83, 1960.

239. MASON, W. A. 'Sociability and Social Organization in Monkeys and Apes', in L. Berkowitz (ed.), *Advances in Experimental Social Psychology*, Academic Press, New York, 1964.

240. MASON, W. A. 'Determinants of Social Behavior in Young Chimpanzees', in A. M. Schrier, H. F. Harlow and F. Stollnitz (eds.), *Behavior of Non-Human Primates: Modern Research Trends*, Vol. 2, Academic Press, New York, 1965.

241. MATARRAZZO, J. D. 'Psychotherapeutic Processes', *Ann. Rev.Psychol.*, 16, 181–224, 1965.

242. MAUDRY, M., and NEKULA, N. 'Social Relations Between Children of the Same Age during the First Two Years of Life', *J.Genet.Psychol.*, 54, 193–215, 1939.

243. MEDNICK, S. A., and LEHTINEN, L. E. 'Stimulus Generalization as a Function of Age', *J.Exp.Psychol.*, 53, 180–83, 1957.

244. MEYER-HOLZAPFEL, M. 'Über die Bereitschaft zu Spiel- und Instinkthandlungen', *Z.Tierpsychol.*, 13, 442–62, 1956.

245. MILLER, G. A. 'The Magical Number Seven, Plus or Minus Two: Some Limits on our Capacity for Processing Information', *Psychol.Rev.*, 63, 81–97, 1956.

246. MILLER, G. A., GALANTER, E., and PRIBRAM, K. R. *Plans and the Structure of Behavior*, Holt, Rinehart & Winston, New York, 1960.

247. MILLER, N. E. and DOLLARD, J. *Social Learning and Imitation*, Kegan Paul, 1941.

248. MILLER, N. E. 'Learnable Drives and Rewards', in S. S. Stevens, (ed.), *Handbook of Experimental Psychology*, John Wiley, 1951.

248a. MILLER, N. E., and KRAELING, D., 'Displacement: Greater generalization of approach than avoidance in generalized approach –avoidance conflict', *J.Exp.Psychol.*, 43, 217–21, 1952.

249. MISHKIN, M., *et al.* 'One-Trial Object-Discrimination Learning in Monkeys with Frontal Lesions', *J.Comp.Physiol.Psychol.*, 55, 178–81, 1962.

250. MISSIURO, W. 'Studies on Developmental Stages of Children's Reflex Activity', *Child Dev.*, 34, 33–41, 1963.

251. MOREAU, R. E., and MOREAU, W. M. 'Do Young Birds Play?', *Ibis*, 86, 93–4, 1944.

252. MORGAN, C. T. *Physiological Psychology*, McGraw-Hill, 1965.

253. MOUSTAKAS, C. E. 'The Frequency and Intensity of Negative Attitude Expressed in Playtherapy: A Comparison of Well-adjusted and Disturbed Children', *J.Genet.Psychol.*, 86, 309–25, 1955.

254. MOWRER, O. H. *Learning Theory and Personality Dynamics*, Ronald Press, New York, 1950.

255. MOWRER, O. H. *Psychotherapy: Theory and Research*, Ronald Press, New York, 1953.

256. MOWRER, O. H. *Learning Theory and the Symbolic Processes*, John Wiley, 1960.

257. MOYER, K. E., and GILMER, B. H. 'Attention Span for Experimentally Designed Toys', *J.Genet.Psychol.*, 87, 187–201, 1955.

258. MUNN, N. L. *The Evolution and Growth of Human Behaviour*, Harrap, 1966.

259. MUNSINGER, H., *et al.* 'Age and Uncertainty: Developmental Variations in Preference for Variability', *J.Exp.Child Psychol.*, 1, 1–15, 1964.

260. MUNSINGER, H., and KESSEN, W. 'Stimulus Variability and Cognitive Change', *Psychol.Rev.*, 73, 164–78, 1966.

261. MURPHY, L. B. *Methods for the Study of Personality in Young Children*, Basic Books, New York, 1957.

262. MUSSEN, P. H. (ed.) *Handbook of Research Methods in Child Development*, John Wiley, 1960.

263. MUSSEN, P. H., CONGER, J. J., and KAGAN, J. *Child Development and Personality*, Harper & Row, 1963.

264. NISSEN, H. W., *et al.* 'Effects of Restricted Opportunity for Tactual, Kinaesthetic and Manipulative Experience on the Behavior of a Chimpanzee', *Am.J.Psychol.*, 64, 485–507, 1951.

265. NOWLIS, V. 'Companionship Preference and Dominance in the Social Interaction of Chimpanzees', *Comp.Psychol.Monogr.*, 2, 17, 1941.

266. O'CONNELL, R. H. 'Trials with Tedium and Titillation', *Psychol.Bull.*, 63, 170–79, 1965.

267. O'CONNOR, N. and FRANKS, C. M. 'Childhood Upbringing and Other Environmental Factors', in H. J. Eysenck, *Handbook of Abnormal Psychology*, Pitman, 1960.

268. OJEMAN, R. H., and PRITCHETT, K. 'Piaget and the Role of Guided Experiences in Human Development', *Percept.Mot. Skills*, 17, 927–40, 1963.

269. OLDFIELD, R. C. 'Memory Mechanisms and the Theory of Schemata', *Br.J.Psychol.*, 45, 14–23, 1954.

270. OLDS, J., and MILNER, P. 'Positive Reinforcement Produced by Electrical Stimulation of Septal Area and Other Regions of Rat Brain', *J.Comp.Physiol.Psychol.*, 47, 419–27, 1954.

271. OLDS, J., and OLDS, M. E. 'The Mechanisms of Voluntary Behavior', in R. G. Heath (ed.), *The Role of Pleasure in Behavior*, Harper & Row, 1964.

272. OPIE, I. and OPIE, P. *The Lore and Language of Schoolchildren*, The Clarendon Press, 1961.

273. OSGOOD, C. E. *Method and Theory in Experimental Psychology*, Oxford University Press, 1953.

274. OSWALD, I. *Sleeping and Waking: Physiology and Psychology*, Elsevier, 1962.

275. PARTEN, M. B. 'Social Play among School Children', *J.Abnormal Soc.Psychol.*, 28, 136–47, 1933.

276. PARTEN, M. B. and NEWHALL, S. M. 'Social Behaviour of Pre-school Children', in Barker *et al.* (eds.), *Child Behavior and Development*, McGraw-Hill, 1943.

277. PAVLOV, I. P. *Conditioned Reflexes*, The Clarendon Press, 1927.

278. PAWLOWSKI, A. A. and SCOTT, J. P. 'Hereditary Differences in the Development of Dominance in Litters of Puppies', *J.Comp.Physiol.Psychol.*, 49, 353–58, 1956.

279. PELLER, L. E. 'Libidinal Development as Reflected in Play', *Psychoanalysis*, 3, 3–12, 1955.

280. PHILLIPS, R. 'Doll-play as a Function of the Realism of the Materials and the Length of the Experimental Session', *Child Dev.*, 16, 123–43, 1945.

281. PIAGET, J. *The Language and Thought of the Child*, Routledge & Kegan Paul, 1948.

282. PIAGET, J. *Judgment and Reasoning in the Child*, Routledge & Kegan Paul, 1951.

283. PIAGET, J. *Play, Dreams and Imitation in Childhood*, Heinemann, 1951.

284. PIAGET, J. *The Origin of Intelligence in the Child*, Routledge & Kegan Paul, 1953; International Universities Press, 1955.

285. PIAGET, J. 'Response to Brian Sutton-Smith', *Psychol. Rev.*, 73, 111–12, 1966.

286. PIAGET, J., and INHELDER, B. *The Child's Conception of Space*, Routledge & Kegan Paul, 1956.

287. PINTLER, M. H. 'Doll-play as a Function of Experimenter-Child Interaction and Initial Organization of the Materials', *Child Dev.*, 16, 146–66, 1945.

288. PORTMAN, A., and STINGELIN, W. 'The Central Nervous System', in A. J. Marshall (ed.), *Biology and Comparative Physiology of Birds*, Vol. 2, Academic Press, New York, 1961.

289. PRECHTL, H. F. 'Zur Physiologie der angeborenen und auslösenden Mechanismen. I. Quantitative Untersuchungen über die Sperrbewegung junger Singvögel', *Behaviour*, 5, 32–50, 1953.

290. PRIBRAM, K. H. 'A Review of Theory in Physiological Psychology', *Ann.Rev.Psychol.*, 11, 1–40, 1960.

291. PROKASY, W. F., JNR 'The Acquisition of Observing Responses in the Absence of Differential External Reinforcement', *J.Comp.Physiol.Psychol.*, 49, 131–34, 1956.

292. PROVENCE, S., and LIPTON, R. E. *Infants in Institutions*, International Universities Press, New York, 1962.

293. PURPURA, D. P., and SCHADE, J. P. *Growth and Maturation of the Brain*, Vol. 4, Elsevier, 1964.

294. RABIN, A. I. 'Culture Components as a Significant Factor in Child Development', in J. F. Rosenblith and W. Allinsmith (eds.), *The Causes of Behavior: Readings in Child Development and Educational Psychology*, Allyn & Bacon, Rockleigh, New Jersey, 1962.

295. RAZRAN, G. 'The Observable Unconscious and the Inferable Conscious in Current Soviet Psychopathology: Interoceptive Conditioning, Semantic Conditioning, and the Orienting Reflex', *Psychol.Rev.*, 68, 81–147, 1961.

296. RENSCH, B., and DÜCKER, G. 'Die Spiele von Mungo und Ichneumon', *Behaviour*, 14, 185–213, 1959.

297. RHEINGOLD, H. L. and HESS, E. H. 'The Chick's "preference" for Some Visual Properties of Water', *J.Comp.Physiol. Psychol.*, 50, 417–21, 1957.

298. RHEINGOLD, H. L. 'The Effect of Environmental Stimulation upon Social and Exploratory Behaviour in the Human Infant', in B. M. Foss (ed.), *Determinants of Infant Behaviour*, Methuen, 1961.

299. RHEINGOLD, H. L. 'The Modification of Social Responsiveness in Institutional Babies', cited by Mussen, Conger and Kagan (see ref. 263).

300. RHEINGOLD, H. L. (ed.) *Maternal Behavior in Mammals*, John Wiley, 1963.

301. RHEINGOLD, H. L., *et al.* 'Visual and Auditory Reinforcement of a Manipulatory Response in the Young Child', *J.Exp. Child Psychol.*, 1, 316–26, 1964.

302. RIESS, B. F. 'Genetic Changes in Semantic Conditioning', *J.Exp.Psychol.*, 36, 143–52, 1946.

303. RIESS, B. F. 'The Effect of Altered Environment and of Age

on Mother-Young Relationship Among Animals', *Ann.N.Y.Acad. Soc.*, 57, 606–10, 1954.

304. ROBERTS, J. M., *et al.* 'Games in Culture', *Am.Anthrop.*, 61, N:4, 1959.

305. ROBERTS, J. M. and SUTTON-SMITH, B. 'Child Training and Game Involvement', *Ethnology*, 1, 166–85, 1962.

306. ROBINSON, E. 'Doll-play as a Function of the Doll Family Constellation', *Child Dev.*, 17, 99–119, 1946.

307. ROBINSON, R. J. and TIZARD, J. M. P. 'The Central Nervous System in the New-born', *Br.Med.Bull.*, 22, 49–60, 1966.

308. ROSENBERG, B. G., and SUTTON-SMITH, B. 'A Revised Conception of Masculine-Feminine Differences in Play Activities', *J.Genet.Psychol.*, 96, 165–70, 1960.

309. ROWELL, C. H. FRASER 'Displacement Grooming in the Chaffinch', *Anim.Behav.*, 9, 38–63, 1961.

310. RUDEL, R. G. 'Transposition of Response to Size in Children', *J.Comp.Physiol.Psychol.*, 51, 386–90, 1958.

311. SACKETT, G. P. 'Effects of Rearing Conditions upon the Behavior of Rhesus Monkeys (macaca mulatta)', *Child Dev.*, 36, 855–68, 1965.

312. SAMUELS, I. 'Reticular Mechanisms and Behavior', *Psychol.Bull.*, 56, 1–25, 1959.

313. SAPORTA, S. *Psycholinguistics*, Holt, Rinehart & Winston, New York, 1961.

314. SAYEGH, Y. and DENNIS, W. 'The Effect of Supplementary Experiences upon the Behavioral Development of Infants in Institutions', *Child Dev.*, 36, 81–90, 1965.

315. SCHEIBEL, M. E. and SCHEIBEL, A. B. 'Some Neural Substrates of Postnatal Development', in M. L. Hoffman and L. N. Hoffman (eds.), *Review of Child Development Research*, Vol. 1, 481–519, Russell, Sage, New York, 1964.

316. SCHENKEL, R. 'Ausdrucks-Studien an Wölfen', *Behaviour*, 1, 81–130, 1948.

317. SCHERRER, J. and FOURMENT, A. 'Electrocortical Effects of Sensory Deprivation during Development', in W. A. Himwich and H. E. Himwich (eds.), *The Developing Brain*, Elsevier, 1964.

318. SCHILLER, P. H. 'Innate Constituents of Complex Responses in Primates', *Psychol.Rev.*, 59, 177–91, 1952.

319. SCHLOSBERG, H. 'The Concept of Play', *Psychol.Rev.*, 54, 229–31, 1947.

320. SCHMIDT, H. D. 'Das Verhalten von Haushunden in Konflikt-Situationen', *Z.Psychol.*, 159, 161–245, 1956.

321. SCHNEIRLA, T. C. 'Further Studies on the Army-ant Behavior Pattern', *J.Comp.Psychol.*, 29, 401–60, 1940.

322. SCOTT, J. P. 'Critical Periods in Behavioral Development', *Science*, 138, 949–58, 1962.

323. SEARS, P. S. 'Doll-play Aggression in Normal Young Children: Influence of Sex, Age, Sibling Status, Father's Absence', *Psychol.Monogr.*, 65, N:6, 1951.

324. SEARS, R. R., *et al.* 'Some Child-rearing Antecedents of Aggression and Dependency in Young Children', *Genet.Psychol. Monogr.*, 47, 135–234, 1953.

325. SEARS, R. R., MACCOBY, E. E., and LEVIN, H. *Patterns of Child rearing*, Harper & Row, New York, 1957.

326. SEARS, R. R. 'Relation of Early Socialization Experiences to Aggression in Middle Childhood', *J.Abnormal Soc.Psychol.*, 63, 466–92, 1961.

327. SEEMAN, J., *et al.*, 'Interpersonal Assessment of Play-therapy Outcome', cited by Matarazzo (see ref. 241).

328. SIEGEL, A. E., and KOHN, L. G. 'Permissiveness, Permission and Aggression: The Effect of Adult Presence or Absence on Children's Play', *Child Dev.*, 30, 131–41, 1959.

329. SINGER, J. L. 'Imagination and Waiting Ability in Young Children', *J.Personality*, 29, 396–413, 1961.

330. SKINNER, B. F. ' "Superstition" in the pigeon', *J.Exp. Psychol.*, 38, 168–72, 1948.

331. SKINNER, B. F. *Science and Human Behavior*, Macmillan, New York, 1953.

332. SKINNER, B. F. *Verbal Behaviour*, Methuen, 1957.

333. SLIJPER, E. J. *Whales*, Hutchinson, 1962.

334. SLIOSBERG, S. 'On the Dynamics of Play', *Psychol.Forsch.*, 19, 122–81, 1934.

335. SMEDSLUND, J. 'The Acquisition of Conservation of Substance and Weight in Children', *Scand.J.Psychol.*, 2, 11–20, 71–84, 85–7, 153–5, 156–60, 203–10, 1961.

336. SMEDSLUNG, J. 'Microanalysis of Concrete Reasoning', 1, 2 and 3, *Scand.J.Psychol.*, 7, 145–67, 1966.

337. SMITH, K. U. *Delayed Sensory Feedback and Behavior*, Saunders, Washington Square, Philadelphia, 1962.

338. SMITH, K. U., and SMITH, W. M. *Perception and Motion: An Analysis of Space* – Structured Behavior, Saunders, Washington Square, Philadelphia, 1962.

339. SOKHOLOV, N. *Perception and the Conditioned Reflex*, Pergamon Press, 1963.

340. SPERLING, G. 'A Model for Visual Memory Tasks', *Hum. Factors*, 25, 19–31, 1963.

341. STEINER, J. 'Observing Responses and Uncertainty Reduction', *Q.J.Exp.Psychol.*, 19, 18–29, 1967.

342. STEVENSON, H. W. Social Reinforcement of Children's Behavior', in Lipsitt and Spiker (eds.), *Advances in Child Development and Behavior*, Vol. 2, Academic Press, New York, 1965.

343. STEVENSON, H. W., and WEIR, M. W. 'Variables Affecting Children's Performance in a Probability Learning Task', *J.Exp. Psychol.*, 57, 403–12, 1959.

344. SUTHERLAND, N. S. *Shape Discrimination by Animals*, Experimental Psychology Society Monographs N:I

345. SUTHERLAND, N. S. 'Stimulus Analysing Mechanisms', in *Proceedings of a Symposium on the Mechanization of Thought Processes*, Vol. 2, H.M. Stationery Office, 1959.

346. SUTHERLAND, N. S. 'Partial Reinforcement and Breadth of Learning', *Q.J.Exp.Psychol.*, 18, 289–301, 1966.

347. SUTTON-SMITH, B., *et al.* 'Game Involvement in Adults', *J.Soc.Psychol.*, 60, 15–30, 1963.

348. SWETS, J. A. (ed.) *Signal Detection and Recognition by Human Observers*, John Wiley, 1964.

349. Symposia of the Society for Experimental Biology, Number 18, *Homeostasis and Feedback Mechanisms*, Cambridge University Press, 1964.

350. Symposium, Therapeutic Playtechniques, *Am.J.Orthopsychiat.*, 25, 1955.

351. TANNER, W. P., and SWETS, J. A. 'A Decision-making Theory of Visual Detection', *Psychol.Rev.*, 61, 401–9, 1954.

352. TEITELBAUM, P. 'Disturbances in Feeding and Drinking Behavior after Hypothalamic Lesions', *Nebraska Symposium on Motivation*, Vol. 9, University of Nebraska Press, 1961.

353. TERMAN, L. M. (ed.) *Genetic Studies of Genius*, Vol. 1, *Mental and Physical Traits of a Thousand Gifted Children*, Stanford University Press, 1926.

354. THISTLEWAITE, D. 'A Critical Review of Latent Learning and Related Experiments', *Psychol.Bull.*, 48, 97–129, 1951.

355. THOMPSON, G. G. and HORROCKS, J. E. 'A Study of the Friendship Fluctuations of Urban Boys and Girls', *J.Genet.Psychol.*, 70, 53–63, 1947.

356. THOMPSON, W. R., and HERON, W. 'The Effects of Early Restriction on Activity in Dogs', *J.Comp.Physiol.Psychol.*, 47, 77–82, 1954.

357. THOMPSON, W. R., and SCHAEFER, TH., jnr, 'Early Environmental Stimulation', in Fiske and Maddi (eds.), *Functions of Varied Experience*, Dorsey Press, Homewood, Illinois, 1961.

358. THORPE, W. H. *Bird-song: The Biology of Vocal Communication and Expression in Birds*, Cambridge University Press, 1961.

359. THORPE, W. H. *Learning and Instinct in Animals*, Methuen, 1963.

360. THRASHER, F. M. *A Study of 1,313 Gangs in Chicago*, University of Chicago Press, 1963.

361. TINBERGEN, N. *The Study of Instinct*, The Clarendon Press, 1951.

362. TOLMAN, E. C. *Purposive Behavior in Animals and Men*, University of California Press, 1951.

363. TREISMAN, A. M. 'Contextual Cues in Selective Listening', *Q.J.Exp.Psychol.*, 12, 242–48, 1960.

364. TREISMAN, A. M. 'Selective Attention in Man', *Br.Med.Bull.*, 20, 1–16, 1964.

365. TREISMAN, A. M., and GEFFEN, G. 'Selective Attention: Perception or Response?', *Q.J.Exp.Psychol.*, 19, 1–17, 1967.

366. TWITCHELL, T. E. 'The Automatic Grasping Responses of Infants', *Neuropsychologica*, 3, 247, 1965.

367. VALENTINE, C. W. 'The Psychology of Imitation with Special Reference to Early Childhood', *Br.J.Psychol.*, 21, 105–32, 1930/31.

368. VALENTINE, C. W. *The Psychology of Early Childhood*, Methuen, 1942.

369. VERNON, M. D. *A Further Study of Visual Perception*, Cambridge University Press, 1962.

370. VYGOTSKY, L. S. *Thought and Language*, M.I.T. Press, and John Wiley, 1962.

371. WALK, R. D., and GIBSON, E. J. 'A Comparative and Analytical Study of Visual Depth Perception', *Psychol.Monogr.*, 75, Whole N: 519, 1961.

372. WARREN, J. M. and AKERT, K. *The Frontal Granular Cortex and Behavior*, McGraw-Hill, 1964.

373. WEIR, R. H. *Language in the Crib*, Mouton, the Hague, 1963.

374. WEISKRANTZ, L. 'Neurological Studies and Animal Behaviour', *Br.Med.Bull.*, 20, 49–53, 1964.

375. WELKER, W. I. 'Some Determinants of Play and Exploration in Young Chimpanzees', *J.Comp.Physiol.Psychol.*, 49, 84–9, 1956.

376. WELKER, W. I. 'Variability of Play and Exploratory

Behavior in Chimpanzees', *J.Comp.Physiol.Psychol.*, 49, 181–5, 1956.

377. WELKER, W. I. 'Effects of Age and Experience on Play and Exploration in Young Chimpanzees', *J.Comp.Physiol.Psychol.*, 49, 223–6, 1956.

378. WELKER, W. I. 'Genesis of Exploratory and Play Behavior in Infant Racoons', *Psychol.Rep.*, 5, 764, 1959.

379. WERTHEIMER, M. 'Psychomotor Coordination of Auditory and Visual Space at Birth', *Science*, 134, 1692, 1961.

380. WHITE, R. W. 'Motivation Reconsidered: The Concept of Competence', *Psychol.Rev.*, 66, 297–333, 1959.

381. WHITING, B. B. (ed.) *Six Cultures: Studies of Child Rearing*, John Wiley, 1963.

382. WOHLWILL, J. F. 'Developmental Studies of Perception', *Psychol.Bull.*, 57, 249–88, 1960.

383. WOHLWILL, J. F. 'A Study of the Development of the Number Concept by Scalogram Analysis', *J.Genet.Psychol.*, 97, 345–77, 1960.

384. WOHLWILL, J. F. 'From Perception to Inference: a Dimension of Cognitive Development', in Kessen and Kuhlman (eds.), *Thought in the Young Child*, Society for Research in Child Development, 1962.

385. WOLFE, D. L., and WOLFE, H. M. 'The Development of Cooperative Behavior in Monkeys and Young Children', *J.Genet. Psychol.*, 55, 137–75, 1939.

386. WOLFF, P. H. 'Observations on Newborn Infants', *Psychosom.Med.*, 21, 110–18, 1959.

387. WOODWORTH, R. S. *Contemporary Schools of Psychology*, The Ronald Press Co., 1964.

388. WYCKOFF, L. B. 'The Role of Observing Responses in Discrimination Learning', *Psychol.Rev.*, 59, 431–42, 1952.

389. YARROW, L. J. 'Maternal Deprivation: Toward an Empirical and Conceptual Re-evaluation', *Psychol.Bull.*, 58, 459–90, 1961.

390. YERKES, R. M. *Chimpanzees*, Yale University Press, 1943.

391. YOUNG, J. Z. *The Life of Mammals*, The Clarendon Press, 1957.

392. YOUNISS, J., and FURTH, H. G. 'Reversal Performance in Children as a Function of Overtraining', *J.Exp.Child.Psychol.*, 1, 182, 1964.

393. ZANGWILL, O. L. 'Speech', in Field, Magoun and Hall, *Handbook of Physiology; Neurophysiology*, Vol. 3, American Physiological Society, 1960.

394. ZAPOROZHETS, A. V. 'The Origin and Development of the Conscious Control of Movements in Man', in O'Connor (ed.), *Recent Soviet Psychology*, Pergamon Press, 1961.

395. ZEAMAN, D., *et al.* 'Use of Special Training Conditions in Visual Discrimination Learning with Imbeciles', *Am. J. Ment Defic.*, 63, 453–59, 1958.

396. ZEAMAN, D. and HOUSE, B. J. 'The Role of Attention in Retardate Discrimination Learning', in N. R. Ellis (ed.), *Handbook of Mental Deficiency*, McGraw-Hill, 1963.

397. ZEIGLER, H. P. 'Displacement Activity and Motivational Theory: a Case Study in the History of Ethology', *Psychol. Bull.*, 63, 362–76, 1964.

398. ZUBECK, J. P., 'Effects of prolonged sensory and perceptual deprivation', *Br. Med. Bull.*, 20, 38–42, 1964.

399. BLURTON-JONES, N. G., 'An Ethological Study of some Aspects of Social Behaviour of Children in Nursery School', in D. Morris (ed.) 'Primate Ethology', in Weidenfeld & Nicolson, London, 1967.

400. EIMAS, P. D. 'Optional Shift Behaviour in Children as a Function of Overtraining, Irrelevant Stimuli and Age', *J. Exp. Child. Psychol.*, 5, 332–40, 1967.

401. LOIZOS, C., 'Play Behaviour in Higher Primates: A Review in D. Morris (ed.), 'Primate Ethology,' Weidenfeld & Nicolson, London, 1967.

402. POSNER, M. I., 'Short Term Memory Systems in Human Information Processing', in A. F. Sanders (ed.). 'Attention and Performance' North-Holland Publ., Co., Amsterdam, 1967.

403. SMITH, F. and MILLER, G. A. 'The Genesis of Language', M.I.T., 1967.

INDEX

published by Penguin Books

The term 'play' has long been a linguistic waste-paper basket for behaviour which looks voluntary but seems to have no biological or social use. What counts as 'play'? What explanations have been given for it, and how far are they adequate? Why do children and the young of many animal species play? To answer such questions Susanna Millar here discusses psychological theories about play and reviews observational and experimental studies of the play of animals of different evolutionary development, of children at different ages, in different cultures, and in therapy. She relates different forms of play to a number of underlying behavioural mechanisms which modern methods of experimental psychology are beginning to uncover. Susanna Millar argues that play is behaviour which looks paradoxical, but has a variety of biological functions related to childhood development and other specific conditions.

Cover design by Patrick McCreeth, photos by Nelson Christmas. 'Cressida', the chimpanzee, photographed by permission of Chessington Zoo

$1.45

14 0209743